MW00563247

The Physics of Possibility

Victorian Literature and Culture Series

Herbert F. Tucker, Editor

William R. McKelvy, Jill Rappoport, and Andrew M. Stauffer, Associate Editors

The Physics of Possibility

VICTORIAN FICTION, SCIENCE, AND GENDER

Michael Tondre

UNIVERSITY OF VIRGINIA PRESS

CHARLOTTESVILLE AND LONDON

University of Virginia Press
© 2018 by the Rector and Visitors of the University of Virginia
All rights reserved
Printed in the United States of America on acid-free paper

First published 2018

ISBN 978-0-8139-4145-5 (cloth)
ISBN 978-0-8139-4146-2 (e-book)

9 8 7 6 5 4 3 2 1

Library of Congress Cataloging-in-Publication Data is available for this title.

Cover art: From "The Universal Church of the Future—from the Present Religious Outlook," J. Keppler, 1883. (Library of Congress, Prints and Photographs Division)

Contents

Acknowledgments   vii

Introduction: Developmental Logics   1

1. The Lost Futures of the Novel: Negated Potential in
    Richard Feverel   29

2. "The Interval of Expectation": *Armadale* and the History of
    the Present   61

3. "A Nat'ral Born Friend": The Evolution of Community in *Dombey
    and Son*   95

4. George Eliot's "Fine Excess": *Middlemarch*, Energy, and
    Incalculable Diffusion   126

    Conclusion: "The Varying Experiments of Time"   165

Notes   175

Bibliography   203

Index   219

Acknowledgments

This book owes much to the individuals and institutions that have supported its completion. I am deeply grateful to Martha Vicinus for exemplary graduate student mentoring, feedback on articles, and incisive comments on the later manuscript. Her guidance has been instrumental throughout the project. I thank John Kucich for prompting my interest in Victorian literature and culture and for providing meticulous, transformative readings of the book in its early stages. Lucy Hartley gave superlative advice on historical and methodological concerns and sharpened my understanding of Victorian science and literature in particular. Feedback from Yopie Prins helped me to reconceive the dissertation as a book. For fostering my efforts leading to graduate school, I thank Richard A. Levin. Other teachers also shaped my earliest efforts, including Marjorie Levinson, David Halperin, Susan Scott Parrish, and Gregg Crane. Thanks to several friends from Ann Arbor: Korey Jackson, who provided intellectual camaraderie and adroit readings, Christopher Becker, Alex Zwinak, Ari Friedlander, Stephanie Batkie, Joanna Patterson, and LaMont Egle.

At Stony Brook University, I found a vibrant community of scholars and graduate students. I owe my greatest debt to Adrienne Munich, who read the entire book with acute insight, and whose mentorship has been vital to my years as a faculty member. I also thank Adrienne for inviting me to join the Editorial Board at *Victorian Literature and Culture,* which introduced me to a learned group of fellow Victorianists. Other colleagues helped me to refine the book's argument. I am indebted to Michael Rubenstein for clarifying conversations and readings, and for putting me in touch with Justin Neuman at the University of Virginia Press at a key moment in the project's completion. Andrew Newman generously discussed ideas at various stages and also commented on several sections of the manuscript.

My further thanks to Celia Marshik, Peter Manning, Jeffrey Santa Ana, Justin Omar Johnston, Douglas Pfeiffer, Benedict Robinson, Susan Scheckel, Rowan Ricardo Phillips, Stephen Spector, Elyse Graham, Andrew Flescher, Eric Haralson, Ann Kaplan, Patricia Dunn, Ken Lindblom, Stacey Olster, Amy Cook, Eugene Hammond, and the participants in my "New Materialisms" doctoral seminar. I thank Jordan Plavincky, Daniel Irving, and Nicole Savage for expert research assistance. A departmental symposium in 2014 provided the opportunity to share material with a congenial audience. The Humanities Institute, directed by Kathleen Wilson, permitted me to bring Victorianist speakers to campus, resulting in fruitful exchanges about the project.

Others in and outside of academia also deserve thanks. Carolyn Betensky, Elaine Freedgood, David Coombs, and Spencer Hawkins read and improved portions of the manuscript. John Maynard welcomed me to the *VLC* editorial staff and to the New York academic community. Anne Humpherys and Gerard Joseph invited me twice to speak at the CUNY Victorian seminar; my thanks to them and to the other participants. At various points, Chris Palmer, Cannon Schmitt, Herbert Sussman, Marion Thain, Daniel Williams, and members of the V21 first book working group took time to discuss ideas with me. Suggestions from an anonymous reader and from the editors of the Victorian Literature and Culture series, edited by Herbert F. Tucker, shaped the book in its later stages. My deep thanks to Phillip Blumberg, in whom I found a consistently empathetic ear and voice.

Funding opportunities supported my efforts to write and share work. A Faculty Fellowship Award provided dedicated time for research in 2014–15; in 2016–17, a university research grant underwrote the book's completion. A series of departmental travel awards enabled me to present work under the auspices of the MLA, NAVSA, NVSA, INCS, and NCSA; I wish to thank audiences at those venues for invaluable feedback. Support from the Stony Brook College of Arts and Sciences and the English Department enabled me to host the annual Northeast Victorian Studies Association conference in 2014, which occasioned dialogues on the year's theme of "sensation."

Finally, my thanks to the University of Virginia Press and to Eric Brandt for excellent editorial guidance. The Johns Hopkins University Press and the University of California Press gave permission to reprint. A portion of chapter 2 appeared as "The Interval of Expectation: Delay, Delusion, and the Psychology of Suspense," *ELH* 78.3 (2011): 518–35, copyright © 2011, the Johns Hopkins University Press; a portion of chapter 4 appeared as "George Eliot's 'Fine Excess': *Middlemarch,* Energy, and the Afterlife of Feeling," *Nineteenth-Century Literature* 67.2 (2012): 204–33, copyright © 2012, the Regents of the University of California. I thank the journal reviewers for their constructive comments.

Introduction

Developmental Logics

Looking back at the Victorian novel's narrative excesses in 1908, Henry James penned one of criticism's most enduring observations on its form: "What do such large loose baggy monsters," he asked, "with their queer elements of the accidental and the arbitrary, artistically *mean?*"[1] James left the question unanswered, as a charge so transparent as to need no explanation. Those "queer elements" had no meaning at all to him. James's statement implies a range of departures from his ideal of organic form, in which each element contributes to the meaningful whole. A partial list might include the dead ends, digressions, and proliferating minor characters marking much Victorian fiction, which seem hard to reconcile with a functional unity of design. Our own era has come to appreciate formal fragmentation and incommensurabilities as signs of artistic sophistication, but scholars have yet to understand how such "elements of the accidental" corresponded to Victorian theories of realistic representation. *The Physics of Possibility* returns to James's provocation to advance a revised history of the novel. In a significant strain of fiction, it shows that those elements contributed to a newly distributed poetics in British culture: a reorganization of objects, actions, and settings as formal categories within the physical sciences and mathematics and rooted in the calculus of possibilities. The elements of style that James denigrated as "accidental" appear as a meaningful legacy of fiction from this vantage, with expansive ethical and political aims. *The Physics of Possibility* reveals novels' involvement in major sciences, also showing scientific innovation to be aspects of the novel, so as to return meaning to what was once deemed merely bad form.

The transformations at the core of this book have been named "the probabilistic revolution," though the title is incomplete. Historians such as Ian Hacking, Theodore Porter, and I. Bernard Cohen conceived the term to describe how mathematical models of probability invigorated the leading nineteenth-century sciences, above all astronomy, physics, and evolutionary biology.[2] But scholars have yet to locate that transformation within the larger lines of Victorian social formation, when the novel emerged as a mass-cultural phenomenon. I examine a roughly thirty-year span when breakthroughs in statistical thinking transformed the physical sciences, and proceed from a handful of mathematically minded savants in 1850 to a shared understanding of fiction as a vehicle for representing possible worlds. That span marks the last interval in which British novelists and scientists shared a common tongue and cultivated common techniques of representation. The history of their interaction, I show, was often one of alternative possibilities. More and more, investigators found it impossible to depict a single star, an atom, a nerve, or a cell at a given instant. Instead, they sought to approximate the condition of those entities in statistical terms: through a curve of alternative possibilities that sculpted around a norm or a mean. This turn to the representation of temporal difference found creative concentration in novels that sought to reimagine Victorian conventions of living, and indeed to transform them. In tandem with new cosmological insights, novelists sought to activate the prospects for an ameliorated social world.

In specific terms, then, the following chapters rewrite the story of the probabilistic revolution as a tale centrally about the form of historical experience in Victorian literature and culture. Here I build on an influential critical corpus devoted to the rise of statistics in Britain, much of which has elucidated the discursive dynamics of power, risk, and accident in modernity. I share this scholarship's investment in nineteenth-century fiction but depart from its focus on outbreaks of coincidence and accident in narrative.[3] In lieu of attending to diegetic depictions of "chance"—on events that seem to index acausal characteristics of the world—I accentuate how novelists joined scientists, mathematicians, and philosophers in figuring alternatives to the actual. By addressing often-overlooked elements of form and literary technique in this vein, my readings invite a reassessment of fiction's creative agency: how novels contribute to processes of intellectual ideation through their narratological configurations, multiple characterizations, and sentence-level designs. Positing that fictional aesthetics are adept at reimagining historical realities, never simply reifying them, and that scientific innovations are entangled with wider cultural innovations, I hope to enrich our understanding the novel's multivalent, occasionally oblique, and often surprising implication in the ascendant physical sciences of the age.

An afternoon in February of 1873. In a room at the University of Cambridge, the scientist James Clerk Maxwell addressed a group of old friends and acquaintances. Maxwell had recently returned to the university where he had completed the Mathematical Tripos two decades beforehand, having been appointed to oversee Britain's first university-housed physics laboratory. His appointment crowned an illustrious list of accomplishments. Maxwell's fame rested on insights into all aspects of the physical sciences, including the mathematics of electromagnetic fields, the thermodynamics of heat, the properties of light, and the substance of Saturn's rings. On the date in question, however, he delivered a more speculative set of reflections on the grounds of historical understanding. Locating science within "the general stream of thought," he focused on a new wave of statistical studies on matter, energy, and force in the mid-nineteenth century.[4] These studies "seem likely to have a powerful effect on the world of thought," he argued, and on Victorian thinking about social and historical change above all (Campbell and Garnett, 438). Enlightenment-era intellectuals like René Descartes, George Berkeley, and John Locke sought to explain events through a schema of empirical time: "a chronology in which intervals of time are measured," Maxwell explained (436). In contrast, Victorian scientists had begun to dream of other states of affairs in which "the past state and the future state of things" were imagined otherwise (440). The most cutting-edge insights in the physical sciences, for Maxwell, were insights into possible worlds.

At a glance, Maxwell's account exemplifies the liberal virtues that contemporaries attributed to scientific learning: its usefulness in promoting a many-sided subject equipped with a vocational training and rational habits of mind. Yet if science suggests a particular route to middle-class life, then it can create skepticism about the realities of the past and future in general—an implication that would have seemed surprising a few decades before. Through the first half of the nineteenth century, physical science was understood largely as an arena of empirical knowledge, prestigious because it was exact in the data conveyed on optics, mechanics, and electricity. But in a kaleidoscopic range of instances, I show how a new generation of thinkers represented the condition of individual things and relations in negative form: through the looking glass of what might have been, could be, or ought to be. That ambition, among vanguard scientists, joined new and incipient ideas in the general press. So much was clear to Maxwell: scientists were participating in a shared undertaking that included lay journalists and popularizers, "professional philosophers," "the unprofessional man," and the "intelligent public."[5]

The title of my book, *The Physics of Possibility,* names the unnamed transformation that Maxwell identifies in British culture. Central to this efflorescence of ideas was a strain of novels that recast the developmental logic of the bildungsroman. These novels suspend the progressive movement of *Bildung* in order to represent a field of developmental potentials: other ways of being and becoming, of growing in the world and escaping into altered futures. The virtual trajectories in these texts share an approach to realism with the "hard" physical sciences. From George Meredith's unconstellated plotlines in *The Ordeal of Richard Feverel* (1859) to the wayward sensation heroes of the 1860s to panoramic high realism, Victorians conceived of character as a field of possibilities departing from classical norms of formation. These were possibilities poised at the knife edge between the real and the unreal. We will see evidence that their unsettled referential location, in Victorian science, had uniquely evocative implications in novels—particularly in novels that questioned the self-evidence of legal, educational, economic, and domestic institutions. What we are approaching is a tradition of realism couched in the conditional or subjunctive mood. By tracing the scientific orientations of this tradition, I specify something like what Eric Hayot calls a "world-physics" of fiction, although the "physics" I interpret had distinctive origins in Victorian scientific, philosophical, political, and religious discourse.[6]

Each chapter considers how novelists posed a fundamental ethical question: What did it mean to be more than an isolated self? How, in other words, might the individual suggest a matrix of possible paths in relation to the lives of others? Such questions organized a rich circuit of writings involving fiction, physical science, and gender. *Richard Feverel,* for example, uses the counterfactual language of science to rewrite conventions of male formation. It imagines alternative forms of desire and attachment that do not end in marriage: a "kingdom of 'would-have-done' and 'might-have-been'" that dominates the limited space for plot.[7] *The Physics of Possibility* assembles a wealth of cognate narrative strategies in this vein. Within this strain of fiction we will find the play of alternative masculinities, intimate friendships, mentor-protégé relations, and adoptive attachments. In various respects, these stories swerve, suspend, and diffuse what Susan Fraiman calls "the single path of middle-class, male development," supplementing it with a range of discontinuous outcomes.[8] Such strategies have been understood as aesthetic weaknesses at one point or another. I have in mind moments of digression and dilation, occluded plotlines, and other instances in which "narrative enters into a state of deviance and detour," in Peter Brooks's words.[9] By locating those signs of formal excess in historical terms, I retrieve their ties to a cosmopoetic practice infusing much mid-nineteenth-century discourse.

There were many reasons why insights in the physical sciences and mathematics coincided with these experiments in form. Just as novelists imagined a more fluid range of potentials for male and female formation, scientists began to imagine life as a set of virtual possibilities at all levels of becoming—as an ecology of potential relations, unguided and never-ending, rather than a great chain with "man" at the top. Charles Darwin influentially envisioned the chance production of new biological forms, conceiving life as "a swarm of various and variegated materialities," as Jane Bennett puts it.[10] Yet Darwin's writings were joined by many others on the unaccountable flux of physical phenomena, including contributions from Maxwell, T. H. Huxley, William Carpenter, William Clifford, and Francis Edgeworth. In some explicit instances, and in many more implicit ones, the potential recombinations of matter, energy, and force troubled the notion of essential reproductive subjects, suggesting more manifold processes of growth across the threshold of bounded bodies: what Elizabeth Barrett Browning called the "the golden spray of multitudinous worlds" that could be intimated in the "outflow of spontaneous life."[11] In part, these boundary-breaking concerns help to explain the appeal of the hard sciences among *fin-de-siècle* writers who cultivated unconventional gender and sexual postures. One thinks of Oscar Wilde's allusions to the mysteries of chemical transformation, thermodynamics, and evolutionism in *The Picture of Dorian Gray* (1890) or of Olive Schreiner's evocation of deep time scales in *The Story of an African Farm* (1883). The affinities between the hard sciences and queer and feminist political projects have a longer history that begins in mid-Victorian writing, when thinkers first recruited probabilistic methods to depict the unpredictable swerve of material forms.

It is here that my study dovetails with scholarship on the thwarted logic of the Victorian bildungsroman. As the term for a general pattern of development from youth to adulthood, the bildungsroman has been read less as a coherent subgenre than a focus of ongoing experimentation (what Fredric Jameson calls an "experimental construct").[12] In Franco Moretti's account, the novel of formation assumed an antisubversive edge in nineteenth-century Britain, as a practice that tended to collude with dominant bourgeois ideologies. Coming of age involves a melancholic compromise between the hero and prevailing social institutions in Victorian novels, enacted through the twin ends of a private marriage and a public vocation. In this sense, the bildungsroman represents the hero's progress toward becoming a representative English subject—naturally male, middle class, and married—who has learned to surrender less conventional desires.[13] Yet another thesis is that the upheavals of nineteenth-century modernization led to the decline and fall of the classical development plot. Perhaps most influentially, feminist critics like Fraiman and Rita Felski have divulged the failure of *Bildung* in novels by George Eliot, Charlotte Brontë, and other women writers whose ambitions were tied to a phallocentric tradition that they could never claim as their own.[14] Confronted by an absence of institutions for female education and occupational training, these novelists "disperse the individual into a set of trajectories," as Fraiman writes, and set up potentials that never issue in a path to final fulfillment (xiii).

Like these critics, I find that the standard tropes of formation led to more volatile and self-shattering experiments in mid-nineteenth-century novels. But I look beyond the traces of failure or blockage. For many major novelists—including Eliot, Charles Dickens, Meredith, and Wilkie Collins—the representation of disrupted development coincided with less conventional possibilities for growth, ironizing the linear logic of biological time that their novels conspicuously introduce. In *Middlemarch* (1871–72), for example, insights into the persistence of lost energy (of statistical entropy) structure Eliot's tale of lost ambition, as Tertius Lydgate's and Dorothea Brooke's vocational aims are obstructed. Over the course of the novel, their dispersed energies are shown to have uncountable consequences on the totality: an "incalculably diffusive" influence within the group.[15] The novels I examine each "suspend the arduous framework of self-culture," as Elisha Cohn writes, releasing conditional torques that depart from the expected ends of juvenile growth.[16] Exploring the scientific dimensions of these narratives will prompt questions like the following: What did it mean to long for alternatives to the conventions of self-formation (chapter 1)? Why do individuals sense and feel alternatives to the present (chapter 2)? What if personal development was conceived on nonhuman scales—less as an inevitable turn to reproductive adulthood and more as a precarious process of exchanges, flows, and feedback loops with the material environment (chapters 3 and 4)?

But this is not to say that novelists and scientists shared a univocal frame of reference. To the contrary, I show how uniquely unsettled the ontological location of the possible came to be for a short window of time. While often using mathematical methods of probability, Victorian physical scientists had no clear consensus about where those possibilities stood in relation to the facts of the real. Probabilities certainly did not represent real indeterminism (referring to objective randomness), but it seemed clear that they were not mere mental chimeras either (referring to one's subjective level of anticipation). I will elaborate on the issue momentarily but want to begin by observing that this unresolved blind spot became central to the Victorian novel's claims of aesthetic agency. In the novels I interpret, the realm of historical possibilities was something more than an illusion, if less than a plain fact. The counterfactual cadences of these texts reflect the utopian potential for new teleologies of living that might become real: developmental para-worlds that were neither quite true nor quite spurious but impossibly both, and whose moral and emotional geometries have yet to be mapped.

What this means is that latent scientific irresolutions—above all, how the realm of the possible corresponded to the actual—had singular importance in literature and *as* literature. So while I reveal the through lines between novelists and scientists and articulate generative interconnections, I take a qualified view to the notion that literature can spur scientific revolutions, since my focus lies on questions that Victorian scientists left unanswered. (What did alternative historical possibilities represent? To what degree did those alternatives reflect real-world phenomena?) And for this reason as well, my readings always fold back to the form of the novels in question: their multiple temporalities, foreclosed plotlines, moments of extended extradiegesis, and other "queer elements" that have been read en passant. These characteristics articulated a mode of literary thinking distinct from the propositional logic of science. Through their formal organization, novels pose ideas without prescribing truth claims, invite multiple perspectives on what had seemed self-evident, and question what went without saying.

Of course, the story goes on beyond the pages of this book. It continues in investigations into modal logic and counterfactual conditionals, which have contributed to what Niall Ferguson calls a "questioning of narrative determinism" among recent historians and philosophers.[17] The story goes on in science as well. The rise of quantum indeterminism is often noted by feminist science scholars like Evelyn Fox Keller, Donna Haraway, and N. Katherine Hayles.[18] Karen Barad, for example, writes that modernist concepts of relativism are "inherently less androcentric, less Eurocentric, more feminine, more postmodern, and generally less regressive than the masculinist and imperializing tendencies found in Newtonian physics."[19] Such progressive accounts of physics have proven compelling, though I find that the notion of a dramatic epistemic upheaval from Newtonian assumptions to modernist ones has minimized interest in the Victorian interlude I wish to examine. Scholars have yet to trace the acute political energies of modernism, which Barad identifies in broad outline, to their mid-Victorian cultural origins: a period of intensification just before Maxwell's Cavendish Laboratory trained some the earliest professional physicists in the world, when the realm of probabilities had no clear-cut connection to people and things. This transitive moment corresponded with a tradition of novel writing whose formal, affective, and political parameters I seek to understand.

ENSEMBLE EFFECTS: MATERIALISM, TEMPORALITY, AND GENDER

An influential academic archive has traced the Victorians' statistical obsessions to the growth of demographic data, accompanied by developments in insurance, the stock market, and associated techniques of risk management in the period.[20] Despite a continuing clamor of interest in the period's statistical boom, however, no single study has been dedicated to the convergence between the high Victorian physical sciences, mathematics, and fiction that I examine. In part, attention to this nexus has been overshadowed by the practices identified in Michel Foucault's late lectures on governmentality, where he pointed out how an outpouring of statistical data—etymologically, knowledge about the state—served to define and manage modern populations. Central to Foucault's managerial account is "the power of normalization" that emerged with the spread of statistical information on national demographics and territories, which facilitated methods "to try to reduce the most unfavorable, deviant normalities in relation to the normal, general curve."[21] Drawing on new statistical knowledge, medical and legal experts could construe particular species of individuals to be more or less normal, in contrast to abnormal others (representatives of a given class or race, for instance, inferred to have a statistical predisposition toward disease). These insights continue to prove revelatory, and on occasion I will be elaborating on them. Even so, in its focus on protocols of subject formation, subjugation, and risk, criticism has yet to observe significant concepts of historicity that also attended statistical innovations. In addition to calculating risks and disciplining normal and abnormal populations, developments in statistics structured a kind of conditional historicism: temporal paradigms exhibiting what Reinhart Koselleck describes as "a continuous space of potential experience," in which the past, present, and future appeared to teem with alternative trajectories, heterogeneous and unassimilable to the singularity of empirical events.[22]

A related reason for the aporia at the modern emergence of statistics stems from the posturings of Victorian scientists, who often cast themselves as avatars of "scientific materialism." That term, introduced by John Tyndall in 1868, functioned to label contemporary scientists as archpositivists devoted to the virtues of mechanical measurement and objective, unmediated facts.[23] Leading popularizers such as T. H. Huxley, Herbert Spencer, and William Clifford enabled misrepresentations of this kind through their use of deliberately provocative terms, as in Huxley's lecture and subsequent 1869 article "On the Physical Basis of Life," which startled readers already anxious of scientific heresy.[24] Read closely, however, Huxley and other provocateurs cultivated more qualified ontological positions. Huxley espoused what he called "a union of materialistic terminology with a repudiation of materialistic philosophy," and in various registers, experimentally disposed naturalists like Tyndall and mathematical specialists such as Clifford conceded that "material" knowledge was rooted in mathematical principles that, however detailed, remained imperfect mirrors to nature.[25] While religious opponents of science sometimes cast these thinkers as iconoclastic positivists, their writings diversely explore the view that mediation is inescapable and define mathematical models as an adjunct to the inadequacies of observation.

Chance itself, as I have said, was an idea in transition. Up until the mid-nineteenth century, "chance" was widely understood as a metaphysical phantom, an illusion of the mind's eye. It functioned as an umbrella concept for all the causes in existence that could never be observed but that were still assumed to exist. When weighing the probabilities about the outcome of a coin flip, for instance, mathematicians claimed to be weighing subjective states of expectation or abstract frequencies and ratios. Charles Babbage gave an authoritative account of this perspective in his *Ninth Bridgewater Treatise* (1837), defining the "probable and improbable" as the measure of one's own level of expectation about a heads or tails, for instance.[26] Within less than a generation, however, that view was already becoming obsolete. By the mid-1850s, a new wave of scientists started using probabilities to represent real ontological events: everything from the jostling of gas molecules to the meandering movements of the stars. The stage was being prepared for ultimate indeterminism—the position that events are truly stochastic or acausal—although this remained a heterodox position until the twentieth century.

I concentrate on the intellectual interlude between Babbage's "subjective" understanding of chance and Maxwell's more or less "objective" understanding because chance occupied a uniquely free-floating location in Victorian writing. Within the decades I interpret, the domain of historical possibilities stood situated between the material and immaterial, occupying an ambivalent space of both, which was quintessentially that of the novel. On the one hand, alternative possibilities seemed to be epiphenomena: no more than practical projections, serving to compensate for our all-too-human failure to trace the divine telos of each particle and force in the world. On the other hand, those possibilities were often implied to have an actual existence, in the hyperconnected ensembles of movement and interrelationship that scientists intuited in the nether reaches of the real. Solid and substantial things were melting into air, and air into precariously assembled forces. The boundaries of the possible, in the physical sciences, stood somewhere between the mind of individuals and the ontological foundations of the world.

Consider Herschel's landmark contribution to the subject: his essay "Quetelet on Probabilities," first published in the *Edinburgh Review*'s July 1850 issue and republished in the author's 1857 essay collection.[27] The piece attracted attention from major Victorian intellectuals, being admired by Charles Darwin and James Clerk Maxwell while also finding enthusiastic readers in George Eliot, George Henry Lewes, and others.[28] Herschel writes, "The same physical relation—the same historical statement—the same future event—may have very different degrees of probability in the eyes of parties differently informed of the circumstances" (3). The article introduces its topic in socially resonant terms for a new generation of middling readers, many of whom were interested in the gentlemanly pursuit of mathematics but wanted formal training. Note its central concatenation of phrases: "physical relation," "historical statement," and "future event." Strung together without an attempt to parse their connections, the terms result in a curious pileup of glosses in the middle of the sentence. The triplicate suggests general affinities rather than clear-cut logical ties, and in doing so signals a conjunction of ideas in much mid-Victorian discourse. For many British intellectuals, thinking about "physical relations" meant thinking about the very nature of "historical" and "future" possibilities. It meant imagining deviations from a singular present that could call into question the way that things are. Historical determinism is not canceled outright: it is suspended, defused, left hanging by a hyphen.

Novels figure such ideals, latent in Herschel's prose, in terms that remain irreducible to an argument or claim, for fiction "belongs with the sentence without ever being reducible to the sum of its sentences," as Roland Barthes wrote.[29] Works of fiction assemble multiple lifeworlds and temporalities that jostle for readers' attention, opening potentialities that may be foreclosed but never jettisoned fully from a text. To locate these tendencies in individual novels, I introduce the notion of "ensemble" effects. By this I mean moments that break the diegetic frame of a plot to suggest other possible distributions of characters, actions, and settings, and that revise what happens as a multiplicity of alternatives; ensemble effects generate what the narrative theorist Ruth Ronen calls "modal stratifications," or deviations from the coherence of a fictional world.[30] I use the term "ensemble" in several related senses. Conventionally, an ensemble means a collection of heterogeneous elements that form a productively integrated whole. Its root form, *insimul,* moreover, carries the meaning of "at the same time," and is useful in suggesting a composite of different possible plots imagined at a given fictional moment or location. Finally, the word "ensemble" acquired a new scientific definition at the twilight of Victoria's reign, when mathematical physicists in Europe and Anglo-America enlisted it in 1902 to describe *statistical* ensembles: a huge number of virtual versions of a physical system, each expressing a possible state of affairs at a given moment.[31] I introduce the concept of fictional ensembles to comprehend these interlocking meanings and to pinpoint a common logic (indeterminate, counterfactual, antiteleological) behind a general family of aesthetic phenomena (prolepsis, analepsis, digression, delay). In distinction from what Andrew H. Miller describes as the Victorian novel's investment in "unlived lives" and what Catherine Gallagher calls fiction's "modal arc," the term accentuates the scientific subtext within a particular lineage of Victorian writing.[32]

By the dawn of the twentieth century, physics had emerged as a discipline organized around research on energy, ether, fields, and electromagnetism. *The Physics of Possibility* considers each of these subjects, while also affirming the eclectic scope of Victorian physical theories before "physics" began to find legibility with the unification of statistical mathematics and physical theories through the mid-1870s.[33] Beginning with an intensifying interest in probabilities around 1850, the arc of my book follows interlocking developments in astronomy, psychology, geology, evolutionary biology, chemistry, and thermodynamics, culminating in two related developments: the onset of formalist doctrines of art for art's sake in the 1880s and the rise of physics as a specialized research domain (marked, in no small part, by the opening of the Cavendish Laboratory in 1874).[34] Those events signal a growing disaggregation between the two cultures of science and literature, as the labors of scientific specialists became increasingly inaccessible to laypersons at the *fin de siècle*. But before our own modern demarcations between literature and science, I uncover a fascination with possible worlds infusing much mid-Victorian writing. By moving across subsequently bounded bodies of knowledge—"physical" sciences like astronomy and thermodynamics and "life" sciences like evolutionism and neuroscience—the following chapters locate the terms of modern scientific research within a wider distribution of mental and emotional habits in Victorian discourse.

A further word on mediation. In some cases, probabilistic concepts had overt outcomes in novels. In Thomas Hardy's *The Return of the Native* (1878), the dynamics of chance inform the novel's twisting, coincidence-riven plot, its minor moments of dice playing, even its choice of names like Diggory Venn. But it would be imprecise to say that science "shaped" fiction, or vice versa, in an unmediated suturing of concepts. Instead of positing a dialogic conversation between science and literature, I will be elaborating a more fluid model of network relations to theorize the development of ideas, intuitions, questions, and affective patterns. Such an approach accentuates how historical objects converge at a number of simultaneous scales and rhythms, with different intensities and directions of influence at once, encompassing fictional narratives no less than nonfictional writings, technologies, and institutions. This approach, which draws upon Bruno Latour's sociology of science, is integral to my purposes because the growth of probabilistic methods spanned myriad arenas—astronomy, chemistry, thermodynamics, physical psychology, and evolution—that had no independent claim to originating them. My method thus takes up Caroline Levine's suggestion, recruiting the philosopher Roberto Unger, to "see social life . . . as composed of 'loosely and unevenly collected' arrangements, 'a makeshift, pasted-together' order rather than a coherent system that can be traced back to a single cause."[35] For Levine, criticism's habit of interpreting texts through the search for foundational sources of influence has defused its potential to follow more collective chains of association between formal artifacts. The goal here is not to pinpoint the origin of textual meanings but rather to observe how a more massive set of associations is structured at a given moment. This book explores the potential of such an approach.

How did the probabilistic calculus come to invigorate the Victorian sciences? The first half of the book treats this question not by articulating a dialectical twinning of mathematics and physical science in isolation but by assembling a more holistic set of developments involving form, feeling, and historical experience in mid-Victorian culture. Chapter 1 examines a decisive historiographical debate in the late 1850s. Did mathematical models of probability lend themselves to deterministic conceptions of history or to conditional conceptions of what might have been? The chapter surveys a constellation of education manuals, scientific articles and monographs, and philosophical commentaries on this question and concentrates on Henry Buckle's *History of Civilization in England* (1857). One notable contribution from this moment, I show, was *Richard Feverel,* a narrative haunted by the perverse presence of "Miss Random" (155). Although the fitful form of George Meredith's novels has been cast as an aesthetic shortcoming, attributable to Meredith's impulsive experimentation, I begin from an alternative premise: *Richard Feverel*'s form builds upon counterfactual formulations of mid-Victorian science and mathematics. As the novel follows the shortcomings of Richard's maturation, it suspends the forward momentum of the plot in order to chronicle a spectrum of occluded potentials for desire, identity, and attachment that remain unrealized. Ultimately, Meredith's tale of failed formation opens out to a counterfactual history of the novel form, as a genre that might have been less complicit with Victorian injunctions of gender and desire. In lieu of depicting the hero's maturation toward an auto-telic adulthood, singular and inevitable, *Richard Feverel* figures a continuum of what Koselleck calls "superseded futures" and "futures past" that extend to the very act of reading the novel at hand.[36]

Chapter 2 locates the topos of arrested development in sensation fiction, focusing on the temporality of single sensations and perceptions. Although few today would dispute that the sensation novel was a genre of readerly acceleration, I reveal its counterintuitive implication in new statistical studies of postponement. My focus lies with Wilkie Collins's best-selling *Armadale* (1866). From the start, Collins's hesitating hero, Ozias Midwinter, fails to cultivate the virtues of masculine haste and assertive action that Anne-Lise François describes as a general cultural aim: the pursuit of "heroic, goal-oriented energies conditional on a call to permanent vigilance."[37] Instead of moving toward a terminal state of attention and passionate resolve, Midwinter's education in the senses leads him to stand back from the present and to cultivate a kind of negative capability. Precisely by learning to embrace his "effeminate hesitations," Midwinter comes to apprehend a nonunified present that teems with possibilities, a not-now in which the relations between the past, present, and future come to seem more malleable and open to negotiation.[38] I position this ideal within major astronomical and physio-psychological studies of postponement, showing how the novel mediates between them in its intuitions of a nonhomogeneous present. Never quite becoming an embodiment of convention, free and fully formed, Midwinter and his hesitations suggest more conditional counterworlds that make up a greater share of narrative interest.

The second half of the book turns to the two dominant Victorian sciences of evolutionism and thermodynamics and attends to theories of the community and population. Chapter 3 reads Dickensian melodrama through a central crux in Darwin's writings on moral and social transformation. Why did nonreproductive individuals—in particular, altruistic agents like worker ants—persist in communal settings, despite failing to leave lineages of their own? This issue, which seemed intractable in Darwin's formative years as a naturalist, encouraged him to imagine chance variation as a phenomenon loosened from isolated reproductive bodies; nonreproductive sexualities suggested that evolution could be best understood as a continuum of possibilities untied to individuals in the flesh. In resolving the problem of ethical nonreproduction, Darwin came to affirm the open potential for new socialities. This account lends precision to Elizabeth Grosz's claim that Darwin intimates "a future that is unknown in, and uncontained by, the present and its history."[39] More centrally, however, the chapter contends that Darwin's vision was anticipated in fictional form, focusing on Dickens's *Dombey and Son* (1848) and the novel's two beneficent bachelors, Sol Gills and Ned Cuttle. At the outset, Gills and Cuttle appear as minor foils in the tale of little Paul Dombey's maturation. But Paul's untimely death forecloses the plot of juvenile apprenticeship. Whereas readers may have anticipated a saga of his gradual reconciliation with the Dombeyan world of "competition, competition," the novel re-presents itself as a meditation on other possible social conditions.[40] *Dombey and Son* imagines in fiction what Darwin was still struggling to comprehend: through its nonreproductive altruists, it envisions the growth of alternative socialities rooted in fellow feeling.

While chapter 3 is a limit case, situated at the nascent boundaries between "life" science and "physical" science, the culminating chapter reads *Middlemarch* squarely within advances in thermodynamics, showing how statistical studies of energy animated Eliot's mature ethics and aesthetics. Of particular interest to Eliot was the second law of thermodynamics: the entropy law, which states that the sum total of unproductive energy always increases in the world. Whether energy is expended in work or only wasted, it is ineluctably lost to useful applications; its potential is diffused. In the late 1860s, when Eliot began planning *Middlemarch,* her acquaintance Maxwell proposed a major revision to the entropy law. The "law" of diffusion, he claimed, had statistical significance alone: it was a probabilistic statement about a huge number of molecules that could never be observed in isolation.

Historians often note that Maxwell's insights led to the birth of modern mathematical physics, but those insights also informed Eliot's crowning contribution to realism, *Middlemarch.* The statistics of diffusion—what the narrator calls "incalculably diffusive" influence—structure the novel's attention to the continuing circulation of unproductive social impulses (825). Even though Dorothea and Lydgate fail to make a measurable social contribution, their futile actions have unpredictable reverberations throughout the larger commons, as the novel figures through the rhetoric of diffusion. I situate these thematics within Eliot's later conception of art's inutility.

For while Eliot conceived of the novel as a genre uncoupled from "petty politics," in her narrator's words, she conceived it as also exerting diffusive influence on the total population (178). At the origins of the modern rupture between literature and science, Eliot imagined fiction's nonutilitarian value through scientific studies of lost energy, and in doing so, she made Maxwell's much-debated ideas into intelligible aspects of the novel.

Each chapter realigns major scientific writings with a canonical experiment in fiction, focusing on a range of marginal, often abased characters: lower-class men and women, sexual outcasts, bohemian bachelors and spinsters, criminals, and drifters. Meredith and Collins anchor their narratives of acculturation around a single protagonist, while Dickens and Eliot locate the individual in a larger field of relations. But each novelist takes the condition of obstructed development as a foundation for imagining other potential paths of becoming. Their works might be said to complicate the demand for formal resolution in narrative, the "desire for the end" that Brooks calls "narrative desire," often in light of discontinuous temporalities and untaken roads of growth (108). In various respects, they incorporate conventions of gothic and historical fiction, the compassionate marriage plot, domestic melodrama, and romantic epic. I approach these novels not as strict specimens of the bildungsroman, adhering to an essential set of codes, but as stories that draw upon a set of familiar tropes to particular and at times estranging effect. They invite us to understand the bildungsroman as a general pattern present within a range of fictional experiments, illustrating Caroline Levine's point that the collision between formal frameworks can create "instabilities" and "aleatory possibilities" through which other social worlds can be imagined.[41]

The privileged position of gender in my account is motivated by the logic of the novels. As fables of juvenile maturation, these novels narrate the hero's education in masculine and feminine norms and thus make questions of biological essentialism and constructionism inevitable. To what extent are gender identities innate or performed? Do behavioral norms have a somatic origin in the body and its morphological contours, or are they inculcated through social rituals, institutions, and codes of belief? How do familial, educational, legal, and religious structures regulate the formation of character—variously canceling, constraining, and fostering potentials for growth? My selection of novels extends the territory mined by feminist criticism on these questions. In addition to the leading female novelist of the period, George Eliot, I examine male novelists who cultivated an avant-garde aesthetics (Meredith), who positioned themselves as antibourgeois bohemians (Collins), and who valorized unconventional family arrangements (Dickens). Following their immanent critiques of the bildungsroman's conventionally male hero, my readings accentuate the play of alternative masculinities, while also attending to patterns of female formation in a period that often interrogated the patterns in question.[42]

The shaping force of scientific innovation also motivates my attention to gender. Innovations in the modern physical sciences, as Claire Colebrook has argued, lend themselves to antifoundationalist conceptions of gender, in that they invite an awareness of "difference and distance from already constituted images of life as necessarily fruitful, generative, organized, and human." Colebrook specifies a range of insights (including theories of genetic transmission, relativity, and quantum indeterminism) that she collectively calls "queer vitalism."[43] In her attention to the political efficacy of such postindividualist ideals, Colebrook's account runs parallel to my own. But because I aim to reconstruct nineteenth-century innovations in this vein, I prefer Huxley's term instead: "nebulous potentiality." With this phrase, Huxley sought to evoke the open-ended potential for "endless growth . . . through all varieties of matter."[44] Growth is virtual in that it entails a probabilistic process of transformations, spanning multiple *durées* and domains of life, where all roads need not lead to anthropomorphic adulthood, much less to inelastic configurations of gender or race. This virtual understanding of growth informs each novel I interpret, where developmental ruin results in a more recuperative vision of "difference and distance" from the given.

Yet multitudinousness—the accretion of possible plotlines, often occulted or foreclosed in novels—does not necessarily lead to a politics of liberation. That a work of fiction spins out a plurality of directions need not signal an investment in alternative possibilities for living or indicate their nonnormative configurations. To be clear, this book resists the temptation to wager claims about fiction's antidevelopmental torques in general. Its goal is more modest: to specify a certain prevailing Victorian tradition of novel writing that reconceived conventions of growth in tandem with new cosmological fascinations, and that articulated new "possibilities for moving through and with time," as Elizabeth Freeman puts it, "that counter the common sense of the present tense."[45] These novels strive to activate an awareness of liminality through the affective experience of reading, in narratives that define developmental norms *as* norms: as conventions that characters could avert (triumphally) or accept as natural (tragically) and that range tonally from staunch skepticism about the coherence of the past, present, and future to postures of uncertainty and aporetic bewilderment. Together, they invite readers to cultivate creative distance from, and alternatives to, the absolutism of the now.

PHYSICS BEFORE PHYSICS: "THE PHYSICAL SCIENCE OF THE FUTURE" IN VICTORIAN BRITAIN

Mid-Victorian intellectuals had no precise term to designate the relation between physical science and mathematics that we now call "physics," but a loose assortment of terms that bear retrospective resemblance alone: among them, mechanics, mechanical science, and natural history. The most common name for physics before "physics," natural philosophy, speaks to the metaphysical orientation of a science still dominated by polymaths and amateur savants. In 1850, the term "physics" was a linguistic newcomer in English, rarely seen except as a catchall for the sciences as a whole. The word "physicist" had entered English during the 1830s, at about the time William Whewell coined the term "scientist," but its invocations were likewise sporadic and loose.[46] While many Victorians believed themselves to be inhabiting a period of great innovation in studies on matter, energy, and force, the discipline of physics did not take hold until the last two decades of the century. Another gap between language and practice defined the statistics of probability. Then as now, the term "statistics" included all mathematical methods for representing diversely constituted collectives. Strategies for representing mass phenomena had been used in the physical sciences since the seventeenth century, but statistics was not a distinct domain in nineteenth-century Britain. By and large, Victorian thinkers did not view themselves as contributing to a coherent research tradition on probabilities; "pure" probability theory did not exist until long after the First World War.[47]

When I invoke the term "physics of possibility," it is to indicate a conceptual legacy that the Victorians largely built but still struggled to name. This was an unsystematic social physics: less a coherent program of knowledge than an informal lineage of discussion and debate encompassing the work of North British mathematicians, experimentalists, and engineers, professional researchers at universities, popular lecturers in London, lay journalists, and spiritualists.[48] These ties spanned the ascendant mathematical physics at Cambridge, promoted through grueling reforms to the undergraduate Mathematical Tripos degree in the 1820s and again at midcentury, and (to a lesser if still significant extent) the nonmathematical populist science of figures such as Michael Faraday, William Grove, and Tyndall at the Royal Institution. Leading lights such as Tyndall did not publish mathematically motivated accounts as did Maxwell, Sir William Rowan Hamilton, and Peter Guthrie Tait, and for their part, Maxwell and Tait rejected the determinism implicit in Tyndall's vision of mechanical relations, which seemed to leave little room for the autonomy of human thought, faith, and free will.[49] But thinkers without a strong mathematical disposition informed topics that were widely investigated in probabilistic terms and vice versa. Thermodynamic concepts, to take a classic illustration, found codification in the work of engineers and experimentalists like Julius von Mayer, James Joule, and Sadie Carnot in addition to mathematically minded contemporaries like William Thomson and Rudolf Clausius; all of these investigators inherited a legacy of Romantic *Naturphilosophie* that informed their simultaneous work on the energy principle around 1850, as Thomas Kuhn first observed.[50] With the appearance of Thomson and Tait's landmark textbook, *Treatise on Natural Philosophy* (1867), mathematical interpretations of energy, including probabilistic ones, began to assume an authoritative position in Britain—differentiated from experimental proofs on the subject but retaining the shared syntax and assumptions of investigators at midcentury (see chapter 4).[51] The boundaries between mathematical and nonmathematical modes of scientific research remained porous, as did the boundaries between science and the cultural mainstream more broadly.

As aspects of a still-modernizing culture of letters, physical scientific discoveries appeared alongside works of fiction and social commentary in family magazines, in technical journals and specialist forums, as well as in children's books and in public lectures at mechanics' institutes and at the Royal Institution. Insights into electromagnetism and thermodynamics by Faraday, Joule, and Thomson were welcomed as triumphs of middle-class accomplishment, attesting to the nation's privileged status as a world capital of industrialism. New university requirements helped to generate interest in natural philosophy and mathematics, as historians such as Andrew Warwick note, while scientific societies like the Statistical Society of London, the Lunar Society, the Society for the Diffusion of Useful Knowledge, and the British Association for the Advancement of Science gradually gained in prestige.[52] These tendencies found one point of culmination in 1874, with the opening of the Cavendish Laboratory at Cambridge. Its scientists included luminaries like J. J. Thomson, Ernest Rutherford, and later C. P. Snow, who returned to Cambridge to delineate the "two cultures" of literature and science in his 1959 Rede lecture.[53] By and large, however, high Victorian scientific innovations flourished within the mainstream. Natural theological accounts of God's cosmic plan proved influential long after the Bridgewater Treatises concluded in 1837, and amateur cultures of specimen collection continued to attract wide interest.[54]

Scholars often observe the residual power of Newtonian mechanics in nineteenth-century science. But what did Newtonianism mean to the Victorians? Newtonianism is a "classical" construction in that it assumes a stable, one-to-one correspondence between phenomena in the world and their representation. *Hypotheses non fingo,* as Newton vowed: I frame no hypotheses.[55] Every general law Newton introduced, it seemed, could be verified through observation. For a theory to fall short of perceptual verification would leave it speculative and therefore unscientific. The law of gravitation stands as a classic case in point. While Newton had arrived at it via highly rarefied mathematical calculations, it was validated by astronomer's direct observations on the heavens.

Of the myriad assumptions at work in Newton's clockwork cosmos, the most significant for the Victorians were two. First, Newton presumed an unseen universe of atoms and molecules that were absolutely uniform in nature: "matter" was composed of infinitely hard, point-like particles with the exact same size, mass, and volume. In addition, Newton proposed a strict dualism between objects (which were passive and unchanging) and forces (which were active and variable). The material world was inert, while forces like gravitation were dynamic and subject to change. These assumptions fueled the confident certitudes of Newton's vision: because the makeup of the world was more or less stable and uniform, one could anticipate all events higher up on the ladder of creation. So long as one knew the position and velocities of objects in a system at a given moment—the orbits of planets, stars, and comets—one could calculate their behaviors at any moment in history, leaving no room for the "possible."[56]

Newton's vision was widely sanctioned in Victorian appeals to providential design, nowhere more manifestly than in Babbage's *Ninth Bridgewater*

Treatise. "The track of every canoe," Babbage writes, "of every vessel that has yet disturbed the surface of the ocean, whether impelled by manual force or elemental power, remains forever registered in the future movement of all succeeding particles which may occupy its place" (114). For Babbage, "future movements" are planned out as ineluctable consequences of the present. The claim encompasses physical phenomena no less than human bodies and social life; cultural and social phenomena are implicated in the same historical plan for all atoms and particles. Babbage also draws here on studies such as Joseph Priestley's *The Doctrine of Philosophical Necessity Illustrated* (1777) and Pierre-Simon Laplace's *Philosophical Essay on Probabilities* (1801; trans. 1814), which elucidated this ideal in no uncertain terms: "All events, even those which on account of their insignificance do not seem to follow the great laws of nature, are a result of it just as necessarily as the revolutions of the sun," Laplace wrote.[57]

Even so, statements such as Babbage's were becoming hard to uphold, as it became more and more apparent that Newtonian cosmologies were premised upon an aporia. To enable its manifest powers of prediction, the foundations of reality had to be accepted as sui generis: what was "commonly taken" and "well known to all," Newton wrote (938). This was a growing problem among eighteenth-century skeptics. Intellectuals like Bishop Berkeley and David Hume noted the purely conjectural nature of Newton's particles, and of course departures from Newton's materialism were widely available in the two centuries leading up to the 1850s, including the theories of Baruch Spinoza, Gottfried Leibniz, and Immanuel Kant. In unique respects, each of these writers stressed that the somatic substrates of existence might be much more vibrant and fungible than scientists conventionally assumed.

With increasing insistence, Victorians like Michael Faraday and William Grove conceived the microcosmos in terms of shifting interrelations rather than of clear-cut monads. Consider Faraday's breakthroughs on field relations. Faraday, a rising star at London's Royal Institution in the 1830s, had wanted to investigate a recently noted phenomenon: when an electric current was fed through two coils of wire and then the wires were moved next to one another, an additional electric current could be detected. Faraday's ensuing experiments led to a curious finding. As the electrified wire was moved between magnets, or as a magnet was moved between wires, a measurable amount of electricity resulted. Faraday took these phenomena to be a sign of a superintending "field" between the objects. He suggested that objects were not passive building blocks that forces pushed and pulled at a distance; they created zones of influence in the space surrounding them: "lines of force" or "lines of influence," in Faraday's developing lexicon.[58] Eventually, these ideas led him to renounce the notion of point-like particles altogether. Proposing the "mutual penetrability of matter," he began to view space as a plenum filled with interpenetrating "powers": "centers of force" distributed throughout the universe and available at all places and times. Departing from the traditional categorical distinctions between things, actions, and places that structured Newton's world, Faraday's "centers of force" suggested the existence of phenomena that did not fit into those categories at all, and that possessed certain characteristics of each.[59]

The "correlations" in nature's economy were so often observed as to illustrate the totalizing drives that investigators intimated in their objects of fascination. As Mary Somerville wrote in the preface to her influential *On the Connexion of the Physical Sciences* (1834), "modern science" has begun to "unite detached branches [of knowledge] by general principles" such that "identity has been proved where there appeared to be nothing in common, as in the electric and magnetic influences."[60] She goes on to observe a shared sense of anticipation, even an "expectation," that the phenomena of light and heat "will ultimately be referred to the same agent" (1). Forecasts such as these proved accurate by the 1850s with the birth of thermodynamics. As with the theory of fields, energy science suggested energy's transformative potentials: the cosmos was an ongoing nexus of alterations, relays, and reconstitutions of matter and energy through time. These were processes of movement and remediation that could not be exhaustively predicted, reconstructed, or observed.

Such an account was presaged in Grove's best-selling *On the Correlation of Physical Forces* (1846), culled from his acclaimed lectures at London's Royal Institution in 1844. "For purposes of instruction or argument," Grove writes, "it may be convenient to assume isolated matter: many conclusions so arrived at may be true, but many will be erroneous."[61] Behind the appearance of "isolated" things in themselves stood a vibrant realm of force relations, since "no such isolation exists in reality" (14). Grove proceeds to imagine a cosmic ripple effect in which individual human thoughts, actions, and feelings circulate beyond acts of reciprocal recognition: "Wave your hand: the motion, which has apparently ceased, is taken up by the air, from the air by the walls of the room, &c., and so by direct and reacting waves, continually comminuted, but never destroyed. It is true that, at a certain point, we lose all means of detecting the motion . . . but we can indefinitely extend our power of detecting it accordingly as we confine its direction, or increase the delicacy of our examination" (22). Grove's thought experiment extends from circumscribed bodies to a collective chain of interrelations. Individuals can create fields of motion, interacting with other fields in the spaces between them. The individual's influence is "continually communicated" in a process linking hand, air, walls, and room, and it persists in "indefinitely" observable forms, but with no stable structure or end. Far from enshrining the body as a privileged locus of subjectivity, Grove locates it within a general economy of relations—a universal plenum of transfers, exchanges, gains, and losses. The sense of an ending, of final "cessa[tion]," is undercut by an awareness of indefinite potentials across time and place.

A new space was opening for possible worlds. In the details of their language, physical scientists such as Grove imagined processes of becoming untethered from foundational origins, and although he was unconcerned with probabilities and preceded programs of research on energy, Grove's lectures and writings helped to secure the foundations for later developments (see chapter 4). Subsequent natural philosophers—diverse British investigators including William Clifford, Balfour Stewart, Peter Guthrie Tait, and John Tyndall—stressed how energy reverberates in illimitable and unknowable directions over time. Their writings mark a turn to the representation of mass tendencies: in lieu of "isolated matter," one could imagine an ensemble of possible interconnections between individual things, actions, and locations at a given moment.

Indefinite, unpredictable, fleeting: implicitly, these terms departed from conventions of statistical thinking as well. Definite prediction and mass regularities had long defined ideas about the behavior of large numbers. Beginning in the 1820s, the power of statistical averages had captivated British audiences, as continental thinkers like Laplace reported surprising constancies in populations (including everything from the annual number of suicide rates, births, and deaths to letters lost in the mail). It was the iron law of averages that motivated Adolphe Quetelet's theories of the average man in the 1830s and 1840s.[62] Historians have traced the eroding emphasis on statistical averages to vanguard scientists later in the century: a handful of experts such as Maxwell and continental contemporaries who investigated the larger range of outliers or deviations from standard values. But these accounts have tended to understate the role of earlier scientists and intellectuals in fostering the assumptions that precede conceptual change. Thinkers such as Grove might not have identified themselves as contributing to this shift, but in imagining the erratic movement of matter, energy, and force, they nurtured what would later become prevailing patterns of thought.

These developments began to culminate through the 1860s and 1870s, when Maxwell published a series of landmark mathematical papers that translated theoretical accounts of energy into more rigorous mathematical form. In particular, he showed that thermodynamic laws—how hot bodies move to colder bodies over time, for example—amounted to a set of general probability statements about a huge number of actual atoms. As he put it in his 1873 "Molecules" lecture, "There is nothing inconsistent with the laws of motion in supposing that in a particular case a very different event might occur."[63] Interpretation is vertiginously suspended between mental and material possibilities. In investigating possible departures from the norm, Maxwell claimed to be considering more than mental fabrications, even though those departures had no clear correspondence with worldly phenomena.

By the late 1870s, Maxwell's contributions were hailed as groundbreaking discoveries, and they are now understood as a foundation for statistical mechanics.[64] Future scientific research, he proposed, should turn upon possible deviations from a norm, not the ontology of sui generis things: "The physical science of the future," he commented, might concern "the study of the singularities and instabilities, rather than the continuities and stabilities of things," a claim echoed by Francis Galton and others who agreed that subsequent scientists would explore possible deviations through time rather than the average condition of collectives.[65] Newton's world—the world of empirical essences and total prediction—was ceding to theories of possible worlds.

FICTION AND THE CALCULUS OF POSSIBLE WORLDS

As a genre whose cultural dominance seemed to be everywhere evidenced, the Victorian novel's conceptual functions ranged from the synthetic to the prefigural, often at once. Scientists such as Herschel, Maxwell, Tait, and Clifford flaunted their learning in unpublished poems and creative commentaries on literature, while writers of fiction exhibited an abiding interest in the physical sciences. One thinks of Dickens's justification of spontaneous human combustion, for example, and of scientific characters like Lydgate, Job Legh, and Swithin St. Cleeve. At times, I interpret granular allusions and characterizations in novels: Austin Feverel and his scientific "system" of education in *Richard Feverel* and the scientific professionals and amateurs that populate Eliot's and Collins's narratives. And when warranted by the archival record, I infer immediate biographical and textual connections as well. But because I wish to develop a thickened understanding of influence, I also observe less direct degrees of association, where the correspondences resist reduction to a prestanding source: shared questions, themes, and rhetorics that transcend individuals and circulate within a given intellectual habitus. What cultural mechanisms made for such diverse and occasionally oblique connections?

Several mechanisms involved the dynamics of popularization. Beginning around the 1860s, when it became possible to make a living through scientific journalism, writers like Grant Allen, T. H. Huxley, Henry Maudsley, and Herbert Spencer cultivated a mass market of educated readers who hungered to be both entertained and taught, as scholars such as Bernard Lightman have noted.[66] The proliferation of books, articles, stage shows, and lectures around this time amounts to something like what the historian of science Katherine Pandora describes as an "intellectual commons," in which "social and theoretical comment could circulate without regard for scientific propriety."[67] This was a commons that novelists and scientists shaped alongside lay popularizers, philosophers, historians, critics, and cultural commentators. The looseness of these categories reflects a premodern milieu in which terms and concepts could be broadly disseminated. And there were lower-level frequencies of connection as well: patterns of thought and feeling that comprised potential theories but began as preconceptual patterns of writing. When I talk about a common culture of letters, it is to account for this predisciplinary matrix of relations—direct and indirect, intentional and unintentional—in different kinds of writing.[68]

In testing this approach, my premise is that developments in one cultural arena need not always be isolated as a root source of influence on a text, where ideas move like billiard balls. Through the chapters to follow, I model an approach to fictional agency more consonant with Bruno Latour and recent critics including Eve Sedgwick, Sharon Marcus, Caroline Levine, and Rita Felski, who have called for less monological modes of historical interpretation. In their accounts, the search for a master source of influence behind a text (e.g., foundational structures like capitalism, empire, or the nation) has prevented scholars from discerning more capacious circuits of meaning, which are often legible on the surface of novels. Social formation is conceived here as an ongoing process of connections: nothing more or less than "the act and fact of association, the coming together of phenomena to create assemblages, affinities, and networks," as Felski writes, where novels "allow us to imagine the subtle unfolding activity of multiple social forms," in Levine's words.[69] The goal for the critic is to tease out these pervasive if fleeting associations, reassembling the multiple points of contact and disconnection that make up the social. The goal is *not* to heroically divulge a latent ideological impulse that organizes a text and defines its instrumental functions.

I will at times be interpreting modes of creative constraint (the effect of legal censorship and self-policing, for example, and of medical taxonomies of deviance), but for my purposes, I find calls to suspend suspicion useful in identifying the generative valances of what may look like textual absences or occlusions. "Nonhappenings"—alternatives to the constellated chain of events—emerge through this vantage as distinctive features of the Victorian novel, with positive moral and social content, rather than as symptoms of a lack: what is repressed or obfuscated due to ideological controls. As a study that does not aim at the inevitable demystification of novels, my book thus extends Sedgwick's ethos of reparative reading. Like later critics (Marcus, Levine, and Felski), Sedgwick proposes a more active attention to the wealth of affects and emotions elicited in texts instead of looking for their presumed participation in the construction of a normative modern subject. A reparative critic might decline a "strong theory" of subject formation, shown to operate again and again in texts, in favor of an attention to "additive and accretional" implications found in diverse objects of analysis. This approach informs my account of the bildungsroman's obstructed form in particular.[70] In the Goethean tradition most influential in nineteenth-century Britain, maturity tends to come with the individual's incorporation into an unbending social world; the heroes of Tobias Smollett, Henry Fielding, and Daniel Defoe learn to tame their juvenile impulses and accommodate themselves to the institutions of bourgeois adulthood after much pain and struggle. Through the movement to conjugal completion and occupational success, the individual emerges as a representative of his world (one working definition of *Bildung*), however tinged with an awareness that his distinctive desires have been compromised. The novels I study each evoke this tradition but bear closer affinities with the female bildungsromans of the Brontës, Eliot, and others whose heroines' ambitions are spurned. Each of the aspiring protagonists I interpret is a failure. Each is unable to master mid-Victorian codes of masculine action and self-control, and each is beset by irresolution in a period that defined frank sociability as a virtue. And in each novel, the subversion of the individual leads to an exploration of nonnormative potentials that crowd in on the plot, indicating ancillary lines of formation: what I have now provisionally defined as an aesthetic of possibility.[71]

To dream of possible worlds, in mid-Victorian culture, was often to dream of reconstituted class relations. Readers of Karl Marx and Friedrich Engels understood that alterity was much more than a subjective desire; alternatives to the present were latent within the dialectic of history, conceived as "the *real* movement which abolishes the present state of things."[72] That understanding continued influentially in Ernst Bloch's account of "real possibility," for example, in which Bloch theorized sites of utopian potential that were substantial and freestanding in our midst, and it persists in later discussions of potentiality. The writings I interpret bear affinities with these contributions; unlike them, however, they never consolidated into an explicit theoretical agenda that could be applied as a lens or optic on fiction. This book instead charts a tradition of representing possible worlds rooted in informal instances of formal experimentation, appearing as aspects of the novel that look like unpromising resources for thought.[73]

Dreaming becomes a more insistent desire—becomes a demand—when alternatives to the given come to seem materially immanent. *The Physics of Possibility* locates this tendency at the basis of Victorian natural cosmologies. For while the Victorians' assumptions about individual and social formation emerged in close connection with the physical sciences, critics and historians have yet to understand how what Huxley named "nebulous potentiality" informed their meanings.[74] The strategies I interpret often appear as "queer elements" in fiction, including static set pieces, multiplying minor characters, and associated instances of anachronism, asynchrony, ellipsis, and nonfocalization. Considered historically, however, those elements attest to a distinctive intellectual transformation, with significant ethical and aesthetic aims. Each chapter reconnects the form of Victorian fiction with that transformation in the physical sciences and mathematics.

CHAPTER 1

The Lost Futures of the Novel
Negated Potential in *Richard Feverel*

The difficult form of George Meredith's novels has long attracted adverse judgments. Victorian reviewers cast his fiction's fits and starts as by-products of creative abandon: a turbulence too lacking in the restraint that might contain their emotional energies and issue in more cohesive structures of narrative. An early review of *The Ordeal of Richard Feverel: A History of Father and Son* (1859) is representative. The novel's events pile up "at the expense of congruity and probability," Samuel Lucas writes, as the plot strains toward an anticlimactic end. Where we might have anticipated an account of final heroism and self-mastery, "it is pure accident that brings about the ending."[1] More recent critics have helped to soften these observations by pointing out the latent totalities of action buried beneath the surface of Meredith's prose. But it seems to remain the case that the stresses and strains of his fiction resist direct interpretation in themselves.[2]

Perhaps it is inexact, however, to read Meredith in these terms. *Richard Feverel*'s focus on "accident" *does* suggest a resistance to conventional trajectories of male development. But to look through the terms of "probability" might be to disregard some of the fundamental questions that his novels pose. In what sense do alternative possibilities stand as an actual ideal in his writing, actively challenging conventions of formation? How do they trouble the movement from juvenile indecision to knowledge, departing from the drives toward marriage, family, and vocation? My premise in this chapter is that "accident," in Meredith's fiction, becomes an aesthetic of storytelling that defies what the term often implies. To tell a story, it seems, is to order uncoordinated actions into coherent codes of meaning, turning the confusion of lived experience into a more harmonious plot. But such an understanding overlooks the specificity of probabilistic ideas in Meredith's milieu, when thinking about alternative temporalities emerged as an acute fascination. Meredith's deviations from design represent a strategic replotting of the bildungsroman through the counterfactual vocabularies and motifs of late-1850s British writing. This strategy served to revise conventions of sexual and social formation, articulating alternatives without upholding a single, master model in the end.

The present chapter reads Meredith's fiction within the discourse of *negated potential*, as I call it, in mid-Victorian culture: the feeling of possibilities that might have been, but never flowered into historical existence. Feelings of negated potential informed the writings of Victorian scientists, logicians, and mathematicians for whom the goal of the investigator was to express one's internal sense of historical difference. To represent the world in this way was to question the rigid realities of the present: What might have happened if the Goths hadn't vanquished Rome? What if Britain never emerged as a national formation? These thought experiments echoed across an influential lineage of writings that included Meredith's novel. By articulating a nested spectrum of negated potentials, Meredith recast the novel of formation as a tale of opportunities for what might have been.

The novel's temporal form had specific salience after the Obscene Publications Act of 1857. With its passage in the midst of *Richard Feverel*'s composition, the line between licit and illicit fictions was subjected to new state protocols of censorship, making the ideological norms of formation all the more rigidly enforced.[3] *Richard Feverel* reacts to these strictures by locating transgressive patterns of development in a field of negated pasts and futures. Ultimately, what might have happened for characters within the story issues in the larger question of what might have been for fiction proper. If the rise of the novel had helped to confirm conventional Victorian virtues— above all, the binary regimes of public and private labor, of masculine action and feminine passivity—then Meredith makes it clear that this state of affairs was far from given. While scholars have observed that discourses of the norm and deviation began to distinguish normal and deviant identities in late-Victorian culture, Meredith challenges precisely those taxonomies. He enlists the language of probability to suggest that desire is natural and prior to its cultural configurations and that attempts to constrain it will have tragic costs.[4]

A final terminological consideration. The language of probabilistic thinking, as I have said, remained somewhat porous in the decades before its emergence as an autonomous arena of research. I use the term "statistics" to designate large numbers. During the 1830s, statistics began to connote a quantitative social science, though the term was widely applied in the major physical sciences as well; there, it could mean any large number or technique used to interpret those numbers.[5] Further ambiguities inhered in "probability" and "chance." The former rose to prominence through the late eighteenth century, when Pierre-Simon Laplace introduced the phrase "calculus of probabilities" as an alternative to the "doctrine of chances." Laplace had hoped to make it clear that "probabilities" implied subjective states of belief or expectation, since "chance" had undesirable connotations of irreducible randomness. Yet the words appeared interchangeably in mid-Victorian Britain, creating confusion even among trained scientists. When I use the terms "probability" and "chance," I hope to clarify what was indicated in a given instance. The term "probabilism" and the phrase "the theory of probabilities" were used, increasingly in the early twentieth century, to talk about both subjective degrees of belief and objective randomness. I see no problem following this tradition, in keeping with the precedent of Theodore Porter and Ian Hacking.[6]

"WHAT WOULD OUR HISTORY HAVE BEEN?": A THEORY OF NONHAPPENINGS

The rise of a unified mathematics of chance was driven by an international republic of thinkers in France, Germany, and Belgium. These thinkers shared a conviction that supposed signs of unruliness could be tamed through the purity of numbers, revealing regularities throughout God's well-designed cosmos. By the first decades of the nineteenth century, their methods had become a shared source of intrigue in European letters. Often, writers used examples involving lotteries, gambling, and game playing, which lent specificity to their abstract mathematical models. Perhaps no example had a greater distinction, however, than Pierre-Simon Laplace's "demon," which was introduced in his *Philosophical Essay on Probabilities* (1801, trans. 1814). Drawn from a set of introductory lectures on the subject, the text sought to attract nonspecialist readers with a heuristic preface, in which Laplace conjured a being of infinite intelligence. He writes: "Given for one instant an intelligence which could know all the forces by which nature is animated and the respective situation of the beings who compose it—an intelligence sufficiently vast to submit these data to analysis—it would embrace in the same formula the movements of the greatest bodies in the universe as well as those of the lightest atom" (4). From its vantage of perfect perception, Laplace's being could represent the total history of the universe: "For it," he continues, "nothing would be uncertain and the future, as the past, would be present to its eyes" (4). Its "formula" is all-encompassing. But to imagine such an omniscient observer, for Laplace, was to conceive just what the probabilist was *not*. Whereas "nothing would be uncertain" to the demon, all things within "the future and the past" were uncertain to humankind. Our own formulas, he explains, entail the calculus of uncertainty. This point is intimated in the halting conditionals of Laplace's sentences, so distinct from the demon's unqualified confidence. The task of the scientist is to weigh the odds of alternative futures and pasts, so as to provide a reliably good guess about the truth of the real.

When Laplace introduced his thought experiment, the calculus of probabilities had already emerged as a ubiquitous continental concern. Major innovations followed from the work of Jacob Bernoulli, Thomas Bayes, and Abraham de Moivre, whose *The Doctrine of Chances* (1763) contained the first mathematical demonstration of probabilities. Linking these contributions was an elegantly illustrated point: a huge number of events, each haphazard in isolation, tended to resolve into the same bell-shaped distribution of averages. This eventually became known as the classical probability distribution but went under a collection of names at the time, including the "curve of chances" and the "error curve." It was revised and rechristened as the "normal curve" in 1809, in part because de Moivre termed its focal point the "norm"; modified versions of the formula appeared with the "personal equation" in 1823 (my focus in chapter 2), in Francis Galton's "correlation" theorem in the 1870s, and in Karl Pearson's subsequent "correlation coefficient."[7]

The earliest investigations placed chance in scare quotes: "chance" designated only one's degree of feeling, for example, that a balanced coin would land on its head or tail. "Chance," de Moivre wrote, "is a sound utterly insignificant: it imports no determination to any mode of existence." The meaning of chance lies in its absence of meaning: it "can neither be defined nor understood; nor can any proposition concerning it be either affirmed or denied, except this one, 'that it is a mere word.'"[8] The reticence of intellectuals like de Moivre helped to avoid religious ire. To affirm the insignificance of chance was to confirm that Providence really did have dominion over all atoms and forces, controlling "the movements of the greatest bodies in the universe as well as those of the lightest atom," as Laplace put it (4). So chance was born out of its emphatic erasure as a topic: that which is meaningless cannot be opened to debate.

But the subjective model of chance was unsettled not long after its introduction. As a calculus of feelings, the subjective model made sense as applied to a finite set of outcomes: one's level of anticipation about the potential outcome of a tossed coin or rolled die. Beginning in the last decades of the eighteenth century, however, investigators discovered that the formulas used to represent those topics could also be used to treat more complicated issues in the physical sciences: the uncertain location of a single star, the rotation of the Earth, the movements of a molecule. The probabilities used to represent these physical phenomena had no relation to one's level of anticipation or belief about them. And yet the subjective model endured on increasingly brittle grounds. For while the model was incoherent as applied to these phenomena, no undisputed alternative emerged to supplant it. The collapse of the subjective view was left implicit until the close of the nineteenth century and was noted only then by thinkers like C. S. Peirce at the edge of the mainstream.

We may locate the first stages of this transition among astronomers during the 1780s. To find the position of a star or other object in space, a team of observers would take measurements through the crosslines of a telescope. Individual measurements were often varied (due, it was thought, to mechanical fluctuations, discrepancies in vision, and varying degrees of skill). But astronomers discovered that the same mathematical methods that de Moivre had used to find a norm could also be used to find the most probable position of objects in space. The discovery was announced by Laplace, in what came to be called "astronomer's error law." In the decades to follow, Laplace extended the error law into numerous social and scientific topics, ranging from annual birth rates to average temperatures and patterns of rainfall. But in introducing these findings, he claimed to be merely manipulating general frequencies; his probabilities were not to be understood as tied to material realities. They were abstract ratios with no indexical correspondence to the world. When he rechristened the mathematics of "chance" as the "calculus of probabilities," it was to underscore this point. Yet those terms assumed an unruly life of their own. By the 1830s, scientists such as Siméon Denis Poisson returned to the distinction between "chance" and "probability" to assert that statistics dealt with both chance *and* probability, both subjective aspects of the mind and objective features of the world.[9] Frequencies were spilling out everywhere into the world that Poisson and others sought to comprehend.

These continental breakthroughs reached England in incremental fashion. Scholars have argued for the influential impact of the Belgian astronomer Adolphe Quetelet in early Victorian discourse, although there are reasons to nuance this picture.[10] By the mid-1830s, Quetelet had developed a sweeping positivist philosophy rooted in the astronomer's error curve. Building on Laplace's insights, he used new statistical information—including annual rates of birth, death, and crime alongside demographic data on weights and heights—to posit what he called the "average man." The average man was the superintending Platonic form of a given race; for Quetelet, individual human beings were to be understood as "errors" or deviations from the transcendent golden mean. Quetelet's theories were widely discussed in France and Belgium and occasioned more than one English translation in the 1830s and afterward. Still, his average man had less immediate force in British settings, in part because Britain had neither a long-standing archive of demographic data nor an educational system structured around mathematics. An added barrier was the tradition of British natural theology, which affirmed a direct appreciation of God's clocklike cosmos. Charles Babbage had famously tried to reconcile religion with chance in his *Ninth Bridgewater Treatise,* as we saw in the introduction; for Babbage, what looked like "chance" should be understood within a larger pattern of providential design. Still, most British theologians insisted on the direct apprehension of God's contrivances and understood "uncertainty" as dangerously close to unbelief.

To address this perceived paucity of understanding, a loose community of British intellectuals undertook to introduce the mathematics of probability to a growing middle-class reading market.[11] Among them were respected polymaths including Augustus De Morgan, John Lubbock, and John Elliot Drinkwater Bethune. For these thinkers, as Porter writes, "it was evident that England had fallen far behind France in probability theory and it would be a great achievement simply to introduce it."[12] Without wanting to make a theoretical breakthrough of their own, they extended the arcane formulas of mathematicians into a wider class of social and philosophical issues. In doing so, they consistently ignored Quetelet's focus on the average man and on normal social states and instead stipulated how probabilism could extend readers' ethical and emotional capacities for tolerating other viewpoints. The formal models of mathematicians in this sense provided a tool for what Elaine Hadley calls "liberal cognition": they offered a portable *form* of thinking about dissonant viewpoints, histories, and habits of living, but with no innate ideological content.[13]

Foremost among these writers was John Herschel, whose extended essay on probabilities appeared in the *Edinburgh Review* in 1850. Like Laplace, Herschel begins by imagining a mode of perfect perception: "In the contemplating mind," he begins, "the past and the future are linked by a bond as indissoluble as that which connects them in their actual experience" (1). There is no such thing as historical contingency: here Herschel understands the causal chain between events in the past, present, and future as absolute. What we call "chance" reflects no more than the inadequacies of human observation. "Chance" is "an internal feeling . . . drawn from the inward consciousness of our nature" (1–2). From this inaugural psychological position, however, Herschel's language evokes a more material point of view. He writes: "In fact the *non-happening* of an event is in itself an event; and in the case of a balanced state of mind this event is held to be as probable as the other; so that the unit of certainty must be taken as equally divided between them. In reference to this state of neutrality, then, the words 'probable' and 'improbable' present a meaning" (4). How can a nonhappening exist? Ostensibly, Herschel's point is that the mind makes sense of phenomena in negative terms: think of an event, and you must inevitably think of other outcomes. A disposition toward the counterfactual seems to be built into psychic life itself. But the parallel form of Herschel's syntax defines nonhappenings as *more* than subjective features of the mind: they have the weight of ontological events in themselves, so that "happenings" and "nonhappenings" become mutually constitutive categories. In essence, deviations define the norm and vice versa.

The question remains, then: How can what never happened have a claim to exist? This question, the paradigmatic condition of fiction, leads Herschel to stray from his intended interest in Quetelet. For while Quetelet had argued that "deviations and anomalies" are erroneous echoes of "the normal state," Herschel continues to define deviations—nonhappenings—in more substantive terms.[14] "An average," Herschel writes, "gives us no assurance that the future will be like the past." Contra Quetelet, he stresses that an average cannot dictate the shape of things to come. "All the philosophical value of statistical results depends on a due appreciation of this," he writes (23).

So an article that began by championing the rule of the average elicits an antithetical implication. Probabilism's "philosophical value" lies in an awareness that the future might depart from the conventions of the past.

Our psychic pull toward other futures and pasts, which so fascinates Herschel, was worked out as a topos of statistical studies before and after him in Britain. Notable among them were Augustus De Morgan's article-length encyclopedia entries and two full-length monographs on probability: his *Treatise on Probability* (1835) and subsequent *Essay on Probabilities* (1838), which were among the most influential British contributions before John Venn's *The Logic of Chance* (1866). Like Herschel, De Morgan had risen to the upper echelon of the Royal Astronomical Society in the 1830s, although he devoted some of his most mature efforts to mathematical and philosophical concerns.[15] De Morgan was quick to point out the moral benefits of his subject. Studies in probability encouraged a liberal recognition of other perspectives, training one to explore how disparate individuals think and feel. He gives an illustration drawn from the centuries-old topic of jury verdicts, which J. S. Mill and others had helped to make fashionable again:

> And thus we see that the real probabilities may be different to different persons. The abomination called intolerance, in most cases in which it is accompanied by sincerity, arises from inability to see this distinction. A believes one opinion, B another, C has no opinion at all. One of them, say A, proceeds either to burn B or C, or to hang them, or imprison them . . . according to what the feelings of the age will allow; and the pretext is, that B and C are morally inexcusable for not believing what is true. Now substituting for what is true that which A believes to be true, he either cannot or will not see that it depends upon the constitution of the minds of B and C what shall be the result of discussion upon them. (7–8)

Even the most sincere intentions can be blinded by custom and habit; individuals are all imprisoned by intolerance, in that what one "believes to be true" is too seldom separate from the "feelings of the age."[16] Criminals (B and C) hold decidedly different opinions from their judge (A), but the judge is no better arbiter of justice, since his perspective is also mired in inherited dogmas. The predicament can be resolved through an education in probabilistic reason, De Morgan suggests. As a practice of overcoming one's perceptual limits, it suspends the search for objective truth in order to weigh different degrees of belief (what A, B, and C believe in relation to one another). Here the mathematician acts as does a writer of realist fiction: the probabilistic mind moves between different centers of consciousness, comparing and collating isolated viewpoints en route to a more sympathetic vision of the whole.

Thus the limitations of legal controls can be remedied by an ethics of other-mindedness, where varied opinions on testimonial evidence, proof, penalties, and rights can be assembled—an ideal that structures Meredith's novel as well. This ideal of moral edification extends to De Morgan's account of social and historical knowledge, where he writes: "Human knowledge is, for the most part, obtained under the condition that results shall be, at least, of that degree of uncertainty that arises from the possibility of their being false. However improbable it may be, for instance, that the barbarians did not overturn the Roman Empire, we do not recognize the same sort of *sensible certainty* in our *moral certainty* of the fact which we have in our knowledge that fire burns, or that two straight lines do not enclose space" (3). Certain physical realities—the burning of a flame, the nature of geometric space—are a priori, while social and historical realities remain uncertain. In keeping with Herschel, for De Morgan the intelligibility of human history depends upon an awareness that our own world might have been otherwise. And as for Herschel, happenings and nonhappenings become conceptual equivalents: our understanding of the fall of Rome is limned by the surreal prospect of its survival. If this looks like a sensationalist case, then De Morgan's point is that it typifies how we understand historical realties in general. Such divergent paths provide clarifying contrasts in the absence of total knowledge and yield relational representations of the world.

What degree of realism can be attributed to these nonhappenings—how do they relate to the material record of history? "Probability," De Morgan writes in his preface, "is the feeling of the mind, not the inherent property of a set of circumstances" (7). The subjective model of probabilities could not be more evidently expressed. And yet the unfurling logic of his argument creates ambiguities at odds with the thesis of historical determinism. He writes: "That fire *does* burn is more certain than the account of the fall of Rome: that fire yet to be lighted *will* burn may or may not be more certain than the historical fact, according to the temperament and knowledge of the individual. And thus we begin to recognize differences even between our (so called) *certainties;* and the comparative phrases of more and less certain are admissible and intelligible" (3). De Morgan has no wish to reason that historical processes are uncertain. His intention is to say something like the opposite: the historical chain of causes and effects is unbending, as certain as all other ontological facts (e.g., that fire burns). But the dizzying conditionals—what "is" and "may be or may not be," what "shall be" and what is not necessarily so—have the effect of obscuring this point, inviting implications that De Morgan would hardly recognize as his own. The fall of Rome might be uncertain not because of the subjective nature of historical understanding but because history is undetermined in essence. While committed to the idea that probabilities are just a state of mind, De Morgan's comparative phrasings cast them in a more material register as the treatise continues. What we might call *semisubstantial* possibilities press up against the world where fire burns and empires fall.

The image of "fire yet to be lighted" captures the warp and woof of a British tradition that had no self-declared experts, à la Laplace or Quetelet in France and Belgium, but that was gathering a deal of popular steam. These writings complicate the notion of a linear progression of ideas moving from science to the lingua franca. In Britain, the work of popularization preceded the onset of a specialized scientific labor force, so that habits of probabilistic thinking were woven into a shared lineage of social and historical thinking from the start. I pause over this fact in order to understand one of the great publishing sensations of the 1850s: Henry Buckle's *History of Civilization in England* (1857–61). The outpouring of ripostes to Buckle, which appeared at the time of *Richard Feverel*'s composition, gave new urgency to the counterhistorical cadences in Herschel's and De Morgan's prose. Presenting himself as Quetelet's British heir, Buckle posited that social progress followed from demonstrably probabilistic rules. These rules were embodied by what he called "the law of averages." Buckle's most notorious example was suicide. Far from a sign of individual deviance, self-annihilation was "a necessary consequence" of "the general condition of society."[17] Like Laplace's demon, he claimed to follow all historical causes and consequences: just as the demon's "formula" could comprehend each force in the past and future, Buckle's calculus of averages promised a total vision of society.

Such was his often-noted ambition at least. Readers of the periodical press could hardly avoid Buckle's book in the late 1850s, which reviewers recommended as "the most important work of the season."[18] During this time, it provided a substantial touchstone for the British intelligentsia—

among them, George Eliot, G. H. Lewes, John Stuart Mill, Thomas Babington Macaulay, Charles Darwin, and Walter Bagehot. But what linked these
writers was the intense skepticism of their reactions.[19] Major intellectuals
including John Acton, James Fitzjames Stephen, Goldwin Smith (named Re-
gius Professor of History at Oxford in 1858), and Lewes launched biting critiques of Buckle's methods. Acton published an 1858 review for the *Rambler*
in two parts.[20] The "law [of probability] is a law of numbers," Acton wrote,
"but not implying any force, or cause, or reason why the things themselves
should be thus rather than otherwise."[21] What we call the "law" of probabilities has no prescriptive function regarding how things must be. Statistical
regularities could be observed throughout the world, but the potential for
different distributions of events—for a timeline that is "otherwise"—is not
foreclosed as a consequence.

In rejecting the thesis of determinism, of an unalterable historical chain,
Acton asserts what had been implied beforehand: the counterhistorical
worlds of the past and future are more than figments of the mind. The point
merits our attention because it resonated through a set of associated observations on the matter. One of the most influential was an article written
by the liberal philosopher James Fitzjames Stephen. Stephen worked with
the same ideas and language of Acton's response, first in a long 1858 review
article for the *Edinburgh Review,* followed by an essay in the *Cornhill Magazine*
shortly afterward.[22] Mill praised the latter in his revised edition of the *System
of Logic* (1843) as "the soundest and most philosophical" of the responses to
Buckle's positivism.[23] As Stephen explained in his first article, a "scientific
view of history, therefore, would be one which would show how and why
all human affairs have happened as they did and not otherwise" ("Buckle's
History" 465). But that view cannot be substantiated through probabilistic
methods, which are rooted in just such signs of an "otherwise." So Stephen
turns Buckle's historicism on its head and gives an example drawn from the
fall of the Napoleonic empire: "How different would the face of Europe be
now from what it actually is, if Nelson had been gratified in his wish of meeting Napoleon on a wind. It is very easy to say that Napoleon was the product
of circumstances, and that if he had been shot they would have produced
another. We very much doubt the fact. It is another form of the old fallacy
that, after throwing all the other throws on the dice, you have a better chance
of throwing sixes than you had at first" (500). Stephen invokes the Battle of
Trafalgar, an ur scene in the British national imagination, to develop a less

linear account of the counterhistorical. Buckle had cast Napoleon as an expression of average social conditions, such that his premature death would have given rise to an exact equivalent. But for Stephen, that view reflects what is known as the gambler's fallacy, where the outcome of one dice roll is thought to influence the next. The error is obfuscating because it blocks our recognition of other temporalities: had Nelson and Napoleon met at sea, we might be living in a different world system, Stephen suggests. The end of the Napoleonic Wars was not preordained, and although Britannia turned out to rule the waves, its victory was far from guaranteed.

The assumption of homogeneous time—time as an unbroken unity of events—is presented as inability to grasp the plenitude of alternate routes between the past and future. Stephen lingers over a range of them. "History is full of such examples," he writes and evokes worlds without the Roman Empire, the British civil wars, the Napoleonic regime, or the United States (501). The counterhistories of Herschel's and De Morgan's work have moved to the cultural limelight. Yet the referential status of those worlds has altered as well. Through the very vehemence of the reaction to Buckle, mid-Victorian commentators represented alternate histories in more material terms than their predecessors. Even when earlier writings ran counter to the subjective model, they did so without the authors' intention, through the play of rhetorical ambiguities and inconsistences. But for Stephen and others writing in the late 1850s, probabilities had an unmistakable kind of ontological heft. Stephen's counterworlds are situated between the material and the merely mental, what is real and "otherwise." "What might our history have been?" he asks.

So instead of a distinct movement of ideas from science into culture, at this moment one observes a network of multitiered associations, direct and indirect, collaborative and critical, also including ideas from scientific popularizers, philosophers, historians, and cultural commentators: what Latour calls a "trail of *associations*" across the developing social field.[24] Theodore Porter notes that "it is far from clear that Darwin or Comte was discussed with greater urgency" than Buckle around this moment.[25] Taken together, we can understand these writings as advancing a new metahistorical sensibility in Britain: a "poetics of history" that resisted the notion of a single, undeviating causal chain.[26] It has become a historiographical truism that "to write history according to the conventions of a novel or play," as Niall Ferguson suggests, is "to impose a new kind of determinism on the past: the teleology of the traditional narrative form."[27] Ferguson has in mind the forward-looking logic of narrative (whether fictional or nonfictional), in which the meaning of individual incidents is to be found in a conclusion set up all along. Paul Ricoeur, in a similar vein, defines the "ultimately narrative character of history" in terms of "the temporal unity of the whole."[28] But what of histories that flout the terminal logic of plot—what narrative forms do they underwrite?

An answer can be gleaned in the poetics of Victorian fiction—specifically, in the fiction of George Meredith, who was richly implicated in this milieu. As a practicing poet and essayist before turning to the novel, Meredith cultivated ties with writers such as Lewes and Eliot, both of whom vocally critiqued Buckle.[29] Several of his earliest poems appeared in the journal Lewes cofounded with Thornton Leigh Hunt, the *Leader,* while Eliot reviewed Meredith's 1856 romance, *The Shaving of Shagpat,* twice (for the *Leader* and the *Westminster Review*). Meredith assumed Eliot's regular reviewing duties for the *Westminster Review* by the October 1857 number, which contained a twenty-four-page critique of Buckle's volume, and his work continued to appear in the *Fortnightly Review* and *Cornhill Magazine* through the next decade.[30] He could hardly have avoided the acute censures of Buckle's work when he began to draft *Richard Feverel* in August of 1857.

The poetics of Meredith's novel, as we shall see, give expression to the shifting form of historical possibilities in mid-Victorian Britain: neither quite physical nor metaphysical, they appear at the impossible crossroads between both domains. But the technical decision to represent alternative possibilities was also, for Meredith, a personal and vocational decision. It marks a turn from the juvenilia of his earliest experiments in fiction to the accomplished antiaesthetics of *Richard Feverel.* As Meredith's first full-length novel, *Richard Feverel* reflects an anxious attention to the weight of the literary past, conjuring up conventions of development under fiery protest, in the key of ironic inversion and pastiche. These problems of literary paternity were recapitulated in Meredith's personal affairs. Like Sir Austin Feverel, Meredith had just seen the birth of his firstborn son with Mary Ellen Meredith in 1858; and, like Sir Austin's wife, she eloped with a family friend shortly thereafter, leaving Meredith to raise the child in isolation during the earliest stages of his novel. His son was less than a year old when its third and final installment was published in July of 1859. In keeping with the inhibited idealist of Meredith's sonnet sequence, *Modern Love* (1862), the fictional husband endures the collapse of his marriage in terms that call for an autobiographical reading, so that the alternate lives within the text extend to Meredith's own. Thus understood, *Richard Feverel* appears as an extended meditation on alternative social imaginaries, the forking paths through which we must make sense of the real. The feeling that our world is incomplete, ringed with something other than what is the case: this "feeling of the mind" became central to Meredith's vocation as a professional male novelist.[31]

THE KINGDOM OF "MIGHT-HAVE-BEEN": *RICHARD FEVEREL'S* COUNTERLIVES

Richard Feverel's plot takes an elliptical form. The tale begins after the departure of Sir Austin's wife; spurred by his hatred of women, he invents an all-encompassing program of education for his son, Richard, which stipulates the child's isolation from the opposite sex until adulthood. What Sir Austin calls the "system" proves effective until the adolescent Richard falls in love with a neighboring farmer's relation, Lucy Desborough (16). Sir Austin forbids the two to meet again and sets out to find an aristocratic wife for him. Upon learning of their clandestine marriage, Sir Austin disowns him. Left without his father's counsel, Richard is soon snared in a seduction plot when an acquaintance, Lord Mountfalcon, becomes infatuated with Lucy. Mountfalcon hires a prostitute named Bella Mount to seduce Richard so that he, in turn, can court Lucy without the threat of discovery. After accepting Bella's advances, Richard is too ashamed to see Lucy and their newborn son. The story resolves when Richard discovers Mountfalcon's scheme and challenges him to a duel. Neither man is killed, but the shock sends Lucy to her death.

As an ironic reworking of the bildungsroman, the novel sets up an arc of male maturation only to bend the temporalities of growth, building a curve of alternative masculinities that never find fruition. That arc is identified with Sir Austin's "system," which recalls influential theories of childhood development from Jean-Jacques Rousseau, Herbert Spencer, and the physiologist William Acton. Sir Austin believes that the system will grant him immaculate control over Richard's social and sexual development. Followed to the end, it should produce a "perfect man" (17): an archetype of Victorian virility who will embody the ideals of marriage and aristocratic gentility that Sir Austin sees as threatened.[32] A "perfect man" is Sir Austin's norm, an Archimedean mean that can be engendered through perfect parenting. In contrast to this expected end, however, the story makes uncertainty—the play of other outcomes and unforeseen events—into a privileged ideal, showing Sir Austin's desire for foresight to be in bad faith. The subtitle, "A History of Father and Son," thereby becomes a red herring: the meaning of what happens follows from a wider continuum of lost opportunities snatched back from the realm of enacted events. Offering an ethics of difference without transcendence, change without redemption, Meredith follows the traces of negated potential until they emerge as a central locus of interest, offering an iconoclastic response to the traditional novel and the terms that defined its cultural power in Britain.

These narrative negations unfold from the opening pages, when the system is introduced in light of its possible alternatives. Sir Austin consults a local physician named Dr. Clifford in chapter 2:

> Dr. Clifford inquired whether it was good for such a youth to be half a girl? Whereat Sir Austin smiled a laugh . . . [and] went into scientific particulars which would reduce the reader to greater confusion than it did the Doctor. They then fell upon the question of Richard's marrying.
>
> "He shall not marry till he is thirty!" was the Baronet's Spartan Law.
>
> "He need not marry at all," said Dr. Clifford. "Birth and death are natural accidents: marriage we can avoid."
>
> "On my system he must marry," said the Baronet, and again . . . entered into scientific particulars. (40)

For Sir Austin, "accidents" are anathema to the system, which promises to make marriage as obligatory as "birth and death." But behind his confidence stand the multiple and contested bases of gender. Richard's limited interactions with women might make him "half a girl" rather than "a perfect man" (17), less masculine rather than more so. Sir Austin's allusion to "scientific particulars" only exacerbates this point and generates "greater confusion" about the categories under consideration. Casting uncertainty over Sir Austin's claim that "he must marry," the exchange opens out to the primacy of "accidents" in Richard's development, reminding readers that the plot "need not" end in a romantic contract. As a gentleman amateur at the time of Richard's childhood, set in the 1830s, Sir Austin is ignorant about the emergence of probabilistic reason, which was challenging "our (so-called) certainties," as De Morgan put it, just as he tries to uphold them.[33]

Such scenes of negated possibility find emblematic expression in chapter 7, which moves the action into London at twilight. A man, just in from the countryside, wanders in search of his hotel. The streets are dense with the voices and bodies that make up the expanding metropole, overwhelming his senses with "the shops, the shows, and the bustle of the World" (137–38). As the man is plunged deeper into the gathering crowd, he comes face to face with his own "living past": "He had almost forgotten how to find his way about, and came across his old mansion in his efforts to regain his hotel. The windows were alight; signs of merry life within. He stared at it from the shadow of the opposite side. It seemed to him he was a ghost gazing upon his living past. And then the Phantom which had stood there mocking while he felt as other men—the Phantom now flesh and blood Reality seized and convulsed his heart and filled its unforgiving crevices with bitter ironic venom" (138). This is the vision of Sir Austin as he scours England for a woman worthy of his son's hand in marriage. Despite his devotion to the task at hand, the point of the scene is that Sir Austin might have been another man. The gaze through a windowpane is a look into another life, recalling the narrative set pieces that Charles Dickens popularized earlier in the 1850s. Like Ebenezer Scrooge, in the preternatural visions of the *Christmas Stories* (1852), Sir Austin's position outside is juxtaposed to a separate sphere of domestic warmth and conviviality as the elderly bachelor bears witness to his lost felicity. In an inversion of the Dickensian archetype, however, here it is Sir Austin who becomes a "ghost" while "the Phantom" assumes "flesh and blood reality" in his stead. What is terrifying about this moment, for Sir Austin, is the shock of recognition, though it is not self-recognition per se. Rather, the scene turns upon the phantasmic power of one's other lives, registering an awareness of how those specters might overwhelm the individual, "seiz[ing]" and "convuls[ing]" one's sense of a singular life (138). The historian J. C. D. Clark sees such voided possibilities as characterizing the low-level allure of nostalgia. "The theoretical structure of nostalgia may be little more than an awareness of options not taken and potentialities never realized," Clark writes.[34] But in Sir Austin's glance through the window, reminiscence about what never happened leads to unsettling, vertiginous terror. "In the morning," notes the narrator, "he remembered that he had divorced the World to wed a system, and must be faithful to that exacting Spouse" (139). The language of that observation only intensifies what was lost, preserving a sense of forsaken happiness. In the act of repudiating his counterlives, he calls attention to the unnecessary nature of what drives him: the search to find a "Spouse" for his son.

Different distributions of character and context such as this—what I have termed ensemble effects—coincide with the counterhistories of "agents, arrangements, and motives" that scientists such as Herschel had imagined.[35] But the novel explores the emotional and ethical significance of those investigations in fiction and *as* fiction. They cast a long shadow over the plot, often in the tenor of longing and lament. In chapter 4, for example, the narrator draws on Dr. Clifford's rhetoric of "accidents" to retroject another past for Richard and those connected to him: "Very different for young Richard would it have been had Austin [Wentworth] taken his right place in the Baronet's favor: but Austin had offended against the Baronet's main crotchet: . . . to ally oneself randomly was to be guilty of a crime before Heaven greater than the offense it sought to extinguish; and he had heard that his nephew was the one seduced" (32–33). Uncle Wentworth's affair with his mother's serving woman typifies the kind of "randomly" created connection that the system aims to prevent. Conceived as a moment of sexual weakness, Wentworth's offense is an offense against Victorian codes of masculine self-containment. This is an unpardonable transgression for Sir Austin, who consequently denies Wentworth's "right place" as tutor to Richard. But in the act of observing this denial—the father's prohibition against random relations—the novel opens up a spectral alternative to the plot, in which the morally benevolent Uncle Wentworth would have helped to guide Richard's education. A more desirable state of affairs is impressed into another past, shaping the reader's sense of misgiving when we finally meet Wentworth's substitute, the self-serving Adrian Harley.

Nowhere are these hybrid temporalities more manifest than in the scene in which Richard meets Lucy Desborough, the farmer's niece whom he later marries. The threat of a random alliance, in the cautionary fable of Uncle Wentworth, emerges here as the defining feature of Richard's development. Framed as a carefully contrived romantic pastoral, the scene breaks from the novel's satirical tone beforehand. But if the idiom seems disjunctive, then the disruption serves precisely to mark the chapter as an anomaly, offering a glimpse into a world never to be coherently realized. "Had she stood before Sir Austin among rival damsels, that Scientific Humanist, for the consummation of his System, would have thrown her the handkerchief for his son," the narrator writes, "and could Sir Austin have been content . . . he might have pointed to his son again, and said to the world, 'Match him!'" (129–30). The odd but fitting term "Match" ironically reframes Sir Austin's wishes to find a good match for his son: Sir Austin proceeds in search of prospective partners for Richard; the novel proceeds in search of lost versions of Richard himself. This train of backward glances culminates in a turn to Shakespearean romance, revealing the mismatch between the potential for happiness and its negation.[36] "If the two were Ferdinand and Miranda," the narrator says, "Sir Austin was not Prospero, and was not present, or their fates might have been different" (130). The conditional inflections of the passage serve to lengthen, at the level of narrative discourse, what appears as an abbreviated instant in the plot, when Austin rejects Lucy and Richard's love. For Sir Austin, the system is given greater importance than the happiness of his son, so that he misses what should be the culminating event of his fatherhood.

As the signs of negated possibility mount in *The Ordeal of Richard Feverel*, the "ordeal" of the title is loosened from its initial meaning, becoming contrary to what Sir Austin assumes. At first glance, the term refers to the inward sexual struggle that Sir Austin believes all Feverel males must endure: a cryptic "trial" that ends either in conventional manhood or its undoing (41). And yet, Richard's "ordeal" is shown to be the ordeal of masculine development itself. It refers to the ideological injunctions of gender that he learns to accept to his detriment. "Had he not been bred to believe he was born for great things?" the narrator asks. "He saw himself caracoling on horseback . . . in the cavalry overriding the wreck of empires," the narrator later comments (458). Rather than setting up Richard's emergence as a free and fully formed man, these fantasies tip toward tragic self-dissolution; his pursuit of manliness leads to his seduction by Bella Mount and the final duel that seals his fate. As U. C. Knoepflmacher writes, "By falling back on his notions of heroism and honor, [Richard] escapes the harder task of reconciling himself to his own faults."[37] And if he "shows himself to be his father's son" (124), then the lesson of his education is that this need never have happened.

The problem of failed formation was widely theorized in medical circles through the 1850s, as Sally Shuttleworth and Sven-Johan Spanberg have written. Commentators like William Acton warned that adolescent intercourse and masturbation might block the passage from youth to adulthood, arguing in 1857 that "the premature development of the sexual inclination" in a male child could spell out "danger to his dawning manhood."[38] Yet such contingent conceptions of gender also animated Victorian discussions of probability in less anxious fashion. As James Fitzjames Stephen wrote in 1858, "One man's choice depended on the improvement of a single opportunity which, if lost, would never have recurred. If William had not conquered England, there is no sort of reason to suppose that any one of his sons would have done so. If, therefore, William I had stayed at home, where would have been the conquest? If there had been no conquest, where would have been the sturdiness? If there had been no sturdiness, where would have been the skepticism? If there had been no skepticism, where would have been Adam Smith?" (505). Standing at the origins of the nation, the reader is exhorted to see that the British spirit has no future destiny. For the particularity of this moment—the "single opportunity" of William I—opens out to a continuum of outcomes in which the vigor of the English racial stock is arrested. Those outcomes define conventional codes of English manliness, including "sturdiness" and skeptical reason, to be just that: standards of living that have hardened into self-evident virtues. There is no essential category of British manhood, Stephen implies, but only certain conventions of identity that now seem sui generis. Ironically, Adam Smith's classic defense of individualism itself can be understood in light of historical divergences from his personage, eclipsed but not forgotten. So Stephen throws the problem of wayward development back a step: male maturation is contingent not just because individuals might depart from the norm but because those norms are themselves conditional formations.

Meredith extends this premise by taking the conventions of fiction back a step: the plot of *Bildung,* of becoming a "perfect man," is set within a field of occluded counterlives (17). One thinks of the friendship between Richard and Ripton Thompson. The son of a lawyer in Sir Austin's employment, Ripton appears throughout the novel as a foil to Richard's development, "the boy without a destiny" to Richard's "boy with a destiny" (109). He embodies an ideal of natural sexuality, curious and unconstrained, in contrast to Richard's education. Sir Austin cannot help but belittle Ripton's effeminate lack of restraint, most memorably when Ripton is caught with the pornographic *Miss Random's Adventures.* "He is a schoolboy. I knew it," he says to Ripton's father, comparing Ripton's errant education to Richard's. "School, and the corruption there, will bear its fruits sooner or later. I could advise you, Thompson, what to do with him: it would be my plan'" (149). The educative function of Sir Austin's system finds an antithesis in the lawlessness of the public school system and the breed of passionate, sexually inquisitive child that it might make. To be a schoolboy like Ripton is to become a lost youth.

But Ripton's uncomplicated candor makes him all the more sympathetic than his counterpart as the two boys mature. In his uninhibited love for adolescent adventures, Ripton embodies a less moribund alternative to the "plan" for Richard's growth and remains more closely aligned with public school heroes like the eponymous youth in Tom Hughes's *Tom Brown's Schooldays* (1857). Their bisecting routes begin in the "Bakewell Comedy" of volume 1. In an afternoon of fighting, hunting, and trespassing onto a neighboring farm, the two children seem to inhabit another novel altogether, so that—for a contained moment—Richard shares the path that Ripton winds up taking in the narrative. And while the thread is cut short when Sir Austin discovers their exploits, Ripton's repeated appearances allow it to persist as a path not taken, gaining in significance as Ripton develops into an "honest" and morally unassailable adult (98). When Ripton confesses to his newly married friend, "I ain't going to get married. I can't see the girl to suit me" (297), the statement shadows over Richard's ordeal as a more desirable alternative. Free to choose, Ripton elects to remain unattached. Eventually, Ripton's beneficent tendencies will leave him one of the few figures to escape the tragic judgment of the conclusion. ("That poor young man has a true heart" [492], as Sir Austin's cousin, Lady Blandish, observes.) Like Sir Austin's ethereal gaze through the windowpane, or the negated scene of happiness between Lucy and the two Feverel men, the comparisons between Richard and Ripton speak to other histories impressed on our experience, challenging our sense of who we are and all that we might have been.

Having studied the dynamics of negated potential in these registers, we may now specify their ties to the marriage plot. Critics such as Andrew H. Miller, Hillary P. Dannenberg, and William Galperin have shown that one of the British novel's characteristic operations is to weigh different domestic futures.[39] Early novelists like Samuel Richardson, Daniel Defoe, and Tobias Smollett depicted individuals who could calculate their fortunes with several potential partners, doing so in a manner that defined marriage as a rational and self-motivated goal for bourgeois readers. Miller writes that these acts of projection were heightened in nineteenth-century culture, when middle-class marriage and the modern family structure flourished as institutions. Marriage invites counterfactual reflection in Victorian novels "in part simply because it promises a certain kind of life, in which our singularity is escaped" (124). It is unique in content (defined by the particularity of whom one marries), and common in form (defined by the generality of the marital bond), so as to foster fantasies of substitution and exchange. Jane Eyre's struggle to choose between two unassimilable futures, suspended between St. John Rivers and Rochester, becomes an ever more common condition in Victorian fiction, where auxiliary prospects are appraised before tapering down to a singular conclusion.

But what if novels did not introduce these prospects only to push them out in the end? In Meredith's novel of frustrated growth, romantic possibilities spin out long after Richard and Lucy are wedded, shifting the novel's focus from marriage toward possible alternatives to conjugal completion. We may understand this as an extension of practices central to female formation novels, where the pursuit of nuptials is often offset by a recognition of other options that Victorian social institutions and practices have foreclosed. In novels like *Mill on the Floss* (1859) and *Villette* (1853), growth toward womanhood "involv[es] not one but many developmental narratives," as Susan Fraiman writes, where the pull toward marriage is suspended and ironically critiqued (xiii). *Richard Feverel* reflects such a practice through Richard's trio of prospective marriage matches: Clare Doria Forey, Carola Grandison, and his wife to be, Lucy Desborough. For even as these characters set up deviating routes to marriage, the story casts conjugal closure as a restrictive goal—one option for fulfillment onto which others are superimposed.

Clare, Richard's initial love interest, finds that objects of desire can be spurned as soon as they are named. We first meet her upon Richard's sexual awakening in chapter 7, as "the young experiment" speaks to an acquaintance named Ralph Morton: "'Do you know,' Ralph continued, throwing off the mask and plunging into the subject, 'I'd do anything on earth for some names—one or two. It's not Mary, or Lucy. Clarinda's pretty, but it's like a novel. Claribel I like. Names beginning with "Cl" I prefer. The "Cl's" are always gentle and lovely girls you would die for! Don't you think so?'" (223, 125). Naming and signification appear as incitements to desire, in the sense that language serves not only to represent but also to construct one's objects of longing. When Richard goes on to proclaim his love for Clare's name, it is as a product of homosocial struggle, in a kind of rhetorical agon with his rival. "What business, pray, had Ralph to write to her?" Richard asks himself. "Did she not belong to him, Richard Feverel? He read the words again and again: Clare Doria Forey. Why, Clare was the name he liked best: nay, he loved it" (127). Behind the façade of romantic attraction are the operations of mimetic desire: the desire to have what Ralph might have, driven by the pull of possessive ownership or "belong[ing]." Insofar as Clare figures within this exchange, her significance is arbitrary: "All were the same to him; he loved them all," the narrator explains (125).

And yet the story refuses to relinquish her prospects out of hand, in a manner that registers resistance to Richard's later life. Ever absent as the plot presses on, Clare remains present at the lower levels of dialogue and narrative discourse. The foreclosure of their marriage organizes the scene of Richard and Lucy's betrothal, as he brushes by Clare en route to their clandestine wedding. In his surprise at stumbling into Clare and her mother, he loses Lucy's ring only to have it fall onto Clare's finger. "The Ring slid down her thin long finger, and settled comfortably," the narrator observes (286). The scene becomes even more charged when we recall that Clare's mother, Mrs. Doria, had long been "casting about in her mind the future chances of her little daughter and . . . marked down a probability of her marrying Richard" (31). Whatever the material movement of the story toward marriage and domestic completion, the story recalls this sedimented "probability" with increasing conviction, layering on an additional life in which Clare marries Richard instead. The indirect narration of the passage picks up on the potential: "'It does [fit]!' Mrs. Doria whispered. To find a Wedding-Ring is open to any woman; but to find a Wedding-Ring that fits may well cause superstitious emotions. Moreover, that it should be found while walking in the neighborhood of the identical youth whom a mother has destined for her daughter, gives significance to the gentle perturbation of ideas consequent on such a hint from Fortune" (286). The ring that fits squeezes uncomfortably into the tale of Richard's marriage, pressing in on the scene that heralds his transformation from "youth" to adulthood. It is a moment made at "the expense of congruity and probability," in the words of *Richard Feverel*'s reviewer, though this seems less like a failure than the goal of the passage at hand.[40] If the system can decree only one partner for "the young experiment," then the story references a wider continuum of canceled loves. And although Clare eventually accepts the realities of the marriage market and a proposal from the elderly John Todhunter, a potential life with Richard remains through her death. That potential, signaled in the rhetoric of "Fortune," "chances," and "probability," will lead to a more encompassing point in turn. Clare's hushed reticence, like Richard's brusque aggression, are products of social conditioning, not the innate impulses that they come to seem (286, 31).

Clare's sudden demise appears as a tableau of these voided opportunities. When she dies as the victim of an arbitrary sickness, it is to underscore the senselessness of her marriage. Upon her death, she is found wearing two rings, one from Richard and one from John Todhunter, as if to give literal expression to the superimposition of opposing plots. Richard finds an explanation of the rings in Clare's diary, a text that both begins and ends with his name: "I shall not be alive this time tomorrow. I shall never see Richard now. I dreamed last night we were in the fields together, and he walked with his arm round my waist. We were children, but I thought we were married and I showed him I wore his Ring, and he said—if you always wear it, Clare, you are as good as my wife. Then I made a vow to wear it for ever and ever" (445). Linking the past and the present, the dream retrojects a very different direction for Clare and Richard's lives. To remain children, in marriage, is to escape from the twin cultural educations that have come to define them: the lessons of Clare's suffocating mother and Richard's domineering father, respectively rooted in the demands of the marriage market and ideological dictates of the system. As an indictment of Victorian gender codes, the dream reaches toward a more loving world in which Richard's masculine possessiveness, like Clare's feminine passivity, never came to be. The moment is all the more striking in light of Clare's reflection, a few sentences beforehand, on Richard's wanton enmity, his "hat[red] of cowards" and insistent self-assertion (445). But the dream is more than an ephemeral fantasy, there and then not there. Above the shadow of Richard and Clare's lives, it looms as a memorial to their obstructed joy, marking Richard's development by censuring the future that he has chosen.

No doubt all narratives court interest in the play of divergent outcomes, as the reader infers how each moment might or might not contribute to the total design. And certain characteristic features of the novel motivate this process: metacommentary and descriptive details, indirect discourse, and dialogue, as well as red herrings and loose ends that remain tangential to the plot. These techniques can create distinctions between what Barthes called "consecutiveness and consequence": zones of fictional meaning loosened from the constellated chain of events that tend to solicit acts of prediction and feelings of expectation or retrospection (251). My premise has been that *Richard Feverel* assigns a greater share of narrative real estate to those spaces;

neither refusing realism nor faltering in its efforts at it, Meredith's novel contributes to a burgeoning interest in alternative temporalities in Britain. As De Morgan asked, "What are we doing but endeavoring to represent that which actually exists?" (4). Scientists, mathematicians, and logicians like De Morgan suggested that the truth of what "actually exists" might be best represented within a continuum of counterfactuals, of predictions and retrodictions about the world.[41] This principle of realism, implicit in the formal logic of mathematics, becomes explicit in a novel that represents individuals, actions, and settings in light of other developmental possibilities. By way of comparison, we might consider John Lubbock and John Eliot Drinkwater's *On Probability* (1830), a formative treatise on the subject. The authors stretch the semantic rules of language in imagining nonlinear temporalities: "When we endeavor to discover whether an event $\frac{\text{did}}{\text{will}}$ happen, we review the different cases which are possible. If the favorable cases are more numerable than the unfavorable, we $\frac{\text{believe}}{\text{expect}}$ that the event $\frac{\text{did}}{\text{will}}$ take place."[42] The superimposed set of terms illustrate the goal of representing possible pasts and futures in comparative form. Mixing mathematical and nonmathematical languages, the authors twist the temporality of their prose, creating multiple *durées* and composite perspectives. The sentences not only rehearse the theoretical premises of scientists and mathematicians; they incorporate the algebraic structures of mathematics into the English lingua franca.

The hybrid organization of Lubbock and Drinkwater's prose corresponds to Meredith's poetic of fiction: using terms that had become powerfully charged in the late 1850s, he furnishes an account of multitemporal strata and possible plots, of "different cases" within a narrative. Building on those terms, moreover, *Richard Feverel* also alters their meaning. Scientists in the 1830s and 1840s went to great lengths to stress that their alternative historical possibilities had heuristic value alone, as abstractions with no ontological relation to the world. But because Meredith wanted to question the notion of an unbending causal chain, his alternative possibilities assume a more substantive edge. In imagining things otherwise, the novel has stronger loyalties to the writings of Stephen, Acton, and others who also challenged the prospect of a singular futurity, and who also assembled a greater plentitude of counterhistories. Deviations are the materials out of which Meredith's novel is built—a resource that he marshals, a means of summoning up worlds that never existed and that are never entirely erased when the action ends.

"THE TRUE EPIC OF MODERN LIFE":
LITERATURE'S LOST FUTURES

As the traces of negated potential continue to mount, the domain of "'Would-have-done,' and 'Might-have-been'" extends to the history of the British novel. We see such recursive gestures, for instance, in Ralph's profession of love for Clare ("It's like a novel," he says), in Richard and Lucy's ensuing Shakespearean pastoral, and in the stylized epistolary prose of Clare's journal (125). In keeping with Meredith's central concern with negated potential, these moments set up an account of fiction as a medium whose conventions might never have hardened into being. If Richard comes to seem shallow and untethered, then this is in part because he tries to live up to reified modes of literary heroism that are found wanting.

Richard Feverel is shot through with the signatures of the literary past. Sir Austin's book of aphorisms, The Pilgrim's Scrip, is a pastiche of antiquated literary fashions, typifying his preference for custom and convention over unmediated social bonds. Sir Austin's brother, Uncle Hippias, nicknamed "The Eighteenth Century," has long researched fairy mythologies, while Uncle Wentworth unsuccessfully tries to shame Richard by pointing out an episode from Rousseau's Confessions. So strong are these allusions as to diminish the novel's reality effect at times—for instance, in Mrs. Grandison's claim to be descended from the hero of Samuel Richardson's novel The History of Sir Charles Grandison (1753). But the reflexive function of these allusions is not to align the novel with a canon of desirable forebears, for what unites them is the fact that none of the characters comes off well as a result. Sir Austin's literary predilections betray a substitution of fiction for lived relationships, most notably, while Mrs. Grandison's fixation on Richardson's domestic novel reinforces her mechanical devotion to the idea of Carola's marriage.

In this sense, the aesthetic allusions betray the seductive power of fiction to shape social experience. And against their compulsions, Meredith retrojects an alternative lineage for the novel in Britain. This dynamic finds emblematic expression in the inset text of Miss Random's Adventures, an erotic send-up of Tobias Smollett's The Adventures of Roderick Random (1748).[43] Hidden within the covers of Ripton's heraldry book, Miss Random's Adventures reconceives the meanings of Smollett's novel: "Mr. Thompson, without any notion of what he was doing, drew the book from Ripton's hold; whereupon the two Seniors laid their grey heads together over the title-page. It set forth in attractive characters beside a colored frontispiece, which embodied the promise displayed there, the entrancing Adventures of Miss Random, a strange young lady" (145). The threat of "random" desire at the outset of *Richard Feverel* returns here in an actual work of fiction. For whereas the hero of Smollett's novel had ended as a respectable adult—as a gentleman and genteel husband, happily reunited with his father—the title of *Miss Random's Adventures* denies any ascent to social incorporation, instead advertising a picaresque compendium of erotic experiences. "One of the very worst books of that abominable class!" Ripton's father exclaims, leading to the narrator's comment that "brazen Miss Random smiled bewitchingly out, as if she had no doubt of captivating Time and all his veterans on a fair field" (149). Meredith's satirical eye is directed not at Ripton's reading material but at "the two Seniors" and their prurient reactions to it. The fathers' joint encounter with the text, as they stare at the "attractive characters" of the title page, exacerbate their failure to establish a more tolerant bond based on their experiences of child-rearing. Paternal outrage here signals an absence of self-regulation, as Mr. Thompson acts "without any notion" of control. Efforts to police the line between good books and "the worst books," it turns out, are rooted in impulsive whims that inhibit a more loving understanding of others.

Meredith is being flamboyant about the increasing polarization of literature and obscenity. There is no absolute moral code behind the pleasure of reading, he suggests, but merely what people find reprehensible. It was well publicized that Mudie's Lending Library refused to circulate Meredith's novel in the climate of the Obscene Publications Act, passed just before the novel appeared in print. In the language of the lord chief justice John Campbell, the legislation was aimed at publications thought to be "corrupting the morals of youth," posing a threat to "the common feelings of decency."[44] Meredith refuses to answer the law on its own terms. Rather than distancing itself from the taint of moral corruption, *Richard Feverel* accentuates how the line between writing and indecency might have been drawn differently. If the novel's respectability in Britain came through the consolidation of patriarchal structures and an attendant division of labor between women and men, private and public spheres, then *Miss Random's Adventures* implies a different direction that the novel might have gone, looking back to the loosely plotted bildungsromans of Laurence Sterne and Frances Burney. *Richard Feverel* neither accepts new publishing regulations nor repudiates them; true to its heterochronic impulses throughout, it introduces an anteriority in which it might have issued in different structures of thought, feeling, and expression.

As the novel develops these implications, *Miss Random's Adventures* circulates as a talismanic source of fascination. When Sir Austin looks back at his defeated system, he sees Ripton as someone who "stood for human nature, honest, however abject," and admits that "Miss Random, I fear very much, is a Necessary Establishment" (330). An indecent text might produce a good-natured adult, defined by "honesty" and plainspoken earnestness, not the corruption that Sir Austin had assumed. The admission, however backhanded, is brought home when Ripton finds himself at a dinner party with Richard, Lucy, and a group of prostitutes that Richard has tried to rescue from the streets. "The Aphorist would have pardoned Ripton his first Random extravagance had he perceived the simple warm-hearted worship of feminine goodness [that Ripton] had," the narrator comments. "It might possibly have taught [Sir Austin] to put deeper trust in nature" (377). Rather than pursuing corruption, Ripton projects the same earnest enthusiasm that typified his habits of reading, interacting avidly with his fellow guests but leaving unaccompanied. It is Richard who, having been brought up in accordance with Sir Austin's system, elopes with the prostitute Bella Mount (introduced as "a sister to Miss Random" [369]). The bifurcation between the licit and illicit in *Richard Feverel* leads consistently to its incoherence as a moral goal.

Increasingly, the narrative registers the potential for erotic experiences untied to a romantic contract—first in Richard's gender-bending charades with Carola Grandison and later with the cross-dressing prostitute Bella. "A girl so like a boy was quite his [Richard's] ideal of a girl," the narrator says (200). Carola figures as a supreme embodiment of this "ideal." Introduced as "the daughter of a System," Carola seems a perfect match for Richard (200). Both bear the marks of their respective pedagogies and are pushed into an arranged marriage with one another. The irony is that neither youth wishes to become man and wife. Instead, their interactions look back to an alternative order of development. "Are you a girl?" Richard asks her, at which point Carola "immediately became pensive":

"Yes," she sighed, "I'm afraid I am! I used to keep hoping once that I wasn't. I'm afraid it's no use. . . ."

"But what do you want to be?" he asked, scrutinizing the comical young person.

"A boy, to be sure." (197–98)

Carola's refusal of gender protocols is introduced only to be spurned as an impulse of "no use." Reified as an absolute, social convention cannot be changed or undone. At the same time, the desire for an alternative remains as a residue of Carola's past, registering resistance to the terms of their systematic upbringings. "If I call you Richard, you'll call me Carl, won't you?" asks Carola. "That's the German for Charles. In the country the boys call me Charley" (198). While left largely incomplete, Carola's desire to be something other than a girl gains a spectral reality in the scene, preserved and intensified in the face of the plot. That the episode was expunged from later editions reflects the overdetermined nature of their interaction.[45] "After this conversation," the narrator says, "Richard informed his father that he thought girls were very like boys" (200). The scene conceives of gender as a kind of ongoing temporal improvisation: "a constituted *social temporality*," in Judith Butler's words, in that gender norms are constructed and reinscribed through their performative enactments over time.[46] Playfully troubling those norms, Richard and Carola attest to their potential revision, even though the alternatives do not issue in new forms of living. Those alternatives are relegated to a largely *unconstituted* temporality that the plot leaves in its wake. Richard's momentary reprieve from his developmental scripts continues to define him, even as he accedes to more conventional postures of manhood in the end.

That fate hardens into being through the final chapters, in which he fashions himself variously as a pastiche of Byronic heroism, working toward Italian unification, as a chivalric courtier, and as a rescuer of fallen women. These conventions of masculine achievement underscore Richard's lack of a more coherent identity or vocation; failing to see an alternative to Sir Austin's paternalism, he embraces a set of traditional templates for a manhood that never quite suits him.[47] "He swallowed it comfortably," the narrator reflects (459). The more he tries to incarnate them, the less room Richard has to grasp the realities in his midst. His occupational quests come at the expense of Lucy and their newborn son, who live apart from him for much of the third volume. "Belief" in Victorian manhood makes him a pastiche of a man; interpolated into the system, he expresses the very violence of its injunctions.

Richard's interactions with Bella provide the novel's clearest critique of those injunctions. In his attempts to save her from the streets, he reveals the faulty foundations of his most charitable impulses. "She's very like a man," Richard explains, "only much nicer. I like her" (382). For her part, Bella embodies the kind of backward glances at attributed gender categories that had defined Carola Grandison. "Wasn't it a shame to make a woman of me when I was born to be a man?" she asks (398). Bella takes on a new alias altogether with Richard, in the indeterminate figure of the "supreme dandy," Sir Julius (398). The narrator writes, "They went hand in hand and had great fits of laughter at her impertinent manner of using her eye-glass, and outrageous affectation of the dandy. . . . When he beheld Sir Julius he thought of the lady, and 'vice versaw,' as Sir Julius was fond of exclaiming" (398). As a "painted" lady, Bella typifies the creative production of gender, parodying the norms that structure and subvert the plot of male maturation (404). These implications culminate as something that can never have occurred. "'We'll drink to what we might have been, Dick,' said the Enchantress" (408). The toast leads directly to Richard's affair with Bella, as he abnegates his responsibilities to Lucy. But in another register, "what might have been" points away from Richard's development as a hero up to this moment. It ironizes his growth in a manner more in step with the gender-reversing scenes with Carola, so as to question his hardening assumptions about what a man might be and do.

The conclusion brings Richard to the edge of contentment. Upon his extended excursion from Britain, Richard learns that Sir Austin has finally accepted his marriage to Lucy; the news spurs him home, fueled by an awakening hope of moral regeneration. On his arrival, he meets Lucy and their newborn son at Sir Austin's estate. The grounds for final happiness are secured. Lucy has rejected Mountfalcon's advances just as Richard has broken his ties to Bella Mount. Sir Austin renounces the system, admitting that "science does not accomplish everything," while Richard announces that he has "cast aside the hero" (475, 468). But these tokens of felicity are set up as a prelude to their more emphatic erasure. As in the earlier swerve from the pastoral mode, the novel veers away from a comic conclusion. When Richard discovers that Bella was hired by Lord Mountfalcon, in a ploy to distract him from Lucy and then to seduce her, he returns to the masculine archetypes he had tried to embody. "That infamous conspiracy to which he owed his degradation and misery," writes the narrator, "scarce left him the feelings of a man when he thought of it" (483). Richard cannot help but embrace the manhood that he has struggled throughout to attain. The narrator writes: "Had not the finger of Heaven directed him homeward? And he had come: here he stood: congratulations were thick in his ears: the cup of happiness was held to him, and he was invited to drink of it. Which was the dream? his work for the morrow, or this? But for the leaden load he felt like a bullet in his breast, he might have thought the morrow with Death sitting on it was the dream. . . . That leaden bullet dispersed all unrealities" (477). Death and dreams, cold lead and the tonic of happiness: the two have become impossible to tell apart. For Richard, the line between reality and "unrealities" no longer holds, leaving him an embodiment of convention. Upon his final duel with Mountfalcon, which brings about Lucy's brain fever and death, Richard assumes the manhood that the reader knows to be merely a bad choice.

The duel gains meaning through a failed attempt to stop it. Mountfalcon first attempts to stand down and asks Ripton to act as an intermediary with Richard. "We'll stop the damned scandal, if possible," Mountfalcon says to Ripton (473). That message, however, stops at the ears of Richard's tutor, Adrian; the "possible" resolution remains an idle exercise. Richard, for his part, tries and fails to imagine an alternate ending:

> [Richard] had come to see his child once, and to make peace with his wife before it should be too late. Might he not stop with them? Might he not relinquish that devilish pledge? Was not divine happiness here offered to him?—If foolish Ripton had not delayed to tell him of his interview with Mountfalcon all might have been well. But Pride said it was impossible. And then Injury spoke. . . . A mad pleasure in the prospect of wreaking vengeance on the villain who had laid the trap for him, once more blackened his brain. If he would stay he could not. So he resolved, throwing the burden on Fate. The struggle was over, but oh, the pain! (486–87)

The passage signals Richard's acceptance of gender as "fate," while opening an alternate portal to a world where "all might have been well." The train of questions seems to function as indirect discourse—we seem to overhear Richard's thoughts on what else the future might hold. But then his mechanical embrace of "vengeance" and "Pride" leaves it unclear what he has considered after all, as if those prospects had eclipsed his awareness. Far from recapitulating the education of its hero, the reader of Meredith's novel has been trained to discern the curve of other outcomes that Richard cannot see. When he concedes that "the struggle was over" and that the alternatives are "impossible," his failed formation marks the reader's strongest sense of dissident futures.

Like the duel, the decisive catastrophe of Richard's life—Lucy's sudden passing—is framed from a distance that reinforces its conditional status. In a chapter that shifts to epistolary narration, Lady Blandish (Sir Austin's erstwhile love interest) reports that the duel has resulted in Lucy's fatal shock. "Had [Lucy] seen her husband a day or two before—but no! . . . Or had she not so violently controlled her nature as she did, I believe she might have been saved" (490). The observation leaves Lucy blameless while folding her into the novel's larger cultural critique. Had she rejected the tenets of female passivity, then she might have been saved. And in this ironic fashion, the deaths of both husband and wife underscore the damage attendant upon their scripted norms of male action and female inaction, of self-assertion and self-suppression. Because the tragedy is communicated through Lady Blandish's handwritten letter, the significance of the ending becomes bound up with the mediated form of its telling, so as to turn reflexive interest to the constructed nature of events.

With this resolution, *Richard Feverel* departs from former models of probability and fictional form. In numerous eighteenth-century fables of education, as Douglas Patey has argued, the protagonist proceeds by learning to infer a set of probable relations between each element in his growth, moving upward to the total, interrelated meaning of the natural order—the "larger economy of nature"—as arranged by God (185). The result of these inferences is an apprehension of natural unity incarnate in formal terms: the form of a narrative where "the topics of 'place, time, thing and person'" are integrated into a unified system of meanings (26). *Richard Feverel* declines such a systematic map of the world. Instead, its ethics and aesthetics follow from the play of negated possibilities that remain unassimilable to what happens in the end. In this, the failed education of Meredith's hero also revises conventions of tragic form. According to Aristotelian poetics, what happens in a tragedy matters most in its contribution to the end, such that "the displacement or removal of any one [event] would disturb and dislocate the whole," as Aristotle explained.[48] Thus "episodic" tragedies—tragedies in which "the episodes or acts succeed one another without probable or necessary sequence"—were to be judged the lowest kind, in contrast to those that underscore the foreclosure of opportunities for renewal (29). Yet in tandem with scientists, mathematicians, and cultural commentators in the late 1850s, *Richard Feverel* defines "pure accident" (in the words of the novel's 1858 reviewer) as an aesthetic ideal in its own right.[49] The final hyperabundance of other options is all the more cause for lament. When Blandish comments that "Richard will never be what he promised" (492), it is to look back to all the other Richards that have not gained full admission into the plot.

Such is the purity of accident: the purity of possible characters, actions, and conditions of life that never were but might have been. As the narrator says at one point, "Now surely there will come an Age when the representation of Science at war with Fortune and the Fates, will be deemed the true Epic of modern life" (237). Meredith's novel represents just such an epic, not because Sir Austin's system wins against "fortune and the fates" but because the novel assembles an ensemble of other possibilities that defines what happens. Through its disenchantment with the British novel's cultural legacies, it offers a more ethically expansive vision of fiction's lost promise and ameliorative potential. *Richard Feverel* aims to restore some semblance of that promise. It explores the undefined terrain between realities and "unrealities," representing alternate trajectories of development that might find fulfillment in the world outside its covers (477). That aim is rooted in the poetics of a novel that moves forward through the disruption of plot and finds in nonhappenings the grounds for a more perfect mimesis.

CHAPTER 2

"The Interval of Expectation"
Armadale and the History of the Present

Make 'em laugh, make 'em cry, make 'em wait.
                    —Wilkie Collins, personal motto (attributed)

Historical sense has more in common with medicine than philosophy;
and it should not surprise us that Nietzsche occasionally employs the
phrase "historically and physiologically."
                    —Michel Foucault, "Nietzsche, Genealogy, History" (1977)

The history of sensation fiction has been most often told as a history of
speed. Beginning with Victorians who first identified its heart-pounding
rhythms, readers have tied the genre's relentless action to the turbulence of
an accelerating British nation. Associating sensation fiction and emergent industrial technologies, Nicholas Daly writes that "we can see in the sensation
genre an attempt to register and accommodate the newly speeded-up world
of the railway age." For Daly, these accommodations come from the novels'
"deployment of nervousness," the instantaneous transmission of feeling
from texts to readers' bodies.[1] The genre's defining term is its speed: through
the novels' immediate impact upon the nerves, audiences are trained to
operate within a frenetic social system of the kind that Georg Simmel and
Walter Benjamin diagnosed in modernity's kinetic hum. From this vantage,
the experience of reading reflects a set of pervasive phenomena in Victorian
culture: a rapid influx of stimuli brought by scalar increases in urbanization,
global commerce, and technological innovation.[2]

But literary historians' emphasis on sensation's speed has obscured vital
connections between sensation novels and the shifting tempos of British
experience. In the decades leading up to the genre's 1860s pinnacle of fame,
scientists redefined sensation through the terms of slowness, suspense, and
lag. The scientific problem of postponement—conceived as the individual's

belated reaction to physical stimuli—was widely investigated, albeit with little consensus about its nature. Romantic-era astronomers understood it as having either environmental or mental causes and devised statistical tools to average out the resulting variations. More empirical explanations began to appear around 1850, when Hermann von Helmholtz measured the velocity of the nerves and revealed—to much surprise—that sensation itself was slow. Human perceptions were residues of the past, he demonstrated: a world gone while we apprehended it. For medical writers in his wake, moreover, excessive postponements appeared as a symptom of mental malaise, bespeaking the languor and irresolution of effeminate men. Yet what I term the new *sensorial* account, among mental scientists, did not displace the established *statistical* account among astronomers; the two continued to thrive in uneasy tension, resulting in ambiguities about the shortest *durée* of historical experience.[3] Were individuals who sensed and felt alternatives to the present beset by delusions? Or did their sensitivities have legitimate, material foundations in the world writ large? Through the 1860s, the questions lingered in want of a single solution.

Collins's fiction joins this genealogy of the temporal present in counterintuitive terms: not by accepting the truth of a given account but by manipulating contrary constructions of its meaning, making the tension between them intelligible as narrative.[4] In elaborating this thesis, I begin with the dictum often attributed to Collins: "Make 'em laugh, make 'em cry, make 'em wait."[5] For Collins, the compulsion to "wait" is not opposed to the thrills of sensation fiction but is its culminating term; it defines the very experience of sensation. That ethos finds full elaboration in *Armadale* and its dispirited hero, Ozias Midwinter. At the outset, Midwinter's "effeminate hesitations" look pathological: a failure to steel his nerves and to live in the now, in contrast to his more impulsive friend, Allan Armadale (157). But then the story turns upon itself by disclosing how Midwinter's hesitations are empowering. They enable him to avert the scheme against him and Allan in ways that cannot be understood as mere mental confusion. Alternating scenes suggest that Midwinter's postponements are a sign of malaise *and* a sensitive attunement to forces from beyond the pale, forces that might lead to adjusted conditions of living. Precisely by becoming more withdrawn instead of spontaneous, preoccupied rather than responsive, Midwinter creates circumstances in which his intimate friendship with Allan can thrive. In the process, the proliferating timescapes of the 1860s emerge as more than a symptom of illness alone. They evoke a present tense that brims with unassimilable directions, open and undecided, that could veer from the constraints of the past to altered futures.

The aim of genealogical critique, for literary studies such as mine, might be briefly defined as an excavation of the myriad historical conjunctures behind assumptions that seem now intuitive and inevitable. Its goal is to trace a contested field of relations through time: "an unstable assemblage" of interactions that make up "the history of the present," as Foucault put it.[6] This goal informs my account of the temporal present because its meanings spanned a wealth of discontinuous ideas, institutions, objects, and genres in Victorian culture, including sensation novels. How can criticism grasp fiction's implication within this field? To get at the temporal torques of Collins's fiction, I will be drawing on recent attempts to understand literature's multichronic scales. Working across different historical arenas, scholars such as Lauren Berlant, Carolyn Dinshaw, and Elizabeth Freeman have stressed fiction's potential to trouble modern notions of time as empirical, homogenous, linear, and shared. In their accounts, literature can create a plural understanding of the present, where "different time frames or temporal systems collid[e] in a single moment of *now*," Dinshaw writes, so as to suggest "forms of embodied being that are out of sync with ordinarily linear measurements." For Freeman, too, "temporal misalignments"—instanced in the narrative fabric of interruption, ellipsis, analepsis, and prolepsis—"can be the means of opening up other possible worlds," where new forms of desire and social relations can be imagined.[7] Much of this work builds on earlier insights in feminist and queer studies, which have shown how one prevailing regime of time (linear, rational, universalist) tends to privilege specific gendered subjects (men geared toward commercial production and patriarchal reproduction). By reading for narrative moments that complicate these hierarchies, these critics seek to recuperate alternative temporalities of living, or what Dinshaw calls "the multitemporal world of the *now*" (10).

Collins suggests such a "multitemporal world" through the aesthetics of fiction: its intricate structure, style, pacing, and characterizations. In narrating Midwinter's development, as we shall see, the novel locates him within a curve of temporal possibilities and associates him with a heightened "historical sense" (in Foucault's terms), an awareness of other potential directions through the past and future.[8] This sensibility builds on the feelings of negated potential that we encountered in chapter 1 and brings me to a final consideration. In the decades leading up to 1850, probabilistic techniques tended to be introduced in subjective terms. They were said to reflect one's feeling of anticipation about the outcome of a coin toss or dice roll. But in a growing range of arenas, probabilities were understood to represent real things and frequencies of behavior as well. As John Venn noted in his landmark *The Logic of Chance* (1866), published in the same months as *Armadale,* probabilities often expressed "the behavior of *things.*" From that premise, he wrote, followed the "whole theory of Probability as a practical science."[9] The statement marks an implicit revision to assumptions that "probability is the feeling of the mind, not the inherent property of a set of circumstances," as De Morgan wrote.[10] Such shifting boundaries between subjective and objective orientations had distinctive resonance in Victorian temporal thinking, particularly in novels devoted to the speed of sensation. More than eliciting immediate thrills, *Armadale* meditates on the construction of the historical present itself and imagines "other possible worlds" in our midst.[11]

"A KIND OF RESTIVENESS IN ALMOST EVERY ONE'S MIND": POSTPONEMENT AND PERSONHOOD

In 1815, Friedrich Bessel—well-known Prussian astronomer, mathematician, and director of the Königsberg Observatory—became immersed in an antiquated set of records on the flight paths of the stars. Whenever two individuals recorded the time that a star passed through the cross wires of a telescope lens, Bessel found that the results varied by at least one-tenth of a second. The problem was alarming because simultaneous observations of this type had become central to the work of astronomers across Europe; they were thought to yield the most precise data about celestial objects, and careful concentration was vital: a small slip of attention could be calamitous, leading to huge mismeasurements of an object's speed and location. But Bessel reported that postponements were both ubiquitous and impervious to remedy. What was more curious, he discovered that the interval of lag time was often constant in each observer. No matter how well trained or attentive the person, a distinct degree of postponement marred each observation of the heavens.[12]

Bessel defined the problem of "constant difference" as an astronomical issue in need of practical redress, not as a mental or physiological concern.

For this reason, a probabilistic solution seemed adequate to treat it. Similar methods had been incorporated into observatories from the later eighteenth century onward, when astronomers first recruited mathematical models to calculate the probable position of stellar objects. The astronomer's error curve, which we encountered in Pierre-Simon Laplace's investigations, gave astronomers a uniquely powerful instrument for managing mismeasurements due to "random" causes (causes without a single source). Through it, investigators could average out random results of all kinds, allowing them to infer the location of celestial bodies that defied direct observation.

But Bessel's problem called for a more nuanced approach. For while Laplace's error curve could average out "random" errors, it was imprecise in situations where "constant" errors stood present—errors, in other words, that fell outside the typical range of probabilities and that therefore seemed to have a single cause. These sorts of errors could considerably skew results, and since Bessel's postponements appeared constant in individuals, he reasoned that they were of that kind. He pondered the issue with his renowned German contemporary, the astronomer and mathematician Carl Friedrich Gauss, while working toward a satisfactory formula in 1818. "We have only very recently reached the stage where we explore small errors or deviations outside the limits of probability," Bessel wrote, "with the same attention as previously accorded to the bigger ones; both point to a physical source (in nature itself, in the instruments[,] or the observer) and we only now consider the discovery of this source."[13] The statement alludes to Gauss's groundbreaking research in the previous decade, when he found international acclaim for his hand in formulating the normal curve (also called the "Gaussian distribution"). The normal curve reduced the importance of wild or incongruous data and allowed investigators to factor in the relative significance of "small errors" and "bigger ones." Bessel imagines his work as advancing this tradition by isolating one specific subset of errors: deviations in the time of observation. Whether those temporal deviations turned out to result from atmospheric, technological, or personal causes—"nature," "instruments," or "the observer"—remained as yet unknown. But bolstered by Gauss's work, he anticipates developing a practical tool to minimize their impact.

Bessel's excitement was warranted. After he published the "personal equation" in 1823, British and continental astronomers hailed his formula as a major, even epochal, innovation—a judgment confirmed by more recent historians, who see it as a milestone in the onset of probabilistic methods.[14] The equation elicited immediate and sustained discussion in the 1820s, when it was adopted as a standard astronomical resource. Notwithstanding the technical success of the equation, however, it notably left the "physical source" of postponement undefined. Astronomers aimed to minimize errors so as to gather reliable results about the heavens, not to isolate the source of the errors in question. So instead of concerted investigations into the origins of postponement, one finds a smattering of causal speculations among astronomers. Bessel posited eleven possible causes for "personal time," including atmospheric events, mechanical meltdowns, slips of attention, and differences in aptitude and training; in Britain, the Astronomer Royal John Pond and his successor John Airy contributed similarly provisional musings that noted the aporia without attempting to offer an empirical explanation.[15]

To stand outside the present, then, was as a common fact with no clear-cut relation to individuals. Consistently, astronomers at this time took pains to avoid the misconception that postponement had to do with only "personal" or psychological causes. Bessel was reluctant to accept the term "personal equation" at all when Pond, the acting director of the Greenwich Observatory, introduced it in 1833. He preferred phrases like "constant difference" and "difference in the moments of observation": more neutral names that included nonpersonal sources of postponement. For his part, Pond took care to define the personal equation as referring to "the difference in the times of noting" events as opposed to differences in individuals.[16] Postponement, the historian of science Simon Schaffer writes, remained "a new variable whose meaning was ill-defined"; while widely noted, its precise origins were nowhere to be found.[17]

Soon after the personal equation's emergence, leading scientists such as William Whewell, John Herschel, and William Carpenter observed its interest for educated British readers, often by underscoring postponement's obscure origins. Carpenter discussed the enigma in his influential *Mechanical Philosophy, Horology, and Astronomy* (1844). "It is a remarkable circumstance, " wrote Carpenter, "that some persons see the passage of a star, or make any other similar observation, a considerable part of a second earlier than others."[18] Postponement intrigues Carpenter as an unaccountable "singularity." It is "independent of [observers'] instruments" and remains "not easily to be accounted for" (395). Drawing attention to the experience of rail travel, he builds an analogy with motion parallax: viewed from within the carriage, distant objects appear to pass slower than those close at hand. Carpenter uses the example to note that the human perception of time is imperfect, although he stops short of wagering whether individual differences derive from the mind, body, or environment; the phenomenon is of singular interest because it is ultimately unaccountable.

So the issue persisted: What did it mean to be out of step with the present? Behind Carpenter's avoidance of a connection between postponement and personhood was the simple fact that commentators could not hope to time the speed of sensation. Because sensation had long been assumed to move at or near the speed of light, it seemed impossible to calculate it accurately. The noted German scientist Johannes Müller commented on the impasse in his *Elements of Physiology* (1833–40, trans. 1838–42): "The attempts made to estimate the velocity of nervous action have not been founded on sound experimental principles."[19] It was Müller's former pupil, Hermann von Helmholtz, who successfully took up this experimental challenge. Working with a pair of electrodes attached to a frog's leg, Helmholtz announced in 1850 that he had calculated the rate of nervous propagation at about fifty meters per second—far slower than current electricity.[20] Helmholtz's findings were widely published in Britain by the early 1850s, in writings that altered assumptions about human and animal bodies. Far from fine-tuned machines, seeming to incarnate the clocklike precision of God, we were subject to a set of haltingly slow signals to and from the world. Just as Helmholtz demonstrated the precision of an experimental approach to the nerves, he confirmed the inherent imperfection of observation.

Psychological writers of the 1850s and 1860s translated this discovery into the English lingua franca, even as the astronomer's account maintained currency as well. Alexander Bain's *The Senses and the Intellect* (1855), for example, enlisted Helmholtz's discovery of "a certain delay" to affirm physiological approaches to the mind.[21] Bain begins with a metaphorical connection between sense stimuli and the signals of a telegraph. Current electricity, he notes, travels with "inconceivable rapidity." But this metaphorical connection between information technologies and neurophysiological networks resolves into catachresis: as it turns out, it points precisely to what sensation is *not*. He writes, "The nerve force is propagated far more slowly" than current through a wire: "there is always a certain delay" in sensation (64). In a similar vein, James Sully identified "duration" as a major issue in his *Sensation and Intuition* (1874). Sully, who had studied both at the University of Göttingen and at Humboldt University, foregrounded the importance of recent experimental insights in a chapter titled "Recent German Experiments in Sensation." "It is probable that there exists some limit of duration below which nervous change fails to produce a sensation," he writes, reasoning that "any advance towards the proof and measurement of this minimum interval would be of great value in helping one to determine the minimum duration of a definite and recognizable sensation."[22]

For both Bain and Sully, research into postponement carried the promise of empirical insight into the mind. More recently, Lorraine J. Daston and Peter Galison have confirmed the importance of this research in the history of mechanical objectivity—namely, in seeming to offer objective knowledge about consciousness itself.[23] It is debatable, however, whether the influence of the experimentalists' work was immediate in Britain, since both the statistical and sensorial models continued to flourish at midcentury. Well into the 1870s, postponement continued to be understood through the mathematical métier of deviations from the norm, even as it also assumed psychological valences, as the historian Jimena Canales notes. The entanglement of vocabularies speaks to this fact. Mental scientists often described postponement as "personal time" and "individual difference" (appropriating the terms of astronomers), while astronomers described it as "reaction time" (using the terms of mental scientists). Scientists shared vocabularies of postponement while claiming to be talking about different things, thus heightening the ambiguities around the topic from the start. As Canales has argued, these scientists worked neither in active antagonism nor in the hopes of collaboration; they simply stressed the virtues of their own respective approaches in issues internal to their own programs of research.[24]

The tension between the two accounts can be glimpsed in occasional attempts at a reconciliation. One attempt came from Hippolyte Taine, the influential French philosopher and art historian, who tried to align the terminologies of statistics and sensation in his lay treatise, *On Intelligence* (1870, trans. 1871). Taine's work drew inspiration from the synthetic studies of Bain, Herbert Spencer, and George Henry Lewes and was read in turn by Walter Pater and other intellectuals in Britain.[25] At a pivotal moment, Taine aligns the new experimentalism of physio-psychologists with astronomers' mathematical models: "Other people do not have our sensations exactly when and as we have them: but they have our possibilities of sensation; whatever indicates a present possibility of sensations to ourselves, indicates a present possibility of sensations to them, except so far as their organs of sensation may vary from the type of ours. This puts the final seal to our conception of the groups of possibilities as the fundamental reality in Nature. The permanent possibilities are common in us and to our fellow-creatures; the actual sensations are not."[26] Taine's language shuttles back and forth between sensorial and statistical registers. He begins by locating postponement in the material "organs of sensation." But the resulting "possibilities of sensation" are increasingly indeterminate. His focus shifts from "our possibilities of sensation" to our own inklings about them: the "possibility of sensations *to ourselves*" and again to "*our conception* of the groups of possibilities" (284). In this line of abstraction, the passage proceeds from actual sensations to our conception of their "possibility" and then to more general compendia of possibilities that are "the fundamental reality in Nature." The result is a paradox. Possibilities both do and do not refer to "actual sensations" (285). In this, Taine's equivocations exhibit a fault line running across Victorian thought: the unstable nature of temporal possibilities as more than a mental chimera but less than an accurate representation of worldly phenomena.

Notwithstanding these limitations, writings such as Taine's served to introduce the science of postponement to the middle-class audiences for whom Collins wrote, articulating the social and philosophical salience of a potentially esoteric concern. Particularly influential in the 1860s was the work of Henry Maudsley, whose ideas stood distinctively in tension with Taine's. Widely renowned as a medical commentator, Maudsley defined postponement as a masculine failure to act. He built an elaborate typology of what we may call the *delayed reactor* and diagnosed postponement as an affliction requiring modern medical management. Astronomers like Bessel and Airy imagined a set of value-neutral norms and deviations from the present; Maudsley imposed a new line of demarcation between normal and deviant categories of personhood. That agenda informs his *The Physiology and Pathology of Mind* (1867), published around the same as *Armadale*. "This time-rate of conduction," Maudsley writes, "varies in different persons, and at different periods in the same person, according to the degree of attention; if the attention be slight, the period is longer and less regular, but if the attention be active, then the period is very regular."[27] Concerted attention leads to an even and efficient pulse of experience, while distraction results in an irregular, sluggish sensorium. But "whether the attention be great or little," he concludes, "a certain time must elapse" (370). Postponement is a condition that can never be eradicated but only made manageable through the individual's perpetual vigilance and self-control.

The powers of concentration, in self-accomplished individuals, find their corollary in the benighted nerves of lagging, less competent others. "Although no such researches into the cerebral centres as those have been made into the conditions of conduction by nerve have been made," writes Maudsley, "we may not unfairly apply the analogy to psychical activity" (371). The work of "analogy" links the specific speed of sensation to the operations of the mind and brain. Maudsley focuses on the effects of "overwork," "emotional anxiety," "hereditary taint," and "direct injury," all of which may result in a "deviation from the normal state" of embodied experience (377). Like Taine, he draws upon probabilistic terms to explain sensation but breaks from the tenets of the statistical account. Here we are approaching an understanding of "deviation" as an unmanly failure of self-management. Maudsley links male enfeeblement to "an innate feebleness of nerve" (377); for him, excessive postponement appears as a metonym for derangement and developmental arrest. Writing to a middle-class audience that valorized an ethos of male assertive action, productive labor, and vigorous self-control, Maudsley conceives of postponement as a gendered problem for habitually languid, indolent men.[28]

Maudsley's rhetoric of the "time-rate" is significant: in his language, one sees the material measurement of nervous velocities turned toward the goal of normalization (370). To stand apart from the immediacies of the world, for him, is a pathological problem in need of diagnosis and therapeutic treatment. Here he aligns himself with John Locke's associationism, in contrast to the natural philosophical contributions of Bessel, Airy, Carpenter, and others. "'There is,' says Locke, 'a kind of restiveness in almost every one's mind.' Sometimes, without perceiving the cause, it will boggle and stand still, and one cannot get it a step forward; and at another time it will press forward and there is no holding it in" (371). The potential for perversion appears in "almost every one's mind," Maudsley explains. "The oppression of mental suffering is notably attended with great sluggishness of thought, the train of ideas seeming to stand still, and even perception being imperfect" (371). Sensory lag indicates "great sluggishness," a cognitive lassitude that is in turn symptomatic of "mental disease." Likeness (between one's nervous "time-rate" and the operations of the mind) slides still closer to correspondence (370). He concludes: "In many cases of affection of the brain . . . a considerable time must elapse between a question asked of the patient and his reply: there is, as it were, a sluggishness of the mind, which perceives and reacts more slowly than natural. Such facts, proving beyond all question that the rapidity and success of mental processes are dependent upon the physical condition of the supreme nervous centers, prove also that time is an essential element in every mental function" (371). Maudsley imagines an entire experimental scenario where these habituated forms of delayed reaction can be investigated. In the scene of Maudsley's physiological plot, the scientific expert elicits responses from the nervous patient and observes the time taken to react. By thus diagnosing and working upon the unnaturally enfeebled mind, brain, and nervous system, this scientist could claim to diminish delay and engender a more integrated individual.

In Maudsley's therapeutic scenario, "affection of the brain" could be traced to the patient's rate of "react[ion]" (371). But this fantasized scene was far from anomalous. It appeared at the dawn of an explosion in reaction-time experiments during the 1860s and 1870s. Those studies—from figures such as Franciscus Donders (in the Netherlands), Wilhelm Wundt (in Germany), and Francis Galton (in Britain)—established new techniques for measuring and evaluating reaction rates.[29] What was in Maudsley's text a general diagnostic concern became a distinct object of research and an impetus for the first psychological laboratories in the 1870s and early 1880s. Defined as the difference between sensory stimuli and their apprehension in consciousness, "reaction-time" became the key metric for understanding a wide range of psychic phenomena and an experimental foundation for modern neuroscience.[30]

Reaction times thus promised an ostensibly objective means of interpreting consciousness. From this moment, as Daston and Galison write, "psychologists could avail themselves of 'objective time determinations' of mental processes."[31] Through these "time determinations," as Wundt had called them, experimentalists could claim to parse out elemental units of thought, feeling, sensation, and perception. Francis Galton devised an assortment of techniques for finding reaction times in his famed anthropometric laboratory, where he sought to lay the foundations for a eugenic society. Similar techniques were developed by Sigmund Exner and Emil Kraepelin (known for establishing the modern distinction between neurosis and psychosis) to study the effects of mental confusion.[32] For scientists such as them, the bare fact of postponement offered an impartial index into psychic health and perversion. Taking up Wundt's laboratory methods, they published on the effects of alcohol, morphine, and other substances upon mental processes; forms of mania, melancholia, fatigue, and insanity could all be traced to abnormal time rates of nerve conduction. The scientific popularizer Joseph Jastrow summarized these findings for English-speaking audiences at the century's close. "Change of reaction times in insanity has been frequently observed," Jastrow reflects. "It seems probable that in most forms of mental disease, and particularly in melancholia, there is a considerable lengthening of the reaction time. . . . In the excited forms of disease, such as mania, a shortening has been observed."[33] The mind is an erratic agency: it stands still and presses forward of its own volition, as in Maudsley's account, with unprovoked pauses and spurts of action that are deemed deranging. By measuring these errant temporalities, the scientist could claim to discover their latent etiology en route to a cure.

The prestige of the experimental ethos in Britain was signaled by the opening of two psychological laboratories in 1897, at the University of Cambridge and the University of London; those institutions attest to psychological science's ascendancy as a discipline devoted to the new experimentalism. Despite the consolidation of mental research programs within these institutions, however, it is important to accentuate the heterogeneity of ideas in high Victorian culture, which was "filled with dispute and without settled lines of theory or protocols for investigation," as Rick Rylance notes.[34] Rylance's observation provides a corrective to progressive narratives about the eventual "domination of the experimental paradigm" in psychological science (8). Instead of assuming a linear movement toward the rise of psychological laboratories, he underscores "the porousness and loose-weaving of psychological debate in the nineteenth century that allows specific creative activities to take place" (148). And although Victorian writings on postponement fall outside the scope of Rylance's account, they reflect just such a loose set of cultural concerns, in which the triumph of the sensorial or statistical account remained far from given. The creative, compound, nonteleological orientations of Victorian discourse appeared even and especially in ideas about the temporal present.

In what manner did Collins join these augmented accounts of the present? Literature and science studies often observe that scientific innovation—particularly before the emergence of the modern disciplines—was fueled by innovations in literature. Jane Austen's narratives of sexual struggle and inheritance gave familiar form to successive theories of evolutionism; Alfred

Tennyson's elegiac meditations on waste and persistence played a role in the acceptance of thermodynamics; Walter Scott's peripatetic historical novels fostered notions of slow geological change.[35] In instances such as these, literature can be said to contribute to the habits of mind that structured scientific revolutions. But in what follows, I resist the thesis that Collins's sensation novels functioned in this regard—namely, in promoting the soon-to-be dominant framework of experimental psychology. Certainly, Collins's rhetoric of sensation and perception aligns him with the leading tradition of mental science in the 1860s, when psychological theorists began to calculate the "time-rate" of the mind, brain, and nervous system (Maudsley, 370). By the *fin de siècle,* the empirical experiments of psychologists flourished just as statistical studies of "personal time" began to wane. Yet Collins's novels remain ambivalent artifacts of that transition. Often observing the prejudices and inadequacies of mental experts, *Armadale* subverts their claims to providing an authoritative account of character. The novel's investment in postponement is skeptical and multivalent: troubling what look like untroubled truths, it stops short of an unified explanation. Instead of positing literature's dialectical ties to reaction-time studies, then, I will be showing how *Armadale* manipulates modes of thinking about alternative temporalities in *non*dialectical form. While *Armadale*'s critique of mental science makes it congenial to the perspectives of physical scientists and mathematicians, the novel ultimately upholds the value of fiction in negotiating between competing observations on the present. It mobilizes diverse vantages without ever ending in a single, composite claim of truth.

A nonfictional example will help to illustrate the processes of oblique association and intensification I have in mind. Consider Walter Pater: the "impressions of the individual," Pater wrote in 1868, "are in perpetual flight, all that is actual in [experience] being a single moment, gone while we try to apprehend it, of which it may ever be more truly said that it has ceased to be than that it is."[36] At first glance, postponement is a fault of the mind and brain alone: the individual's alienation from the realities of the present, in keeping with the psychological lineage of Bain, Sully, and Maudsley. And yet Pater goes on to reimagine that condition in a manner at odds with Maudsley's therapeutic prescriptions. Rather than urging us to accelerate toward the now, he advocates the opposite: "Our one chance lies in expanding that interval, in getting as many pulsations as possible into the given time" (302). The expansive experience of postponement, of shrinking from worldly immediacies, underscores the leitmotifs of revival and temporal returns that he would later elaborate in *The Renaissance* (1873). The past stands ever present.[37] I invoke Pater's oneiric musings because, without responding to a particular theorem, his writing informed subsequent scientific appraisals of postponement. As T. H. Huxley commented in his 1893 Romanes lecture and essay "Evolution and Ethics," "No man can, with exactness, affirm of anything in the sensible world that it is. As he utters the words, nay, as he thinks them, the predicate ceases to be applicable; the present has become the past; the "'is' should be 'was.'"[38] Huxley appropriates Pater's terms and Pater's reflexive focus on the temporalities of speech and writing in order to evoke the eternal presence of the past. And through those terms, postponement becomes something other than a problem of mental malaise for Huxley as well. He goes on to affirm the "nebulous potentiality" of cosmic change, which includes human minds and bodies but is not limited to them (9:50). Such an account complicates the supposed scientific materialism attributed to contemporaries like John Tyndall, William Clifford, and Huxley himself, who were occasionally critiqued as subordinating human faith and free will to the mechanical operations of the universe. Just as Tyndall took pains to distance himself from charges of crude materialism and preserved space for "latent powers" within what he called his "higher materialism," Huxley drew upon Pater's words to distinguish himself from an unqualified materialist reductionism, stating that "what I may term legitimate Materialism—that is, the extension of the conceptions and of the methods of physical science to the highest as well as the lowest phenomena of vitality—is neither more nor less than a sort of shorthand Idealism."[39]

Pater and Huxley neither embrace nor reject particular propositions of knowledge. And yet their language generates forms of understanding temporal experience at variance with the theories of mental scientists. The sensuous lyricism of their prose, which accentuates the continuum between what "was" and what "is," leads to a nonpathological conception of existing outside of the present and solicits what Elisha Cohn calls "a diffusive, atmospheric experience" of reading that suspends linearity.[40] Collins joined these creative contributions as the leading practitioner of the most influential genre in the 1860s, writing often on the sensational temporalities of fiction. He explained in his 1861 preface to *The Dead Secret* that "after careful consideration, and after trying the experiment both ways, I thought it most desirable to let the effect of the story depend on expectation rather than surprise."[41] This "experiment" continued to define Collins's approach to characterization and plot. One thinks of Franklin Blake's listless, somnambulistic dream states in *The Moonstone* (1868) or of Marian Halcombe's tortured diary entries in *The Woman in White* (1859). "I count the hours that have passed since I escaped to the shelter of this room, by my own sensations—and those hours seem like weeks," Marian writes. "How short a time, and yet how long to me."[42] Both a symptom of delusion and its circular cause, postponement appears as an unambiguous loss of self-control for Marian; its experience is unnerving.

Postponement also appears unnerving for *Armadale*'s young protagonist, though its nature becomes more defiantly fugitive. It is introduced as a symptom of Midwinter's "hysterical" nerves and "sensitive feminine organization" (122, 265). But as the action advances, his irresolution is reinscribed as a heroic virtue, looking less like an illness than an alternative goal of formation that ironizes the transition from youthful indecision to adulthood. In this, the novel departs from the conventions of male development that it invokes. Scholars have pointed out that sensation novels tend to resemble bildungsromans whose heroes demonstrate their manhood through feats of spontaneous action (in the manner of Walter Hartright, for instance).[43] And as if to suggest that *Armadale* will follow suit, Collins's title conjures up associations with the best-selling male bildungsromans of the age, such as *Pendennis* (1850), *David Copperfield* (1850), and *Phineas Finn* (1867).[44] But the connection is rendered ironic from the opening pages, which introduce no less than five Allan Armadales—a referential plenitude that speaks to the intertwining of names, identities, and destinies throughout the text. It increasingly becomes clear that Midwinter (whose birth name is also Armadale) will be no conventional figure of male maturation, moving from stultification to rational self-mastery, marriage, and family. Far from narrating Midwinter's triumph over inaction, the novel redefines postponement as an alternative regimen of self-care. And through it all, the topic is claimed as one that is best suited for the professional male novelist, conceived as an expert in "mak[ing] 'em wait."[45]

THE NOT-NOW: A POETICS OF POSTPONEMENT IN *ARMADALE*

Published after the commercial successes of *Basil* (1852), *The Woman in White* (1859), and *No Name* (1862), *Armadale* secured Collins's reputation as a leading light among nineteenth-century novelists. Its composition, however, was singularly protracted. The first monthly part saw publication in November of 1864, nearly three years after Collins arranged terms with *Cornhill Magazine*. Subsequent installments were interrupted by family difficulties, bouts of rheumatism, and a growing addiction to laudanum, all of which impeded its progress for nearly two more years.[46] "My mind is perfectly clear—but the nervous misery . . . is indescribable," he wrote to his friend Edward Pigott in 1864.[47] Collins recorded these ills in the preface to the first single-volume edition, where he observed that the book "was not hastily meditated, or idly wrought out" (4).

The plot exhibits a reflexive recognition of this struggle to write, as if Collins was working through his authorial anxieties in the content of the tale at hand. From the outset, it appears as a story within a story. Its frame narrative centers upon a deathbed confession by the father (Allan Armadale Sr., formerly named Matthew Wrentmore) to the son (Allan Armadale Jr., who later assumes the name of Ozias Midwinter). In his confession, Wrentmore admits to murdering a rival and former friend, Fergus Ingleby (to whom the Allan Armadale namesake also belonged), who had attempted to steal Wrentmore's inheritance. Wrentmore relates all this to his infant son, Midwinter, as the novel begins. "I see danger in the future," says the dying father, "begotten of the danger in the past" (54). Earlier evils threaten to be transmitted to the next generation of Armadales, so that Midwinter and his new friend Allan Armadale (the sons of Wrentmore and Ingleby, respectively) might recapitulate the initial bloodshed. In the previous generation, Midwinter's father had killed the father of Allan Armadale Jr. In the current one, Midwinter (né Alan Armadale) worries that he is doomed to repeat the same sequence of events with his friend, the son of the murdered man.

As the tale unfolds, the distinction dissolves between the two generations of Armadales. By repeating its initial ur plot in different registers, *Armadale* asks how earlier experiences can conspire with current ones; it posits an indistinction between prior perceptions and sensations and immediate conditions of living. There can be no immanence of action for characters caught at this threshold, only a series of parallels and associations with what has happened before. The "blank place" in the father's letter (19), in which he relates the murder to the young Midwinter, is thus a void that can never be filled and remains a touchstone for the ensuing events. "As long as there is a page left," Midwinter says, "I shall read it. And, as long as I read it, my father gets the better of me, in spite of myself!" (127). The father's confessional letter functions as a kind of toxic text, a figure for the compulsive consumption of narratives and their effects upon the mind. It elicits a captivation by the past—a "parallel between the past and the present" (150)—and indicates the dangerously disorienting effects of that experience.

As an initial framework, then, the prologue dissolves the distinctions that it builds between the experience of the past and an impending future. But it also sets up a more specific trajectory toward the 1860s science of postponement. By bracketing the action between the Wildbad public baths (at the outset of the novel, set in 1832) and Dr. Downward's private sanatorium (at the ending, set in 1851), the narrative looks toward new taxonomies of deviance identified in terms of mental speed. But in *Armadale,* the meaning of postponement never fully coheres with mental science alone, as the narrative observes how social conditions can conspire to define illness. More than an indication of pathology, postponement also adduces a mode of what Anne-Lise François calls "recessive action": it becomes a minimal means by which the immediacies of Midwinter's world can be suspended and reworked, allowing him to escape the "Fatality" of earlier events (338, xiv). Through his very irresolution, Midwinter avoids the paternal template of impulsive violence and arrives at a more mutual future for himself and Allan.

Midwinter's intense inwardness is presented through these dual registers from the start. He appears after being discovered in a field, disheveled and confused, by a passing stranger. The narrator emphasizes his "singular perversity":

> Ozias Midwinter, recovering from brain-fever, was a startling object to contemplate, on a first view of him. . . . Mr. Brock could not conceal from himself that the stranger's manner was against him. The general opinion has settled that if a man is honest, he is bound to assert it by looking straight at his fellow-creatures when he speaks to them. If this man was honest, his eyes showed a singular perversity in looking away and denying it. Possibly they were affected in some degree by a nervous restlessness in his organization, which appeared to pervade every fiber of his lean, lithe body. (73)

Startling, singular, and perverse: looking right at Midwinter, no one can describe him well. The disclosure of his disordered body works first to establish the assumed abnormality of his "nervous restlessness" and then to hold that assumption up to another, ironic interpretation. Midwinter is introduced "in a disordered state of mind" that looks like "downright madness" (67).

But the passage proceeds to trace the tensions between his confused condition and the "madness" that the onlookers ascribe to it.[48] Through the turn to indirect discourse, his description is filtered through the "general opinion" of his "manner" (73). That opinion is formed as much by his "nervous restlessness" as by his "foreign look" (73, 67), by his "preoccupied" appearance as by his status as a loosely racialized male "vagabond" (73). Insanity is defined by draconian social assumptions, not by an objective observation of facts.

The constructed nature of Midwinter's malaise is underscored in the tale of his upbringing as he proceeds to tell it. "Everything Ozias Midwinter said, everything Ozias Midwinter did was against him," the narrator notes. "There he sat—his face averted; his hands mechanically turning the leaves of his father's letter. . . . With . . . a strange mixture of recklessness and sadness in his voice, he began his promised narrative" (104). Withdrawal appears as a defining attribute of Midwinter's speech. His "sardonic indifference" and "insolence" repel the sympathies of his audience (104). But the passage then turns from the vantage of "any man" to those who observe his early sufferings. Midwinter's passivity reappears as a learned response to the beatings and humiliations of his youth. "Did you ever hear of a dog who liked his master the worse for beating him?" he asks (107). "I don't wonder at the horsewhip now. . . . Natural penalties all of them, sir, which the child was beginning to pay already for the father's sin" (105). Midwinter's manner of self-reproach at once echoes and undermines his audience's antagonisms; in his very disavowal of sympathies, he calls attention to listeners' irrational refusals of them.[49]

But postponement has empowering effects as well: stretching the boundaries of realism, it issues in an augmented awareness of how, in Elizabeth Freeman's words, "temporal dislocation might produce new orientations" to the world (16). Consider the death of Midwinter's adoptive "gipsy father," as he recounts it:

> He made the dogs yelp first, and then he called to me. I didn't go very willingly—he had been drinking harder than usual, and the more he drank the better he liked his after-dinner amusement. He was in high good-humor that day, and he hit me so hard that he toppled over, in his drunken state, with the force of his own blow. He fell with his face in a puddle, and lay there without moving. I and the dogs stood at a distance, and looked at him: we

thought he was feigning, to get us near and have another stroke at us. . . . It took me some time to pull him over—he was a heavy man. When I did get him on his back, he was dead. (108)

"I didn't go very willingly": with this tale, Midwinter's hesitation is situated within a larger life narrative that revises its desultory connotations. At first, his failure to dodge the blow looks like a weakness, aligning him with the same brutalities that the dogs have learned to endure. But while positioning him as an inert center of action, the upshot of the account is to endow Midwinter's ennui with an asocial aura of power. His inhibition leads to his father's self-defeat, so that torpor is made more generative than any fleet-footed reaction could ever be. The implication is reinforced by Midwinter's physical "distance" and detachment from the father's dying gasps. This is the first lesson of Midwinter's education in the senses: disengagement from the present can trigger a break from its routine realities, opening portals to altered social circumstances. For the death of Midwinter's father begins his movement to the genteel landscape of Thorpe-Ambrose, the lateral friendship between him and Allan, and the professional pursuit of writing. Here and elsewhere, postponement becomes less a metric of blockage than the gateway to improved conditions of living.

But Midwinter's "policy of waiting" (798) is neither neutralized nor transcended through his ties to Allan; as the very friendship that his father had warned him to avoid, his inhibition is all the more heightened as a consequence of it. Their friendship reflects a structure of complementary differences: Midwinter's untutored state of "nervous restlessness" (73) finds its inverted image in Allan's conventional public school virtues of frank sociability and physical prowess. The discrepancy makes Midwinter seem stunted by contrast. But as their friendship blooms, we learn that Allan's charismatic élan reflects an absence of depths. This plays out in Allan's fixation on train schedules and departure times and in his repeated fluster while waiting out odd moments of static fixity between destinations. Alan, as the narrator explains, "would infinitely have preferred starting . . . in a violent hurry" (399). In his unthinking haste, Allan emerges as a "flighty" example of social correctness (221), nailed to the temporality of the clock. By comparison, Midwinter grows by learning to refuse the present's sovereign rule. His sense of what Freeman calls "temporal dislocation" and "the slow time of delay and deferral" is intensified as the friendship blossoms, growing in accordance with his superstitious sense that the past is haunting him (16, 18). And with this sensibility, he resolves to avoid the attitude associated his father's homicidal rage: in so many words, he avoids "violent hurry."

We see in miniature here a cluster of themes within mathematical models of time. As in the statistical account of "personal time," two individuals experience events at syncopated tempos and have fundamentally different relations to the present. So writes Francis Baily, a founding figure and president of the Royal Astronomical Society: "I believe that it seldom happens that two persons . . . will agree precisely in their measures," he writes, "but there will almost always be some slight difference between their results."[50] In keeping with Collins's multitemporal plot, the present is understood as a composite creation, not a sui generis fact. And in keeping with Collins's plot, the scientist's task is to compare dual perspectives on it without positing the correctness of either one. Baily stresses that temporal differences need not reflect attributes of personhood: "Each individual," he goes on to explain, "has some real *or* imaginary cause . . . which may differ from that other person" (28). The cause of temporal difference may be external (rooted in "real" environmental conditions) or internal (rooted in "imaginary" mental conditions) but in either case can never be definitively revealed.

It is on this point that the mysteries of time, in natural philosophical arenas, find creative concentration in *Armadale*. For Collins also imagines the prospect of bisecting timescapes situated somewhere between the "real" and the "imaginary." He imagines them not as an argumentative claim, à la Baily's report, but through the techniques of sensation fiction: through the tempos of dialogue, narrative discourse, perspective, and plot. My thesis, as I will be arguing through the remainder of this chapter, is that these techniques do distinctive cultural work: they evoke the propositional claims of scientists but more expansively exploit the ambiguous referential nature of alternative temporalities. The terra incognita between the "real" and the "imaginary," in scientific studies of temporality, emerges as the central landscape of Collins's novel. This point is relevant to two topics that will lead us deeper into *Armadale*'s temporal form: first, the onset of standardized systems of timekeeping in mid-Victorian Britain and second, Collins's counterintuitive ideal of heroic growth.

The fantasy of a collective order of time is introduced at a dinner party in volume 2, when Midwinter finds an elaborate clock of Major Milroy's design. Milroy, Midwinter's acquaintance at Thorpe-Ambrose, displays his handicraft as a reproduction of a famed Strasbourg clock. That clock was widely celebrated as a model of temporal precision in the Victorian periodical press, and Collins had seen the original with Dickens in 1853.[51] The fascination of Milroy's clock lies in its synchrony with the prototype: "They both show what they can do on the stroke of noon," he says (267). In this regard, the spectacle of coordinated clocks is one of a time that stands independent and a priori: "the novelty of precise and ubiquitous time reckoning," as Sue Zemka describes the Victorians' early enthusiasm for standard time.[52] But the defining feature of Milroy's model turns out to be its suggestion of temporal dissonance. Watching the first three chimes, Midwinter and the other guests look on as the figurines tumble to the floor: "[The figures] tottered out across the platform, all three trembling in every limb, dashed themselves headlong against the closed door on the other side" (270).

A provocative idea gets packed into this short span: marching out of time, the figurines evoke a present that has no reality except as the sum of our individual relations to it. This is an intuition that Midwinter recapitulates in turn, when his histrionics force the gathering to spin out of control. Leading up to this point, he had tried to overcome his melancholia and to cultivate a more sociable disposition. But the attempt to harmonize himself with the group falters when the contraption breaks down, and he has a "strange outbreak of gaiety" all the more jarring than his usual self-absorption (264). If Milroy's mechanical figures fail to line up in time, then how could individuals with minds, brains, and nerves?

The meaning of the tableau resides in that question and not in its significance to the succeeding train of events. For what happens in it has little bearing upon the plot per se, so that its untimeliness extends to the formal machinery of the novel. Certainly Collins was fond of unintegrated spectacles such as this, as Victorian critics noted when lamenting sensation fiction's unplotted peregrinations and accumulations of incident upon incident.[53] But the content of the scene invites another assessment of its functions, less as a fall from the totalizing order of narrative than a comment on the very demand for formal regularities. We might understand this demand in the terms that Georg Lukács introduced in his influential essay "Narrate or Describe?" For Lukács, aesthetically successful novels tend to *narrate*. Each element of dialogue, description, and action bears upon the intertwined destinies of individuals in the end; through their cohesion, those elements foster a dynamic, unified understanding of social relations amid tumultuous historical change. In contrast, less successful novels *describe*. Lacking "epic concentration," they tend toward minutiae with only oblique relation to the plot, resulting in what Émile Zola called "a hypertrophy of real detail" in Lukács's example.[54] What aligns such static moments to the formal totality is often nothing more than "crass accident": for instance, fortuitous parallels between names, locations, and actions elsewhere in a novel (112). *Armadale*'s clock scene matters little to the plot; although it indirectly parallels the novel's finale, which turns upon another unruly clock, its only operative function is to depict an early encounter between Midwinter, Allan, and Milroy's daughter, Neelie, who will emerge as Allan's love interest. Yet it would be imprecise to regard the scene as a merely unincorporated incident, important to the narrative only through such serendipitous associations, for what motivates it is precisely its intimation of competing temporal logics. Through its ironic resistance to linear synchronization, the scene underscores what *Armadale* as a whole has so strenuously affirmed: a novel could complicate rather than uphold a functional, uniform order of temporal relations, troubling its aura of self-evidence and activating a more dynamic "historical sense."[55]

Several historically specific reasons exist for Collins's concern with these teeming, evanescent timescapes, perhaps none more significant than the inception of standard time regimes. Literary and cultural historians have shown the 1850s and 1860s to be pivotal years in the transition from regional timekeeping, with town clocks set to the movement of the sun, to a coordinated national standard. And although the shift from solar or "natural" time to standard time escapes a precise date, the most important events overlapped with Collins's development as a novelist. In 1846–47, the British railway adopted Greenwich Mean Time, resulting in the synchronization of formerly local times according to national train schedules. By 1855, nearly all of Britain's public clocks had been set to the same standard. As a result of "rail time" and related technological, administrative, and infrastructural changes, we can observe a more singular present beginning to take hold in high Victorian discourse, as Zemka observes when writing that "many Victorians experienced their lives as subject to a temporal regimentation that was new, drastic, even humorous."[56] Within this milieu, time could be understood as autonomous and unified across local topographies. This understanding gained further legitimation through a Smilesian ethos of economy and efficient labor, as famously parodied by aesthetes like Pater and Oscar Wilde at the century's close.

In *Armadale,* Collins also interrogated time's reification within middle-class culture. On numerous occasions, juxtaposed viewpoints suggest a non-unified order of events, extending beyond the novel's depiction of Midwinter in this regard. At one moment, the narrator contrasts the slow chimes of a local church clock, which Mr. Bashwood hears in Thorpe-Ambrose, with the speed of Midwinter's departing train; elsewhere, the reader is invited to compare the velocities of a telegraph signal and another train: "While [Allan and Midwinter] were on their way back, a somewhat longer telegraphic message . . . was flashing its way past them along the wires, in the reverse direction" (430). Train, telegraph, clock, characters: different temporalities coexist in an asynchronous narrative moment, to which we might add the temporalities of reading and narration. With these intersecting timescales, Collins deploys the tools of multiplot narrative—the representation of competing perspectives on an event and of different events happening at once—to provide an experience of reading that mirrors Midwinter's own sense of disjointed time. Establishing when things happen, in reading *Armadale,* means mediating between an abundance of tempos, rhythms, and just-noticeable differences within the present, none necessarily delusional or rational in themselves. Increasingly, as we shall see, the question of what postponement "is" for Midwinter—the experience of something personal or extrapersonal, pathological or otherwise—turns into the further issue of what the novel "does" to its readership, in *Armadale's* own prolonged patterns of suspense. Through its prodigal temporalities, Collins casts sensation fiction as a genre of mass entertainment whose allure lay in its dangerously distracting powers of influence, its potential to slow down individuals tied to a rapidly accelerating culture.

In lieu of a direct transference of feeling from the text to the reader's nerves, then, the reader encounters varied orientations to time: a kind of proprioceptive present intimated in myriad acts of sensation, perception, and feeling with no singular relation to the world.[57] With characteristically bohemian verve, Collins acknowledged delay's status as a symptom of psychic perversion, only to then offer interpretations that were becoming closed off to more middling sensibilities. Time after time, *Armadale's* conflicted, emasculated hero slips from the immediacies that surround him, and in each case, the novel affirms a wider continuum of temporal rhythms that are shown to be beneficial. The magical outcomes of Midwinter's inhibition, as in the death of his stepfather, should be understood in this light. In its insistence that alternatives to standard time are never *just* illusions, the novel moves in an antithetical direction, fantasizing that an attunement to other temporalities might have disproportionly productive outcomes in the world. At various later instances, this ideal infuses Midwinter's hesitations with an unaccountably aggrandized agency. Standing back from the now, cultivating an awareness of diverse temporalities, turns out to have transformative social benefits, bearing out what Caroline Levine describes as "the pleasures of suspense" in Victorian novels: "Narrative enigmas and delays," Levine writes, "could help to foster habits of hesitation and uncertainty."[58] Collins's novel not only invites a skeptical understanding of the present but invests it with the fantasy of serendipitous social change.

The main fulcrum for the plot is the narrative of Allan Armadale's dream. As a growing obsession for Midwinter, the dream heightens his "superstitious distrust" of others, leaving him all the more morose (332). At the same time, his fixation on it is shown to be legitimate, since it prefigures ensuing events. In the first of the three dream tableaus, the dreamer sinks underwater in the cabin of a ship, as had Allan's murdered father; the tableau anticipates what later occurs in the narrative, when the two friends stumble upon the ship where the murder had happened. "Here, where the deed had been done," the narrator writes, "the fatal parallel between past and present was complete. What the cabin had been in the time of the fathers, that the cabin was now in the time of the sons" (150). The suggestion of a "fatal" course of events throws Midwinter into a state of morbid preoccupation. Yet his reactive withdrawal here confers a solution to the very issue at hand; against the impulsive violence of the paternal pattern, which looms over the scene of the crime, his hesitations open the prospect of divergent trajectories to the future, so that deviations within the present lead to new routes of living.[59]

When Midwinter transcends these holding patterns and steels himself to act, the outcomes are counterproductive. This is the case in his initial rapid-fire responses to Lydia Gwilt. In the prologue, Gwilt had appeared as an unnamed accomplice in the initial murder; here in volume 1, she has reemerged in disguise after Allan inherits an estate at Thorpe-Ambrose and begins to court Neelie Milroy. The reader knows that Gwilt has become Neelie's governess under a false identity. But when Midwinter acquires a physical description of the accomplice and compares it with Gwilt, he acts all too fast. "He was self-possessed enough, in the interval of expectation, before the governess and pupil reached the end of the walk" (334). At the "interval of expectation," Midwinter appears as a model of self-possession and acts for once in the heat of the moment. But it turns out that this "dogged resolution" is futile in a way that affirms his more irrational, irresolute impulses (334). "In all that related, to his position towards his friend," the narrator observes, "he had reached an absolutely definite conclusion, by an absolutely definite process of thought. . . . In the place of the Dream-Shadow, there had stood, on the evidence of the rector's letter, not the instrument of the Fatality—but a stranger!" (337–38). Midwinter's hesitation appears as a state to be overcome by "definite" thought and action. But then the "interval of expectation" is purified of its pejorative implications, since spontaneous action is what lets Gwilt evade detection (334, 337). His haste allows Gwilt to work against Allan and him unobserved as she schemes to marry Midwinter, kill the two friends, and then claim Thorpe-Ambrose for herself (having taken Midwinter's true name, Armadale).

So to endure against Gwilt's scheme, Midwinter must learn to cultivate the "interval of expectation" rather than to leap into action, heightening what may look like an antisovereign condition of the nerves. The limitations of the medical account become clear in the depiction of Dr. Hawbury, the resident physician who rescues the friends from the ruined ship on which the dream occurred. Hawbury embodies an "essentially practical point of view" (173) that the narrator shows to be blinkered by convention: "The one absorbing interest in Midwinter's mind—the interest of penetrating the mystery of the dream—kept him silent throughout. Heedless of all that was said or done about him, he watched Allan, followed Allan, like a dog, until the time came for getting down into the boat. Mr. Hawbury's professional eye rested on him curiously, noting his varying color, and the incessant restlessness of his hands" (166). For Hawbury, Midwinter's intense introspection appears as an unmistakable sign of disorder. "I wouldn't change nervous systems with that man," the doctor concludes, "for the largest fortune that could be offered me" (166). Symbolically linked to the dogs that accompanied him as a child, Midwinter looks like an atavistic outcast. Yet subtle shifts within the passage work to undermine Hawbury's authority as a judge of character. The narrator observes Midwinter's pallor and restless, nerve-racked limbs but then steps back to critique the doctor's parochial

fixation on appearances alone. Hawbury's supercilious statement in conclusion is less a "professional" diagnosis than a personal slight, so that his
pronouncement on Midwinter's nervous system is shown to be in bad faith.
The medical perspective is a personal perspective like any other.

The critique of medical standards here speaks to the novel's resistance
to the trajectories of male maturation more broadly. *Armadale* endlessly suspends its hero's growth toward coordination with an adult social world, only
then to impugn the assumptions of a culture that defines his unconventional
rhythms of experience as abnormal. That project corresponds to Collins's
characteristic subversion of middle-class virtues, whose hypocrisies are exhibited as lacking throughout his sensation novels; but the theme is borne
out with increasing force through the latter half of *Armadale,* as Midwinter's
sensory education issues in intensified forms of drift. Rather than moving
from indecision to spontaneous action and strong social bonds, Midwinter
learns to cultivate a vigilant awareness of other temporalities, a not-now out
of sync with the ideals of his milieu. In effect, Collins reimagines the problem of arrested development by literalizing it, until postponement emerges
as an alternate strategy of living. Through this process, Midwinter's characterization comes to reflect neither a vigorously antiauthoritarian politics
nor a final acceptance of convention but something like what Heather Love
calls a "weak refusal" of the present.[60] Immersing himself in discontinuous
timescales, he learns to stand back from the world that threatens him: "Well,
if I can't laugh," he says, "I can wait" (239).

On this point, the novel's dynamics of stunted growth coincide with *Richard Feverel,* whose wandering hero also stops short of conventional manhood,
and whose shortcomings also invite a narrative recognition of alternatives.
With Midwinter, the formal fits and starts of Meredith's novel are hypostasized
as a foundation for character; self-interruption is Midwinter's signature trait.
Consistent with the reception of Meredith's novel as well, Victorian reviewers
critiqued Midwinter's stalled development as a lapse in narrative design. The
unnamed reviewer for the *Saturday Review,* for example, lamented "the amount
of ability expended upon Midwinter," given that "it is impossible to derive
much pleasure or profit from the spectacle of his feeble mental and moral
evolutions."[61] The drama of enfeebled evolution—of underdevelopment—
has a low level of interest compared to the novel's thrilling events. But behind
the problem of failed formation stands a more dynamic question within the
narrative itself: is Midwinter's sense of temporal difference a mental mirage

or something tied to outward conditions of existence? Midwinter's postponements raise divergent interpretations but leave the question up in the air, suspended in a haze of ghostly traces, dreams, and shadows.

So strongly is Midwinter's character associated with irresolution that it
defines his eventual choice of a vocation. When he takes up writing, upon
his short-lived marriage to Gwilt, that choice heightens his torpor instead
of helping to overcome it. Even in the midst of marriage and a public profession, Midwinter remains a withdrawn visionary whose strength is sapped
"beyond what his brains will bear" (668). "Day after day," Gwilt writes of her
new husband, "the hours that he gives to his hateful writing grow longer
and longer; day after day, he becomes more and more silent, in the hours
that he gives to me" (660). His labors spur him to take up "his old vagabond
habits" and to dream of former days with his stepfather and Allan (660). The
shadow of earlier events haunt him still. And as it turns out, those vagabond
habits have more useful outcomes than Midwinter can know, since they
keep Gwilt at bay. While forging the last links in her scheme to kill him and
Allan, she is unable to manipulate a husband who wills himself to remain
out of step with the world. Despite a visiting doctor's warning to "drop your
pen" (671), his writing keeps him alive precisely because it plunges him into
"the shadow of the past" (147).

But *Armadale*'s multitemporal logics are not embodied exclusively in Midwinter; they also find powerful concentration in Gwilt, his wife and would-be
nemesis. She appears as an explicit authorial figure—a "shadow" (171) who
works to usurp the tale through the manipulation of older melodramatic
conventions. "[Gwilt] persisted in giving a name which was on the face
of it a false one; in telling a commonplace story, which was manifestly an
invention" (94). She appears as a unique character who tells a "commonplace story," a singular voice within a tale that threatens to repeat its initial
ur narrative. Through these self-reflexive gestures, the thematics of "delay
and deferral" in *Armadale* open out to a further problem of interpretation:
coming to terms with the presence of the past, Midwinter must become
effective at identifying former fictions (Freeman, 18).

As she tries to enact her plan, Gwilt is beset by hesitations that mirror
and accentuate Midwinter's own. "The irritation of continued suspense,"
the narrator notes, "had produced a change for the worse in Miss Gwilt's
variable temper, which was perceptible to every one about her, and which,

strangely enough, was reflected by an equally marked change in the doctor's manner" (743). For everyone in her radius, Gwilt's "continued suspense" is an unquestionable illness, despite an absence of clear-cut symptoms. "Perhaps I am overexcited," she asks herself, "by the suspense and anxiety of my present position? Perhaps the merest fancies and suspicions are leading me astray?" (724). As her plan presses forward, "singular hesitation" emerges as Gwilt's most constitutive characteristic (92). "Why am I hesitating? Why not go on to step the third and last?" she asks (538). Willing herself to overcome self-suspension, Gwilt explains in her diary that "I determined to snatch at [Allan's fortune] without allowing myself time to hesitate" (699–700). Jenny Bourne Taylor writes that the diary entries represent a "merging of narrative time and story time," a simultaneity of action and its inscription as text.[62] But we might also note that it compounds the inner drama of her hesitations. In fact, Gwilt's epistolary narration can be understood as offering a composite of postponements: the gap between the time of writing and action, between actions and the time when characters sense and perceive them, between perceptions and the time of narration, and between the narration and the experience of reading. By focusing the reader's interest in these proliferating lag times, the novel offers a vicarious experience of the temporal disorientations it identifies with Midwinter and Gwilt, so as to heighten the strategies we have seen throughout: to read *Armadale* is to be thrown from the present tense in an experience of estrangement from the now.

Like Midwinter, Gwilt is an orphaned outsider whose hesitations appear by turns personal and extrapersonal. But whereas Gwilt aims to minimize her "suspense and anxiety" in order to consummate her scheme, Midwinter learns to expand the interval of postponement and to cultivate a sense of other temporalities. The juxtaposition of their efforts finds an apotheosis in the conclusion, set in the sanatorium owned by Gwilt's accomplice, Dr. Downward. The sanatorium appears as an embodiment of modern medical methods; in its depiction, however, Collins draws on gothic conventions about the madhouse as a site of confusion and reversal, parodying the treatments recommended by Victorian medical reformers such as Joseph Connolly in the 1850s.[63] The doctor's "private snuggery" typifies the rationale of the institution as a whole: "Above the fireplace hung a collection of photographic portraits of men and women, enclosed in two larger frames hanging side by side with a space between them. The left hand frame illustrated effects of nervous suffering as seen in the face; the right hand frame exhibited the ravages of insanity from the same point of view; while the space between was occupied by an elegantly illuminated scroll bearing inscribed on it the time honored motto, 'prevention is better than cure'" (712). Transparent trappings of middle-class domesticity—the ornate bookcase, glass doorways, and portrait-lined fireplace—belie the scientific spectacle of disease. The two portraits at the center illustrate a taxonomical approach to personhood, in which "nervous suffering" and "insanity" refer to fundamental qualities of who and what one is. "And there is my System," Downward explains. "Let other men treat insanity, if they like—I stop it! No patients in the house as yet. But we live in an age when nervous derangement (parent of insanity) is steadily on the increase and in due time the sufferers will come" (713). When Midwinter and Gwilt arrive, their hesitations will expose the "System" as amounting to little more than a system of coercion.

As a program of medical surveillance, Downward's "System" recalls "the system" in *Richard Feverel*. Like Sir Austin Feverel, Downward works against the threat of perversion by disciplining subjects unaware of being manipulated at all. "[The] treatment," he explains, "sedulously pursued throughout the day, follows the sufferer into his room at night; and soothes, helps, and cures him, without his own knowledge" (770). While granting the illusion of autonomy, the system controls one's perceptions and sensations at every moment of their incitement. "A nervous patient who always has his own way," he concludes, "is a nervous patient who is never worried—and a nervous patient who is never worried, is a nervous patient cured" (774). The irony of this ideal is underscored by its association with Gwilt's conspiracy. To be freed from dragging inhibition is just another means of disempowerment. Presentism, the bias toward temporal immediacies, is shown to be an invidious foundation for modern medicine.

Even as the sanatorium serves to distinguish normal from abnormal individuals, then, *Armadale* shows the categories themselves to be incoherent. This is made most striking in Midwinter's and Gwilt's paradoxical position within its walls. Through a process of symbolic inversions, they become both outsiders and also its most fitting subjects, starting with their ploys to gain admission. When Gwilt appears disguised as a nervous inmate (a performance that allows her to obtain the poison for her scheme), she enacts the role all too well. "The prevalent impression," explains the narrator, "was . . . that [Dr. Downward's] first inmate was mad" (770). The continuity between Gwilt's performed persona and actual nervous condition calls her self-coherence into question. For his part, Midwinter's admission to the sanatorium merely marks an escalation in his vaguely nervous condition. His actions at once fit the protocols of the sanatorium and turn them on their head, so as to emphasize its shortcomings as a site of mental management.

By manipulating its entry conditions, then, the characters reveal the institution's inadequacies as an arbiter of mental health and attest to the novel's competitive prestige in imagining more capacious and creative forms of temporal experience. "The English novelist who enters my house," Downward tells Gwilt, "must understand his art as the healthy-minded English reader understands it in our time. All we want of him is—occasionally to make us laugh, and invariably to make us comfortable" (769–70). Downward's ideology runs counter to *Armadale*'s poetics of postponement. His premise—that novels should render readers uninhibited, tranquil, and pliable—indicates the attitude that Midwinter must renounce to survive. Freedom from the irresolution and "continued suspense" becomes a questionable goal that lulls one into an unthinking acceptance of immediacies (743). At the very cultural moment when sensorial studies of reaction time began to flourish, it is instead Midwinter's morbid "policy of waiting" that leads to ameliorated social conditions (798).

The critique of prevailing mental models, incarnate in the sanitarium, sharpens *Armadale*'s sense of liminality. The reader discovers that there is no singular now for Midwinter to inhabit so much as an amalgam of temporal deviations within the present. Against a normative orientation in time, Midwinter is situated within what Harry Harootunian calls "the collision of coexisting temporalities," an interval filled with compound vectors of becoming.[64] Never does this recognition rise to a full vindication of Midwinter's nervous condition; still less does it issue in a statement about how Britain might escape its larger legacies of bloodshed and overseas despoliation, as indexed in the dark skin and biracial heritage that mark Midwinter as a product of Barbados slavery. The suggestions of alterity remain implicit in the reader's affective experience of a novel that repeatedly reveals how Midwinter's hesitations are enabling and that repeatedly reorients the boundaries between the past and future, while stopping short of defining the nature of its "coexisting temporalities" once and for all. *Armadale* activates a recognition of difference at the levels of thought, feeling, and sense experience—what I have been characterizing as a poetics of postponement, an aesthetic of sensation fiction that denies any univocal historical sense.[65]

The ending advances a dual account of "continued suspense" (743), in keeping with the twin interpretations of postponement all along. By turns, Midwinter's hesitations appear as an emasculating illness and also as a generative goal: an unconventional form of agency under conditions of disempowerment. Having been lured into the institution to save Allan's love interest, Neelie, Midwinter moves through a sequence of abstract associations to find her. "His mind," the narrator says, "clouded and confused by disturbing influences, instinctively took refuge in its impressions," while "the sense of an unutterable expectation throbbed in his heart" (796). Beginning with this unaccountable belief in some "hidden danger" (796), his "disconnected impressions" gather around a "vague distrust of what might happen next" (795, 794). These impressions lead to a flash of insight into Gwilt's scheme. In this epiphanic instant, Midwinter realizes that he and Allan, not Neelie, are the true objects of her wiles; she has conspired with Downward to kill Allan while he sleeps, he reasons, a discovery that leads Midwinter to switch rooms with Allan in order to save him. "To reach this conclusion, and to decide on baffling the conspiracy . . . by taking Allan's place, was with Midwinter the work of an instant" (796). This realization appears as a moment of self-realization. "Confronted by actual peril, the great nature of the man intuitively freed itself from the weaknesses that had beset it," the narrator writes (796). From a benighted condition of weakness and delusion, Midwinter is primed for forthright action of the kind that will demonstrate his "great nature" as a man.

Or so it seems. For while Midwinter convinces Allan to switch rooms with him, the climax is anything but instantaneous; his revelation folds back to the position of irrational inaction and distrust that typified him from the beginning, and which is even elevated now into a "policy." "Without a fact that could justify to other minds his distrust of what might happen with the night . . . the one policy he could follow, come what might of it, was the policy of waiting for events" (798). Midwinter has no evidence that the room is set to be filled with poison gas. Proceeding without rational motivation, Midwinter's most assertive action in the finale is an acceptance of "delay and deferral" (Freeman, 18): the resignation to linger in the room, which finally thwarts Gwilt's scheme. When she is nearly finished filling the room with gas, her guilty gaze at her husband drives her to suicide. This fate echoes the death of Midwinter's stepfather, where willful inaction also had disproportionally generative results. Shrinking from the present produces an altered chain of events, as is only accentuated by the scrupulous record of the minutes. For at the center of the drama is not Midwinter but "a clock of the noiseless sort." Introduced as "incapable of offending irritable nerves," the clock ironically intensifies Gwilt's sense of confusion: "Touched the quarter-past one, Miss Gwilt stepped noiselessly into the corridor" (798). "Turning from the window, she looked at the clock. It was twenty minutes past one" (800). "She pondered over it till the minute-hand of the clock pointed to the half-hour. 'No!' she said" (800). "After marking the time by a glance at the clock, she dropped into the glass funnel the first of the six separate Pourings" (801). "The first of the intervals of five minutes was endless. The time stood still. The suspense was maddening" (801). "She was startled into sudden self-remembrance. She turned quickly, and looked at the clock; seven minutes had passed since the second Pouring" (802). "Three out of the next five minutes passed, and again the suspense began to madden her. The space in the corridor grew too confined for the illimitable restlessness that possessed her limbs" (802). "She waited the event. A time passed: a time short enough to be reckoned by minutes on the clock; and yet long enough to take her memory back over all her married life with [Midwinter]" (805). The scene advances a final synthesis between the narrative's representation of postponement and its incitements to readerly postponement; the plot winds down through the characters' compulsive hesitations. In particular, suspense is incited through Gwilt's increasing rate of deviation from the "minutes on the clock." And unequivocally, for once, that state is maddening. This is underscored through the scene's shifting narration, which oscillates between the third person and the indirectly presented perspective of Gwilt. "Oh, the time! the time!" she thinks. "If it could only have been begun and ended with the first Pouring!" (801). The "last interval" of life is the first that she lives in a pure present: "As she gently closed [Midwinter's] fingers . . . and looked up, the last minute of the last interval faced her, recorded on the clock" (806). Overcoming one's hesitation, in *Armadale*, is anathema to becoming an autonomous and fully achieved individual; for Gwilt, attempting to match the tempo of the clock proves fatal.

So the meticulous register of time, in the finale, folds back to an apprehension of the multichronic landscapes throughout the novel. In part, the scenario evokes experiments in reaction time through the 1860s and afterward. As in Maudsley's fantasy of a site devoted to calculating how "time is an essential element in every mental function" (371), the novel envisages an institution for measuring nervous intervals and so seems to anticipate Wilhelm Wundt's opening of the Leipzig Institute in 1879, where "the fundamental dimension of the new science," as Daston and Galison write, "was time."[66] But *Armadale* defines those temporal measurements as an incomplete index into mental life, since Midwinter fails to appear in the scene at all. Suggesting the limited vantage of the medical establishment, the scene instead presents an ensemble effect: it substitutes the hard facts of Midwinter's existence, as an embodied presence in one time and place, with an evocation of different possible relations to the minutes of the clock. In this respect, the appearance of the clock culminates his evasion of its meanings throughout the novel. Midwinter's unassimilable relation to the present becomes most manifest when he vanishes from plain sight.

Ultimately, *Armadale* withholds an empirical explanation of the temporalities that it has conjured up all along. In keeping with the tension between probabilistic (statistical) and physio-psychological (sensorial) accounts, the nature of its timescapes remains multiple and contested to the end. Midwinter's refusal to accept the "rational view" of events in the epilogue leaves him susceptible to the irrational impulses that defined him at the outset (815). Should his asynchronous affects be branded a disease of the modern mind and brain—a sign of wayward development, of stunted growth—or affirmed as a legitimate intimation of "other possible worlds," in Elizabeth Freeman's words?[67] Collins leaves the mystery unresolved. But unlike the writings of contemporary scientists, the novel finds positive value in the ambiguity at hand. *Armadale* manipulates the boundaries between a rational and spurious sense of alternative temporalities; not by embracing a clear-cut theorem but by deploying the unique resources of the novel, it participates in a continuum of ideas about possibilities poised between the "imaginary" and the "real."[68]

So the various clues concerning Midwinter's "historical sense" lead to no final answer about its nature; whatever his gut feeling of alternatives to a homogenous historical time, in the end the taint of delusion lingers.[69] But the novel does clarify its importance to the occupation of writing. This becomes clear in the final lines, which mention Midwinter's ambitions "to take to Literature" (814). No longer tied to deviance alone—to his status as a vagabond devoid of a name or vocation—his hesitations have been turned to socially constructive outcomes. Irresolution reemerges as a trait of the professional male novelist. In this, Midwinter ends where *Armadale*'s author began, as Collins experienced an assortment of debilitating ills in the service of a text "not hastily meditated, or idly wrought out" (4). But the ending exonerates Collins from the prospect of a failed novel: of a self-interrupting narrative whose hesitant hero fails to grow up, overcome his emotionalism, and emerge as a conventional male hero. Those potentials have been revised in triumphal terms, with Midwinter as a less grandiose kind of protagonist than the reader might have anticipated. Having escaped the crushing violence of a patriarchal past, he winds up as a bachelor liberated from a name and family. His "effeminate hesitations" (157) have helped to produce a different future for this generation of Armadales, who will not be brutal rivals but intimate friends. In arriving at this conclusion, the ending also absolves Collins from excessive interruptions in the production of the text itself. For as Midwinter's choice of a vocation suggests, untimeliness is not only common to the act of writing but perhaps its most normative state.

CHAPTER 3

"A Nat'ral Born Friend"
The Evolution of Community in *Dombey and Son*

A "fatal" problem: so Charles Darwin described an explosive enigma in his work. The problem, he wrote in *On the Origin of Species* (1859), appeared as "the one special difficulty that at first appeared to me insuperable and actually fatal to my whole theory."[1] The term "fatal" provides a clear compression of the difficulty at hand. For what troubled Darwin was the problem of nonreproduction—the problem, that is, of evolutionary dead ends. In his earliest writings, Darwin typically explained evolution as a rivalry between self-interested individuals; to win out in the "battle for life" was to advance an isolated stock or seed of one's own, doing so in a heated Malthusian struggle for dwindling resources. Selfish striving was the only game available, or so it seemed. For nonreproductive creatures confounded the rule of internecine personal conflict. Worker ants, for instance, devoted themselves to others' offspring at the expense of independent lineages. Their sacrifice was so perfect as to exclude even the goal of self-perpetuation. And yet these beings continued to thrive generation after generation. Confronted with their paradoxical persistence, Darwin worried that nonreproduction could only be an aporia at the heart of evolutionism, suspending the rules of the game that defined it as a coherent system of knowledge. "I . . . leave the problem as insoluble," his rival A. R. Wallace later wrote to him, "only fearing that it will become a formidable weapon in the hands of the enemies of Nat. Selection."[2] The enigma of nonreproduction threatened to pull Darwin's theory apart before it could be brought into print.

How do transfigured forms of character come into being? Under what circumstances can altered habits of feeling be born and cultivated, resulting in more mutual structures of living? These questions suffused the language of Darwinian biology from its incipience in the mid-1830s. Darwin first identified the "one special difficulty" of altruistic nonreproduction at that juncture, then laboring over it in dialogue with his international network of correspondents. Eventually, he found that selfless creatures could lose in order to win. By abnegating a single reproductive partner, nonreproductive individuals could devote themselves to safeguarding the lives of close relations, thereby advancing a shared stock in communal settings. Individuals of this sort promoted their interests in more mediated fashion, helping all and adding to the general invigoration of the group. The effect of this finding was to redraw the ostensible opposition of sexual success and sexual failure, of egoism and altruism, by affirming their functional equivalence at a higher scale of relations. Far from an exception to the rules of evolution, the growth of moral and social sentiments illustrated its mechanisms in singular form.

Scholars such as Robert J. Richards, Helena Cronin, and Thomas Dixon have examined the theoretical intricacies of Darwin's "difficulty," often situating it within British naturalist traditions. Cronin's account aims at "confining itself to the scientific content of the theories and other matters internal to science," while Dixon adds that the "literary machinations of the metropolis were in sharp contrast with the much more detached life of the naturalist Darwin"; Richards more precisely tracks Darwin's explanation to an isolated insight in June of 1848.[3] But attention to Victorian literary production begs for a complication of this internalist narrative. The present chapter argues for the aesthetic functions of the novel in prefiguring Darwin's solution and in contributing to an emergent fascination with the subject in mid-Victorian culture. Interest in the evolution of altruism became widespread after Darwin's publication of the *Origin;* by the late 1870s, it emerged as a recurrent topic in generalist lectures and articles, philosophical treatises, and political tracts, as Dixon and David Stack observe.[4] But of more formative importance, I show, were the benevolent bachelors in mid-Victorian novels: above all, those in Charles Dickens's *Dombey and Son,* whose last installment appeared in nearly the same month as Darwin's breakthrough. By foregrounding the sensibilities of its marginal men, the "intimate friend[s]" Solomon Gills and Ned Cuttle (260), the novel imagines how abstemious sexual sacrifice could yield more roundabout routes of communal regeneration and unseat the reign of egoism in the hungry 1840s.[5] In doing so, it suggests how that transformation might unfold at all levels of life, linking human and nonhuman agents as "creatures of one common origin" (Dickens 2002, 702).

A rearticulation of the through lines between this chapter and the previous two will clarify its stakes. For chapter 3 turns from major arenas of probabilistic thinking, within the "hard" Victorian sciences, to its central elaboration within the sciences of life. Here we move from leading mathematicians and astronomers, perched atop the Victorian scientific hierarchy, to investigators working with a more eclectic range of methods and concerns. In part, Darwin's account of moral and social transformation helps us understand the informal, heuristic ways in which the mathematics of variation shaped science before more modern partitions of knowledge. It helps us understand evolutionism's emergence at the intersection between the sciences of life and matter: as an arena structured less around monadic reproductive bodies than a general continuum of "chance" variations. Following Foucauldian lines, cultural historians have become astute at linking Victorian biological thinking to the *fin-de-siècle* explosion of discourses about sexuality, when informal sexual behaviors became enshrined as a cardinal feature of the subject. Darwin himself, however, elaborated an account of life that occasionally unsettled the ties between bodily knowledge, sex, and the individual. Looking beyond the fate of isolated sexual monads, he imagined a processural drama of relations rooted in the impromptu mingling of forces, chemical compounds, and vital powers—relations that could issue in provisional modes of living but no fixed forms of existence. So much is cognate with Elizabeth Grosz's point that "Darwin politicized the material world by showing that it is an emergent or complex order that generates surprising configurations," in which the natural economy has no prestanding origin or end.[6] The present chapter specifies the moral and social orientations of this schema and argues for the cultural work of the novel not only in illustrating but actively anticipating its conceptions of community, altruism, and temporal variation.

DARWIN'S "ONE SPECIAL DIFFICULTY": THE NATURAL HISTORY OF MORALS

Less than a month before the publication of *The Descent of Man* (1871), Darwin wrote a letter to his friend Joseph Hooker. The letter is one of myriad communications of the type between Darwin and his scientific correspondents, though it ends with a singular thought experiment. After outlining a handful of issues ranging from spontaneous generation to Louis Pasteur's experiments in chemical combination, he writes:

> It is often said that all the conditions for the first production of a living organism are present, which could have been present. But if (& oh what a big if!) we could conceive in some warm little pond with all sorts of ammonia & phosphoric salts,—light, heat, electricity &c present, that a protein compound was chemically formed, ready to undergo still more complex changes, at the present day such matter would be instantly devoured or absorbed, which would not have been the case before living creatures were formed.[7]

Darwin's pond consists of a loose bricolage of elements that combine to provoke life from matter. In this assemblage lies the origin of all species, it would seem: the ur event that the *Origin* had left undefined. Or not. The thought experiment resolves in the suggestion that the "first production" of life is a one-time event. If the primordial substance suddenly reappeared, then it would soon be ravaged by beings that evolved after it. The history of life cannot be rewound or repeated post de facto, for "changes" are all-encompassing, and beneficial variations in one niche may become unbeneficial in another. But with its emphasis on the limits of historical knowledge, the passage also typifies Darwin's reliance on modes of conditional thinking: what Tina Choi calls his "recurrent language of causal hypotheses, contingency, and alternativity," and on what might or might not "have been the case" through time, given the imperfection of the geological record and the inferential foundation of his arguments.[8]

What provokes the "changes" that Darwin describes? This was a larger riddle that he never answered in full. Over the course of his lifetime, Darwin entertained an array of conceivable causes for variation. These included the long effects of personal will and self-cultivation, artificial breeding practices, and even (in his earliest prose) the indirect hand of God. But behind these individual influences stood the specter of chance. Small variations leap out at erratic intervals, most of which will prove useless. But the sheer number of variations tend, on the greater balance, toward change in all living forms. What Darwin called chance or random variation operated at two levels of evolution. First, chance operated in individuals who were born with new traits or behaviors, the sources of which were due to material mechanisms that Darwin never claimed to understand. Second, chance operated in the natural selection of individuals and groups, as external changes within a niche made one variation or another beneficial. At both levels, variations were due to "chance" in the sense that they were nonteleological, resulting from factors other than providential design. Darwin had worked out these premises in the late 1830s, though he continued to revise them over the two decades leading up to the *Origin,* where the laws of chance variation were accorded a privileged location in its fifth chapter, "Laws of Variation."

It seems clear, then, why historians have placed Darwin's writings at the center of the Victorian's probabilistic revolution.[9] As a member of the Statistical Society of London and the British Association for the Advancement of Science, Darwin was alive to the latest innovations in probabilistic reason. His extensive intellectual circle included John Lubbock, Babbage, De Morgan, Herschel, and other mathematically minded savants that we have seen. While working to prepare the *Origin* for publication, he spoke with admiration about Henry Buckle's *History of Civilization in England* (if only to report his bemusement after meeting Buckle in 1858).[10] He consulted Herschel's 1850 essay on probabilities several times in the decade leading up to the *Origin,* which Darwin dubbed his "big book on variation," and asked for Lubbock's help with the statistical ratios that he thought would lend it an aura of scientific exactitude.[11]

And yet, while Darwin was attuned to probabilistic developments, he marshaled them in informal terms. An 1860 letter to his friend and mentor Charles Lyell agrees on the cogency of this approach: "I shd. think your remarks were very just about mathematicians not being better enabled to judge of probabilities, than other men of common sense."[12] For Darwin, the calculus of probabilities expressed a "common" sensibility, a prevailing form of thought that transcended the work of specialists. The meanings of "chance variation" therefore remained somewhat provisional to him, as aspects of his argument to be worked out in stylistic terms, in keeping with Devin Griffiths's reminder that "Darwin's science is narrative and comparative, relying heavily on formal experimentation" to "conjure the imagined past."[13] From the 1830s, Darwin seemed confident about what chance variations were *not.* They were not signs of God's guiding hand or moral purpose. But he lacked a clear alternative to the tradition that he rejected. All variations *had* causes for Darwin; those variations were "accidental" only in that they were without intention, not that they were without material impetus at all. As he wrote in *The Descent of Man,* "Variations, owing to our ignorance, are often said to arise spontaneously," though they do not in fact.[14] And yet, the opacities of Darwin's language left the concept indistinct. It stood as "one of Darwin's greatest problems" virtually from its inception, as intellectual historians note, which "would not go away" even as he labored to control its referential range.[15] T. H. Huxley diagnosed the issue in 1866, writing that "Darwin is obliged to speak of variation *as if* it were spontaneous or a matter of chance."[16] Darwinian "chance" slides between competing orders of reference, as a phenomenon implied to be both literal and analogical in turn. The potential for variation is ubiquitous but has no precise relation to individuals.

When Darwin opened his transmutation notebooks in the 1830s, he understood himself as advancing Newton's cosmology by translating established doctrines about the heavens into the emergent sciences of life on Earth (geology, embryology, physiology, and comparative anatomy). He writes in a notebook of 1838: "Astronomers might formerly have said that God ordered, each planet to move in its particular destiny.—In the same manner God orders each animal created with certain form in certain country, but how much more simple, & sublime power let attraction act according to certain laws such are inevitable consequen[ces]. Let animals be created, then by the fixed laws of generation, such will be their successors."[17] Darwin posits a God that stands outside the workings of his creation, inaugurating "fixed laws" but ruling in absentia. According to pre-Newtonian wisdom (what astronomers "formerly have said"), God shaped the "destiny" of each object in space and time; in contrast, Newton proposed a clockwork mechanism in which objects obeyed stable, predictable forces like gravitation. This framework could be extended to natural history, Darwin speculates. Against the notion that Providence intervened to adjust species in relation to environmental changes, he imagines autonomously acting laws. The word "attraction" has meanings in the realms of inanimate matter (referring to the Newtonian law of gravitation) and animate life (referring to the laws of reproduction or "generation"), so as to encapsulate Darwin's project: an account of life as harmonious, stable, and predicable as Newton's account of the heavens.

Not long afterward, however, Darwin's attention turned toward more erratic processes of change. One source of inspiration was Lyell, who had studied the "chance transport" of organisms (plant seedlings, for example, that were transported over great distances by the variable movements of wind and water).[18] Another was the Malthusian account of population pressure, which led to a singular breakthrough in 1839. "My principle," Darwin wrote in his fourth transmutation notebook, is "the destruction of all the less hardy [ones], & the preservation of *accidental* hardy seedlings," adding that "there ought to be no weeding or encouragement, but a vigorous battle between strong and weak."[19] This is Darwin's first statement that "accidental" change can result in higher modes of organization.[20] Changes are "accidental" in the sense that they do not result from Providential or human "encouragement." But the repeated "accidental," though shorn of explicit ties to religion, is itself indistinct: an ancillary modifier rather than an independent locus of concern, it is introduced alongside Malthusian concepts of "preservation" and "destruction." Chance is presented "as if" real but is inserted in a passage that leaves it undefined vis-à-vis individual bodies.

These definitional ambiguities persisted through the *Origin,* as scholars including Dov Ospovot and Curtis Johnson have noted, resulting in what Choi calls "ever more complex hypothetical possibilities" in his prose.[21] Darwin writes in the fourth chapter, "Natural Selection": "Can it, then, be thought *improbable,* seeing that variations useful to man have undoubtedly occurred, that other variations useful in some way to each being in the great and complex battle of life, should *sometimes* occur in the course of thousands of generations? If such do occur, can we doubt . . . that individuals having any advantage, however slight, over others, would have *the best chance* of surviving and of procreating their kind?" (164; emphasis added). On occasion, some slight variation will benefit one individual in the battle for life, leading to that variation's inheritance and intensification. In the struggle of each against each, victories tend to be obtained by small, accidental changes in isolated beings. But the precise mechanisms of variation are left opaque. Instead, the passage invites the reader to entertain what might be "improbable" or not, asking what we might or might not "doubt" to be true. Darwin's speculative language converts probabilistic principles from a matter of content to one of form. While stipulating laws of variation in general, he remained mute as to variation's causes.

What seemed safe to wager was that individual variations were rooted in individual beings, whether those variations had physical, behavioral, or mental manifestations. From the early 1840s, Darwin's writings most often defined the struggle for existence as a battle won by minor variations in individuals. "As more individuals are produced than can possibly survive," Darwin wrote in the *Origin,* "there must in every case be a struggle for existence, either one individual with another of the same species, or with the individuals of distinct species" (147). Darwin's focus on individual struggle, in the theory of natural selection, extended to sexual selection's focus on individual reproductive rivalries. When Darwin began to envision a natural history of morals, it was with this focus on individual variation. Of particular influence was William Paley's *The Principles of Moral and Political Philosophy* (1785), which Darwin encountered as an undergraduate at Cambridge. Paley conceded that individuals are disposed to selfish gratifications, only to then redefine gratification in religious terms; for the highest pleasure in the world, he wrote, was the thought of eternal happiness. From this vantage, looking out for the good of others was less an obligation than a pleasurable pursuit in itself, as one acted instrumentally in anticipation of heavenly rewards. "Whatever is expedient is right. It is the utility of any moral rule alone which constitutes the obligation of it," Paley argued.[22] In Paley's doctrine of expediency, self-interest is what guides God's moral plan.

From the 1830s onward, Darwin accepted Paley's conception of self-directed individuals and allowed that egoism might lead to communal bonds of "obligation," while denying Paley's religious rationale. He writes in September of 1838: "I am tempted to say that those actions which have been found necessary for long generation (as friendship to fellow animals in social animals) are those which are good and consequently give pleasure, and not as Paley's rule is then that on long run *will* do good. Alter *will* in all such cases to *have,* and *origin* as well as *rule* will be given."[23] "Alter *will,*" take out "have": these mock emendations turn Paley's language at odd angles from itself. "Paley's rule" decreed the invariable nature of social sentiments (what "will" and must transpire in social life). In contrast, Darwin posits a conditional history of virtue in which the "good" has historically changed. Bonds of "friendship" may be beneficial in securing food, land, and protection, which collectively promote "long generation"; but no innate virtue lies in friendship per se. Darwin refined this position as he read religious and philosophical thinkers like Whewell, Herschel, Harriet Martineau, and James Macintosh in the 1840s, returning to the primacy of self-preservation as a motor of organic change.

At this point, however, he was confronted with a vexing paradox. For certain neuter and sterile classes—nurses and builders among hive bees, for example—could not be reconciled with an account of individual moral variations. "On the theory of natural selection," he explained in the *Origin,* "the case [of sterile organisms] is especially important, inasmuch as the sterility . . . could not possibly be of any advantage to them" (424). In social communities, nonreproductive members embodied the highest principles of self-abnegation. Common sense dictated that such sentiments would perish as more rapacious ones intensified over time. That self-sacrificing behaviors might be "profitable" made sense, it seemed to Darwin in the early 1840s, only through the theological conventions that he disclaimed.

At the center of this problem stood a more fundamental lacuna in the concept of chance variation, as we have seen: the fact that "chance" variation had no particular relation to individuals. Possibilities for social change, which suffused the world, floated free from isolated beings in the flesh. Nowhere was the concept's status as a working model, a set of informal inferences and conjectures, more manifest. Nonreproductive altruism stood as a challenge to Darwin's understanding of chance variation, and thus to his evolutionism more generally, because it marked an otherwise unmarked line of incoherence at its core. Variations, so conceptually prevalent, could not be pinned down to a specific location in nature's economy.

Certainly, Darwin was quick to explain the raison d'être for other nonreproductive forms. He saw some neuter and sterile classes, for instance, as evidence that nature imposed limits on interbreeding and self-fertilization. And he was willing to entertain certain Lamarckian models of altruism as well, according to which repeated behaviors became hard-wired over many generations. But altruistic nonreproduction could not be explained in these terms. Darwin gives a clear account of the dilemma in *The Descent of Man:*

> It is extremely doubtful whether the offspring of the more sympathetic and benevolent parents, or of those which were the most faithful to their comrades, would be reared in greater number than the children of selfish and treacherous parents of the same tribe. He who was ready to sacrifice his life, as many a savage has been, rather than betray his comrades, would often leave no offspring to inherit his noble nature. The bravest men, who were always willing to come to the front in war, and who freely risked their lives for theirs, would on an average perish in larger number than other men. (155)

Nature tends to select organisms best suited to compete for personal needs. But selfless individuals put themselves in harm's way for others, suffering acts of violence without the prospect of returned aid. How could benevo-lent impulses "on an average" continue to thrive, given the universal drives toward personal profit?

A lethal issue, then: it seemed that the existence of selflessness could *only* be explained through appeals to God's moral contrivance. Most influentially, William Kirby and William Spence's four-volume *An Introduction to Entomol-ogy* (1828) had defined the instincts of "those insects which live in society" as strong evidence of God's designing will. The insects were "truly extraordi-nary, and without parallel in any other department of nature" because they "willingly sacrifice their lives" for others, as Kirby and Spence wrote, reason-ing that their instincts must therefore be "indulged by Providence."[24] Upon reading the text in the 1830s, Darwin jotted a note of frustration: "Neuters do not breed! How instinct acquired."[25] He went on in that space to work out several ideas but did not arrive at a satisfactory solution for many years. In the species book that was abridged as the *Origin*, Darwin acknowledged that "it is most natural to believe that the transcendent perfection & com-plexity of many instincts can be accounted for only by the direct interposi-tion of the Creator."[26] How could life exist sans reproduction?

In a tradition dating back to Malthus, British intellectuals had cast the instinct to reproduce as equivalent with the will to survive; both were thought to be fixed and universal in human and animal agents, as Cather-ine Gallagher has argued.[27] That connection had hardened into a virtually axiomatic assumption by the 1830s; it seemed impossible for life to persist without the reproductive impulse. We can see Darwin beginning to pry apart the connection between life and reproduction in June of 1848, when he composed a significant four-page manuscript on the subject. This was the foundation for his eventual explanation of altruism, though Richards notes that it seemed implausible at the time (147). In it, Darwin considered that queen bees might spontaneously produce offspring whose variations benefited the group. In that case, natural selection would operate at the scale of the community rather than the individual. He concludes: "I must get up this subject—it is the greatest *special* difficulty I have met with. More facts are wanted." As if to put the speculations themselves under erasure, the first three manuscript pages are crossed out entirely.[28]

Darwin would wait another decade to accept these effaced speculations. Richards stresses the importance of an analogy with artificial selection that Darwin discovered in late 1857. When livestock farmers found that a slaughtered animal had a desirable trait, the farmers could cultivate it by breeding a near relative. After meditating on this practice, Darwin wrote that "natural selection might act on the parents, and continually preserve those which produced more and more aberrant offspring, having any structure or instinct advantageous to the community."[29] Here Darwin is beginning to theorize the will to reproduce as something that could be controlled and optimized across many generations, as Kathleen Frederickson has discussed elsewhere.[30] He underscored the point both in the *Origin* and *The Descent of Man:* "We can, I think, come to no other conclusion with respect to the origin of the more complex instincts, when we reflect on the marvelous instincts of sterile worker-ants and bees, which leave no offspring to inherit the effects of experience and of modified habits."[31] Those instincts, which Kirby and Spence had cast as "extraordinary" evidence of spiritual design, found distinctively material meaning in Darwin's schema.

As for the ambiguities surrounding "chance variation" itself, Darwin held his tongue. The concept remained a useful abstraction, an umbrella of ideas imprecisely linked to individuals. Yet in the case of neuter insects, variations really *were* nonlocalized, in that they were passed on through mediated modes of inheritance. In this, Darwin furnished a model of communal relations in which potentials for moral change existed everywhere in general and nowhere in particular. No longer a "difficulty" to minimize, the rhetoric of his explanation makes the irony into a shared marvel. This was a significant shift for a thinker sometimes seen as naturalizing laissez-faire economics (incarnating the "competitive, capitalistic, Malthusian dynamics of a poor law society," as Adrian Desmond and James Moore put it).[32] Darwin concludes, "I am bound to confess that, with all my faith in this principle, I should never have anticipated that natural selection could have been efficient in so high a degree, had not the case of these neuter insects convinced me of the fact."[33]

And yet the story of Darwin's breakthrough has yet to be told from a more inclusive vantage. Between 1848 and 1858, as Darwin wrestled with his first musings on nonreproduction, no scientific treatise or article appeared to corroborate them; even his close rival and acquaintance A. R. Wallace remained silent on the matter. This makes it imperative to understand the larger cultural processes that contributed to Darwin's solution—particularly, we shall see, the publication of Charles Dickens's *Dombey and Son,* which captivated British audiences at the time of his 1848 breakthrough. Like the writings of Darwin, Dickens's novels imagine life as a drama of communal relations in which the behavior of isolated individuals can be best understood in relation to the totality. Uniformitarian principles furnished both writers with common structures of expression on this front; a few years after Darwin imagined how "any change may undergo indefinite change" in his transmutation notebook of 1837–38, Dickens's narrator in *Martin Chuzzlewit* (1844) drew on the same conception of slow geological transformation.[34] "Change begets change," Dickens writes: "what was rock before becomes but sand and dust."[35] The illusion of isolated ontological units shrinks to dust through time, an ideal informing the larger narrative structure of *Dombey and Son*. "It's a world of change," in the words of Dombey's sister, Mrs. Chick (448). Such a world tends toward mass spectacles of vitality, in which the individual grows and garners significance through an unfolding web of communal relations.

Gillian Beer speculates that perhaps "Darwin was freed from some of the difficulties he experienced in expressing the relation of man to the rest of the natural order by his reading of Dickens."[36] We may never recover Darwin's debt to particular novels by Dickens, which he relished reading in the 1840s, but it seems safe to observe that the two wrote within an "intellectual commons," where insights circulated in heterogeneous genres at once (Pandora, 491). Without actively collaborating on an account of organic forms, they joined a shared network of writings that exceeded local lines of appropriation and response. The initial issues of Dickens's *Household Words,* for instance, published in March and April of 1850, included serialized excerpts from Elizabeth Gaskell's *Lizzie Leigh* alongside a naturalist account of birds ("Perfect Felicity: In a Bird's-Eye View"), a survey of ancient and modern burial practices ("Heathen and Christian Burial"), and a travelogue of Egypt and the South Seas ("Some Account of an Extraordinary Traveler"), reflecting the magazine's overarching focus on contributions from "men of various professions—barristers and divines, medical men and naturalists, soldiers and sailors," as Anne Lohrli writes.[37] Dickens's novel introduces ideas of nonreproduction within this commons, joining the work of naturalists, natural theologians, political economists, and others in Britain. Its antidevelopmental logic of narrative and the associated formal, linguistic, and characterological concerns of Dickensian melodrama: these features define *Dombey and Son*'s implication in the "one special difficulty" of moral and social change.[38]

"ONE COMMON FOUNTAIN": THE EVOLUTION OF
COMMUNITY IN *DOMBEY AND SON*

Dombey and Son, Dealings with the Firm, Wholesale, Retail, and for Exportation announced a new phase of Dickens's novelistic career. As his first novel written with a plan for individual numbers, it marks a turn from the sprawling, episodic configurations of *Barnaby Rudge* (1842) and *Martin Chuzzlewit* to the more focused institutional satires of his middle period. The story begins as a tale of youthful development, concentrating on old Dombey and his "son and heir" (300). Dombey aspires above all to raise another "perfect Dombey" to inherit his "stock" in the family shipping business. But in doing so, he consistently conflates the drives toward production and reproduction, mixing the domains of Dombey House and home in a manner that reflects the same "master-vice" of self-interest (69, 143, 700). That vice stood as a central problematic of the 1840s, as Dickens diagnosed it: not so much capitalism's endless expansion outward as its encroachments into the domains of family and fellow feeling. Dombey's signature egoism, his pride, converts filial attachments into the terms of financial exchange, reducing all ties to the logic of an economic contract. How might mutuality unseat the unbridled prerogatives of "competition, competition" (52)? In unraveling this problem, *Dombey and Son* reveals the "usual return" of paternal pride (309), showing how an attempt to uphold the Dombey line both defines and ultimately undermines the law of the father.

The tale begins with an image of closure and containment, as Paul Dombey Jr.'s birth announces an apotheosis of the Dombey lineage. "The House will once again," Dombey says, "be not only in name but in fact Dombey and Son, Dom-bey and Son!" (3). The hyphenated noun points precisely to the absence of interrupting influences between father and child and affirms the timeless vitality of the family name, firm, and fortune. In fact, what appears most notable about the infant Paul is the absence of any singular trait at all. As a facsimile of the paternal pattern, he embodies each Dombey past. Old Dombey "had risen, as his father had before him, in the course of life and death, from Son to Dombey," with the expectation of a continuing circle into the future (4). In this sense, little Paul's birth does not imply progress so much as a guarantee of future stasis: there is "nothing of chance or doubt in the course before my son," Dombey says (92).

The keynote paragraph extends these sentiments in ironic fashion. The narrator comments: "Dombey was about eight-and-forty years of age. Son about eight-and-forty minutes. Dombey was rather bald, rather red, and though a handsome well-made man, too stern and pompous in appearance to be prepossessing. Son was very bald, and very red, and though (of course) an undeniably fine infant, somewhat crushed and spotty in his general effect, as well" (11). The narrator's punctual repetitions reinforce Little Paul's status as a miniature model of his "well-made" father. But incommensurabilities lurk beneath these syntactic parallels, not least in the son's "crushed and spotty" distinction from Dombey's "stern" inflexibility. Images of violent opposition subtend their mirroring. Dombey is "a tree that was to come down in good time"; he proceeds to "toast" his son upon the fireplace, and the reader is told that little Paul "seemed, in his feeble way, to be squaring at existence" (11). What defines the son, notwithstanding his innocence, is a desire for passionate self-negation. The differences between father and son culminate through the interjected "of course," which accentuates all that is unexpectedly "off course" (11). "The two," the narrator concludes, were "very alike, and yet so monstrously contrasted" (12).

In these respects, little Paul's birth makes it clear that a genealogical lineage is never quite itself and that "chance" variation is incessant (92). The narrative underscores this point by situating him outside the traditional parameters of *Bildung*: fraught and "feeble," withered before his time, the child looks back to a childhood that never was, as his medical examination makes clear. "'Shall we make a man of him?' repeated the Doctor. 'I had rather be a child,' repeated Paul" (62). Paul's admission signals the tale of youthful cultivation that *Dombey and Son* will not tell. While Dickens displayed an acute grasp of the Goethean developmental pattern (having acquired a copy of *Wilhelm Meister's Apprenticeship* by 1844, in addition to absorbing the examples of Roderick Random, Tom Jones, and Robinson Crusoe), in *Dombey and Son* he declined those models in order to observe how institutions of trade, the public school system, and the marriage market could obstruct one's growth. In lieu of foregrounding little Paul's apprenticeship, the tale traces more collective circuits of growth defined in terms of friendship and self-abnegation.

But no one is more anxious about friendship than the elder Dombey, as the narrator explains: "An indescribable distrust of anybody stepping in between himself and his son; a haughty dread of having any rival or partner in the boy's respect and deference; a sharp misgiving, recently acquired, that he was not infallible in his power of bending and binding human wills.

In all his life, he had never made a friend. His cold and distant nature had neither sought one, nor found one" (61). Dombey's antisocial impulses bar the intrusive influence of others, shoring up the isomorphism between generations at the expense of more lateral attachments. Opposition exists everywhere he turns, making "friend" and "rival" into conceptual equivalents: each evokes a dangerous proximity. Other people cannot help but diminish Dombey's "parental scheme" of management, whose master terms are "respect and deference," "bending and binding." Friendship would weaken the "infallible" unit of Dombey and his double by opening it to potentially limitless lines of affiliation; the boundaries of family are marked through the perpetual threat of their violation.

In the ensuing events, *Dombey and Son* will put this appraisal of friendship to the test, at once observing its validity and offering a different framework for interpretation. That framework is worked out through the juxtaposition between Dombey's paternal estate and the estate of the two bachelors, Ned Cuttle and Sol Gills: between Dombey's desire to convey his family fortune to little Paul and Gills's desire to leave his savings to Walter Gay, Gills's nephew. In the eventual union of Walter and Dombey's daughter, Florence, Gills's influence will win out and so safeguard the couple's future, giving rise to an ethically reconstituted Dombeyan lineage. But as Gills and Cuttle become surrogate fathers for the couple, the boundary between "friend" and family itself will dissolve, so as to affirm the interrelated life of the collective.

The issue that animates Dickens's novel, then, is not who will win out in the struggle for reproduction but rather how isolated instances of sexual failure might be incorporated into larger processes of communal regeneration. For what links Dombey, Gills, and Cuttle is not that they scramble to preserve their lineages against one another; to the contrary they are all constituted as failures. Most notably, little Paul's early death disrupts the Dombey lineage, shifting the story's focus from Dombey's successful paternity to the ensuing evacuation of his household. But equivalent examples abound. Dombey's second marriage to Edith, the new Mrs. Dombey, does not result in a male child either; to the contrary, it instigates a futile rivalry between Dombey and John Carker, the manager, which ends in an absence of children. Dombey's hapless acquaintance in the marriage market at Leamington, Joe Bagstock, fails to marry Louisa Tox, but Bagstock's erstwhile overtures also prevent her from marrying Mr. Dombey. A grotesque caricature of pride, Bagstock is left alone after attempting to court Edith's mother, Cleopatra Skewton. The rapacious Carker, said to be "sharp of tooth" (329), embodies these tendencies in violent form: he pays with his life for courting Edith and is left likewise without a legacy.[39] The upshot of these failures is to turn from the initial plot of male maturation to an encompassing question of sexual breakdown—to the question of those innumerable individuals who, as Darwin also noted at this time, never advance a lineage of their own. How might the failure of reproduction result in wider circuits of social growth?

Shifting from the fall of Dombey's house to the rising fortunes of Gills and Cuttle, the novel shows how erotic and financial failure could have surprisingly productive outcomes. The location of this shift, and the central site of the bachelors' good graces, is the Wooden Midshipman, the naval supply shop owned by Gills, where he lives and works with Cuttle. The shop becomes an adoptive home to a set of otherwise unconnected children: a procession of surrogate sons and daughters including Florence Dombey, Walter Gay, Toots, and Rob the Grinder. As an inverted image of Dombey's house, the Midshipman emerges as a salutary domestic domain—a commons of mutual "friend[ship]," conviviality, and compassion—precisely insofar as it is insolvent. After her expulsion from home, Florence finds it "convenient and orderly, if not as handsome, as in the terrible dream she had once called Home" (652). The shop's careworn appearance is its main attraction, signaling its location at the margins of the marketplace and the imperatives of personal profit. But if the Midshipman offers a haven from competition, then this fact also augurs its collapse, as Gills explains to Walter: "'You see, Walter,' he said, 'in truth this business is merely a habit with me. . . . But competition, competition—new invention, new invention—alteration, alteration—the world's gone past me. I hardly know where I am myself; much less where my customers are'" (52). Faced with the Dombeyan norm of competition in the 1840s, Gills's sympathies can only be bad business. "[I have] fallen behind the time, and am too old to catch it again," he explains (53). In the battle for survival, habits of selfish striving have prevailed, a fact that leaves little room for self-denying individuals like Gills. As the passage proceeds, his selflessness becomes all too literal. "I am only the ghost of this business—its substance vanished long ago; and when I die, its ghost will be laid," he says (53). For the ghostly Sol, selfless sentiments lead to the grave; in his distance from material matters, he is deemed devoid of "substance" altogether.

"I hardly know where I am myself": Gills's words have metafictional meaning within the tale of little Paul's growth. For Gills has come to assume surplus room in a character system set up to orbit around Dombey and his son. Like Cuttle, Gills seems to have no functional importance in the plot that nevertheless continues to feature him. An "old Sol" (47) whose resources "vanished long ago," his very name underscores his aberrance as an elderly bachelor in the novel of youthful formation. He attests to the fact that, as Alex Woloch writes, "*all* characters are potentially overdelimited within the fictional world—and might disrupt the narrative if we pay them the attention they deserve."[40] Against Dombey's ideal of self-extension, Gills—the "sole master and proprietor of that Midshipman" (46)—has given up the prospect of a wife and child in order to raise his sibling's son, Walter, who observes so much in chapter 9:

> I feel you ought to have, sitting here and pouring out the tea instead of me, a nice little dumpling of a wife, you know—a comfortable, capital, cosey old lady, who was just a match for you, and knew how to manage you, and keep you in good heart. Here I am, as loving a nephew as ever was (I am sure I ought to be!) but I am only a nephew, and I can't be such a companion to you when you're low and out of sorts as she would have made herself, years ago, though I'm sure I'd give any money if I could cheer you up. (133)

Praising the good will of old Sol, Walter winds up rubbing salt in the wound, as he perversely points out the material and sexual losses that define his uncle. By caring for Walter, a less immediate relation, Gills has abnegated a "capital" wife, a companion to "manage" his interests rather than reduce them. Making (what "she would have made") assumes transitive and intransitive properties here, indicating both a marriage and what that marriage would have engendered: an actual son and heir, a "partner" akin to little Paul Dombey (61). The very form of Walter's dialogue, which suspends syntactic resolution with peripheral qualifications and embellishments, underscores its account of Gills's life as an ensemble of canceled opportunities. His self-interruptions suggest something like what Garrett Stewart calls "intension," in reference to minor, sentence-level lexical effects that disrupt the momentum of plot and that make the experience of novel reading "both discontinuous and hence all the more intermittently arresting."[41] With its parenthetical asides, its emphasis on how things would be and "ought" to be otherwise, its at once omnipresent and self-effacing "I" and "you": in all of these ways, Walter's language accentuates Gills's negated potentials for felicity. The ensuing narrative will not recuperate these failures, in the form of a wife and child, but will rather revise their meaning. For while Gills continues to diverge from orthodoxies of middle-class success, his deviations become all the more generative than the Dombeyan norm, as the drives toward "competition, competition" yield to more communal conditions of living.

The opposition between Dombey and the two bachelors expresses, as a problem of narrative form, the same theoretical knot that Darwin was working to unravel at the time: What alternatives to egoism might thrive in the face of collective competition? Why should the legacies of Gills and Cuttle persist while Dombey's die out? The questions come to a point through the inaugural incident in Gills's affairs, which involves his struggle to pay a family debt. An "old bond" between Gills and his deceased brother, Walter's father, the debt confirms both Gills's good will and dwindling fortunes (142). "It came of helping a man that's dead now," Cuttle explains, "and that's cost my friend Gills many a hundred pound already" (152). Just as Gills had given up a chance for family in order to raise another man's child, he has also assumed that man's "cost[s]." "I've paid a good deal of it, Ned," he explains. "But the times are so bad with me that I can't do more just now." Confronted with these material immediacies, Gills seems to have no future: the last "fragment" of his inheritance marks his lineage as unfit for survival (142).

As it resolves the problem of the debt, the narrative will convert Gills's "old bond" into a source of mutual gain; as a spur for community and cooperation, it turns out to yield limitless social benefits. Accordingly, Gills's isolation is lessened as the weight of the debt continues to mount, beginning when Walter and Cuttle ask Dombey for a loan. "People," Dombey declares, "had better be content with their own obligations and differences, and not increase them by engaging for other men" (153). Through the screen of pride, Cuttle's and Walter's solicitations appear as a moral failing that attests to their loss of masculine self-direction. In contrast, Dombey sees their request as an opportunity to display dominance over others, as he instructs his son to see "the power of money, and all it can do" (152). After framing the matter in this light, he delegates the decision to little Paul:

> "If you had money now," said Mr. Dombey; "as much money as young Gay has talked about; what would you do?"

"Give it to his old uncle," returned Paul.

"Lend it to his old uncle, eh?" retorted Mr. Dombey. (153)

The reader might be amused upon learning that Dombey cannot conceive of "giving" except as a euphemism for personal gain. But the jest wears thin as the father's belligerence becomes palpable. "Young Gay comes all this way to beg for money," Dombey says, "and you, who are so grand and great, having got it, are going to let him have it, as a great favor and obligation" (153). When little Paul proposes again to give the money away, he not only shows himself to be an imperfect Dombey but also aligns himself with another family. The gift turns an "old bond" between brothers into a new one, substituting Gills's prior obligation into the new brotherly bond between little Paul and Walter. For his part, Dombey tries to convert the gift back into an economy of obligation. "You will consider that this is done for you by master Paul," he decrees, as if indicating what is owed to the boy (154). But the father's statement serves not so much to transform the gift as to disassociate himself from it, establishing distance from an estranging event.

In questioning the narcissism of patriarchal controls, the narrative accentuates how character can shift between generations. The scene intended to make Paul Jr. emulate his father designates him instead as a spiritual son of the Midshipman. Through the agency of the gift, older obligations become an inducement to new family attachments; from this point onward, Walter and little Paul will be remembered as friends and actual fraternal relations. Walter's brotherly bond with little Paul is in turn translated into the mock sibling relationship between Walter and Florence and then into the finally fertile marriage of husband and wife. These bonds are set up in little Paul's dying words to Florence, as she reports them to Walter: "He liked you very much, and said before he died that he was fond of you, and said 'Remember Walter!' and if you'll be a brother to me Walter, now that he is gone and I have none on earth, I'll be your sister all my life, and think of you like one wherever we may be" (293–94). In this extension of family, the story complicates its initial binarisms between failure and development, sexual stagnation and reproduction. Fellow feeling can create family ties, troubling the line between genealogies of blood and more massive structures of affiliation.

With the demise of little Paul in chapter 5, the tale "appears to disrupt or reverse the patterns of *bildungsroman,*" as Lyn Pykett writes; this was a shift that Dickens planned actively, as his working notes record that Paul had been "born, to die."[42] Little Paul, like Richard Feverel and Ozias Midwinter, fails to come of age as a representative of his world. The resulting void is left unoccupied either by Dombey's daughter, Florence (who remains child-like to the end), or by her husband to be, Walter Gay (whose growth goes largely unnarrated). Instead, little Paul's disrupted development leads to a more "wholesale" fantasy of transformation arising from Cuttle's and Gills's self-denials. For even though the bachelors lack a single "son and heir," that absence enables myriad mock sons and daughters to gather around them in the Midshipman—most notably Walter, Florence, and Rob. Released from a strict hierarchy of blood bonds, these children assume a range of intrafamil-ial positions. Florence, for example, variously appears as a "niece" to Cuttle, Cuttle's "ward," and an object of Gills's own "parental reverence" (741, 740, 242). Gills and Cuttle are labeled "brothers"; at the same time, Cuttle acts as a father to Gills's nephew, Walter, who is "almost a son" to him (312, 265). And most manifestly, Florence and Walter become bonded as siblings and remain "brother and sister" until their marriage makes their "false" family real (547, 702). When the two are wedded, there is "no better father than Captain Cuttle" (872), a statement that formalizes the attachments between them.[43] In this process, the narrative transforms the two bachelors' virtual family ties into actual attachments, rotating from Dombey's ideal of self-perpetuation to the interrelated family of man: the "mighty mother" and "the Father" of our shared vitality (700, 702).

Thus affirming the polymorphous potentials of its bachelors, the novel imagines how Cuttle's and Gills's legacies persist within the total commu-nity, whereas egoists like Dombey end in isolation or death. Their selfless sentiments will be preserved through Walter and Florence's child, purify-ing the Dombey lineage of its self-seeking nature. We see the collabora-tive identity of Gills, Cuttle, and Walter assume metafictional form in the tale of Dick Whittington, a child who rose from poverty to marry his mas-ter's daughter and become London's mayor. The two bachelors begin to tell the Whittington narrative when Walter finds employment as a clerk in Dombey's house, and they return routinely to it afterward. In celebration of Walter's new position, Cuttle, Gills, and Walter drink a toast. "We'll finish the bottle, to the House, Ned—Walter's House," says Gills. "Why it may be his House one of these days, in part. Who knows? Sir Richard Whittington married his master's daughter" (142). Through his alignment with Whittington, Walter is associated with an instructive model of youthful ambition: a child who worked up from obscure origins to achieve social and romantic success. But whereas Whittington had labored in heroic isolation, Walter's ambitions will be fostered through the unreturned aid of others. The Whittington tale serves as an inspiration for Gills's and Cuttle's support, so as to invert its individualistic premises in the very telling of it. Walter may be uneasy "when the Captain and Uncle Sol talked about Richard Whittington and masters' daughters," but this only underscores his guardians' enthusiasm for it and him; for their part, Gills and Cuttle ritualistically tell and retell the tale as they bring about its vicarious success (130).[44] Cuttle can hardly contain himself after learning of little Paul's death and informs John Carker, Dombey's business manager: "'Pass the word, and there's another ready for you,' quoth the Captain. 'Nevy of a scientific uncle! Nevy of Sol Gills! Wal'r! Wal'r, as is already in your business!'" (178). Because Walter remains shipwrecked abroad for most of the plot, what brings the Whittington narrative to fruition are the domestic dealings of Cuttle and Gills. For them, to tell a story is to create connections beyond their immediate radius, imagining new lines of affiliation that could lead to transformed futures. Fantasizing something other than the hard facts of the present, Gills and Cuttle create prospects that are, in Gills's words, "already in your business!" (262).

I have been suggesting that *Dombey and Son* prefigures Darwin's understanding of moral and social variation in three ways: the novel grants the seeming self-evidence of interpersonal conflict; it then posits how nonreproductive individuals might offer an altruistic alternative to it; and from that point, it elaborates a more encompassing vision of communal change that attests to the growth of new socialities. In the final section of this chapter, I extend these observations in light of the erosion of spiritual structures through Dickens's middle period. For while Dickens never stopped trying to pull the tokens of "chance" and "doubt" back into a higher spiritual system, his writings began to reveal the constructed nature of those gestures qua gestures, as George Levine has argued.[45] In *Bleak House* (1853) and *Little Dorrit* (1857), Dickens's humanism seems tinged by an awareness that the world has not been shaped for the good of one and all. Even morally compromised characters like Richard Carstone and William Dorrit, who are set up for rebuke, seem excessively punished for their sins, suffering deaths that are hard to reconcile with the sense of felicity that the novels try to impose.[46] *Dombey and Son* evokes these tensions by indicating that the possibilities for moral change might not all line up in a progressive, liberal humanist direction and might in fact have no direction at all.

Such a relational understanding of virtue informs the moral miseducation of the "bad child," Rob the Grinder (333). Dickens had intended initially to make Walter "go bad, by degrees," but shifted that ordeal onto the minor figure of Rob, allowing the novel to explore the transient nature of moralities while still safeguarding the purity of his heroic counterpoint.[47] Yet the outcomes of this exploration threaten to undermine the humanist vision that the novel devotes central space to building, particularly when the sharp-toothed Carker becomes a surrogate father to Rob. In the triangular struggle between Cuttle and Carker for the boy's affections, the story extends the intrigue of friendship and inheritance, which now issues in a contest between two mock patriarchs to govern his morals.

Rob gains distinction in the novel above all as a foil to the other youths, veering from the good moral luck of Florence and Walter. As the son of little Paul's wet nurse, Polly Tootles, Rob is tied to Paul by the "one common fountain" of the mother's milk (32), though this ideal is abhorrent to Dombey. Louisa Tox, a friend of Dombey's sister, explains that Polly "naturally must be interested in her young charge, and must consider it a privilege to see a little cherub closely connected with the superior classes, gradually unfolding itself from day to day at one common fountain" (32). The nurse's hired breast becomes metonymic of shared origins, much to Dombey's chagrin. For this "one common fountain" threatens to undermine any absolute demarcation between natural and artificial attachments, opening the prospect of an anxious, all-leveling sameness. Dombey's anxieties take the form of a changeling fantasy in chapter 2: "His thoughts were tending to one center: that a great temptation was being placed in this woman's way. Her infant was a boy, too. Now would it be possible for her to change them? Though he dismissed the idea as romantic and unlikely—though possible, there was no denying—he could not help pursuing it. . . . Whether a man so situated would be able to pluck away the result of so many years of usage, confidence, and belief from the impostor, and endow a stranger with it?" (31). It is conceivable, Dombey acknowledges, that there may be no neat distinction between kin and kind. Whatever the notional boundaries between sons and strangers, "perfect" Dombeys and "false" ones, in fact family may be rooted only in one's "belief" in its existence (16, 702, 31). Rob's condition as an exchangeable child raises the prospect that others' offspring might also be one's own. This recognition marks Dombey as a "romantic" storyteller of sorts. But whereas Cuttle and Gills accept the premise and aim to make their "false" family real, Dombey disavows it as abhorrent.

The drama of fictional families becomes poignant when Rob spurns his upbringing. His violent treatment at the Grinder's charity school leaves him estranged from the apple-faced Tootles clan and leads to a chain of other attachments. An alien presence at home, Rob is said to have gone "on the wrong track," having jumped his family line to meander throughout the social system. "You could hardly be off hearing of it somehow," his father says, "and it's better I should out and say my boy's gone rather wrong" (309). In wandering from the Tootles family, Rob has become errant in another sense, as "Robert Tootles" is replaced by the changeling child Rob the Grinder. His education involves less a series of hurdles en route to adulthood than a learned refusal of self-cultivation; he drifts from an idealized household to the terrors of the charity school, from the school to the streets, and finally to the clutches of the rapacious Carker, where he is hailed as the "bad son" that he will remain (333). These peregrinations extend an idea implicit in little Paul's depiction: character might have no providential or biological basis and might amount to no more than an unguided conjunction of events. Whatever the fixed nature of characters like Toots and Bagstock, here Dickens attends to the prospect of moral mutability without end.

As an embodiment of suspended growth, Rob is shadowed by a set of occluded developmental "tracks"—counterlives he might have had at home and school—in keeping with the alternate temporalities that attend Richard Feverel and Ozias Midwinter's development. Later in the century, Darwin extended this ideal in explicit engagement with Dickens. In *The Expression of the Emotions in Man and Animals* (1872), he invokes the mob scene from *Oliver Twist* (1837) to reinforce his claim that the history of emotions follows the selection of chance variations. But the more relevant passage occurs in *The Descent of Man*: "If, for instance, to take an extreme case, men were reared under precisely the same conditions as hive bees, there can hardly be a doubt that our unmarried females would, like the worker-bees, think it a sacred duty to kill their brothers, and mothers would strive to kill their fertile daughters; and no one would think of interfering. Nevertheless the bee, or any other social animal, would in our supposed case gain, as it appears to me, some feeling of right and wrong, or a conscience" (122). Darwin's changeling children, like Dickens's own "bad son," have been raised to hate (333). In a social setting governed by violence, we would doubtless grow to have "some feeling" or "conscience." But that feeling would run counter to traditional liberal sentiments. Within the domain of the hive, hatred has the same social purpose as love among humans; the two are functionally equivalent. The message is anathema to the moral universalism of Cambridge theologians like Paley and William Whewell, which Darwin so stridently rejected, and is implicit in Dickens's own changeling thought experiment: for no rational reason, Rob is interpolated into Carker's world, where enmity reigns as a sovereign good. Insofar as the individual has a field of potential "tracks," there may be no higher explanation for why one is traveled and all the others remain untaken.

To pull these implications back into a schema of moral design, in the final volume the narrator asks a question that has been everywhere implied: "Was Mr. Dombey's master-vice, that ruled him so inexorably, an unnatural characteristic? It might be worthwhile, sometimes, to inquire what Nature is and how men work to change her and whether in the enforced distortions so produced, it is not natural to be unnatural. . . . Vainly attempt to think of any simple plant or flower or wholesome weed that, set in this foetid bed, could have its natural growth or put its little leaves forth to the sun as God designed it" (700–701). The passage's function is to generate sympathy for Dombey before his moral metamorphosis. His egoism might be no fault of his own, because it is "natural" to have been shaped by a pulverizing material milieu. But this suggestion leads to the prospect that there might be no inherent moral meaning anchored in "Nature," since natural moral characteristics and "unnatural," immoral ones are interchangeable. Turning to God's good intention only exacerbates the problem: what "God designed" may be nothing more than what we "vainly attempt to think."

The contradictions within this natural history of virtue are amplified when the narrator assumes the role of "those who study physical science" (700). Surveying the world from above, he observes our common creaturely pedigree:

> Oh, for a good spirit who would take the house-tops off, with a more potent and benignant hand than the lame demon in the tale, and show a Christian people what dark shapes issue from amidst their homes, to swell the reti-

nue of the Destroying Angel as he moves forth among them! For only one
night's view of the pale phantoms rising from the scenes of our too-long
neglect; and from the thick and sullen air where Vice and Fever propagate
together, raining the tremendous social retributions which are ever pouring
down, and ever coming thicker! Bright and blest the morning that should
rise on such a night; for men, delayed no more by stumbling-blocks of their
own making . . . would then apply themselves like creatures of one common origin, owning one duty to the father of one family, and tending to one
common end, to make the world a better place! (702)

This well-known passage encapsulates, in miniature, the novel's contrary
conceptions of how new socialities are born. For the recognition of our
shared somatic condition has yielded not one but two theories of moral
development. At first, the narrator makes morality out to be a product of
individual volition. Morals are bred within the secret recesses of the heart
and home, so that sin is of individuals' "own making." And yet morals are
also interpreted in structural terms. Virtue is shaped by the "sullen air" of
urban filth and pollution, which wafts outside the domain of self-control.
Critics such as Catherine Gallagher and Andrew Sanders have noted these
tensions, though their meaning gains distinctive cultural importance in light
of Darwin's shared ambivalences around the same time.[48] For both writers,
the potential for social change is ubiquitous, indeed central to the ethical
evolution of a community, but with no clear ties to the life of its individual
members.

In lieu of a resolution to these explanatory tensions, the novel furnishes
a more general observation on our shared humanity: the "one common
origin" and "one common end" of the totality. That observation is abun-
dantly borne out through the finale. The fallen woman Alice Marwood, for
example, is discovered to be Dombey's niece from his first marriage, while
old Mrs. Brown is revealed as Dombey's sister-in-law. Such connections cut
across hierarchal divisions between social classes to reveal the tangled relations of the communal order. But no character more fully exemplifies these
relations than Dombey's daughter, Florence. Defined as "base coin" in the
Dombey household, Florence embodies several significant meanings of the
term. As the female inhabitant of a patriarchal household, she is deemed a
"bad Boy," representing the perverse presence of women within the homosocial order of Dombey and Son (13). But the very pathos of the father's

aversion suggests an added reason for her devaluation, as Diane Sadoff and Hilary Schor have observed: the prospect of an adulterated genealogy. We see this in several scornful comments upon her lack of resemblance to Dombey, as when Mrs. Chick laments that she is "her Mama, all over" (57). Marked as the product of another family lineage, she threatens to dilute the Dombey "stock."[49] Florence's love for her deceased mother, Fanny; her actions on behalf of her sickly brother; and her affection for Walter, Gills, and Cuttle: for Dombey, all these selfless impulses indicate the threat of dispersion, of mixing Dombey's house and home with exogenous elements. When Florence is cast out of his household, following the departure of her stepmother, Edith, it is to enter the public arena in which she has always threatened to circulate.[50]

Florence's expulsion, however, has the effect of inverting the opposition between Dombey and the two bachelors. It defines Dombey as a bachelor devoid of children or a wife. ("Mr. Dombey and the world are alone together," the narrator observes [781].) And at the same time, it makes a new family unit of Florence and Cuttle. "Homeless and fatherless" upon her arrival, Florence is insistently identified as Cuttle's new charge (736). "The Captain was not troubled with the faintest idea of any difficulty in retaining Florence, or of any responsibility thereby incurred," the narrator notes. "If she had been a Ward in Chancery, it would have made no difference at all to Captain Cuttle" (740). The upshot is to invest Cuttle and Gills as heads of an alternate family. When Cuttle helps her buy a dress, he calls attention to their newly constituted bond: "At the word 'niece,'" the narrator comments, "he bestowed a most significant look on Florence, accompanied with pantomime, expressive of sagacity and mystery" (741). The "pantomime" underscores the make-believe of an attachment, while expressing actual affection that is communicated in his "most significant look." When Cuttle confers his meager savings to Florence, it is not so much to quantify their relation as to disregard the metric of personal loss and gain altogether. "'It an't o' no use to *me*,' said the Captain. 'I wonder I haven't chucked it away afore now'" (742). From Dombey's ethos of (re)production, Florence settles into a family of "compassion and gentleness," sympathy and self-sacrifice (402).

Walter's return from abroad, after her arrival, confirms her identity in this reinvigorated family order. Cuttle develops the connection between the two mock siblings in his very refusals to inform her of his presence. "'He was older than you, my lady lass,' pursued the Captain, 'but you was like two children together, at first; warn't you?'" (738). By perversely pointing out Walter's loss, Cuttle accentuates their bond while laying the foundation for its reconstitution as a romantic one. The understated "at first" serves less as an affirmation of their initial identity as brother and sister than a testament to the seemingly misplaced potential for an adult sexual bond. After Florence rues the death of "my brother," Cuttle notes that Walter "*was* your nat'ral born friend like, warn't he Pet?" (737). The term "friend" floats between familial and romantic registers: it picks up on the adoptive attachment (the two are "nat'ral born" together), while pointing to an ensuing erotic tie, and so reworks the threat of intimacy that Dombey identified with friendship. When Walter enters, it is to extend their former family bond in new directions. "I have not a brother's claim," he says. "I left a child. I find a woman" (769). What had been an artificial sibling connection can no longer persist; the effect of their dialogue, however, is to reimagine rather than entirely disavow their initial connection, as Florence suggests. "All I ask is, Walter, in the name of the poor child who was your sister once, that you will not struggle with yourself' (768). This new bond derives from the ashes of the older one, transforming their mock relation as "nat'ral born friend[s]" into a real relation of marriage.

In the scene of their reunion, then, Walter and Florence's fiction of family becomes real. Cuttle's overwrought reaction serves to accentuate this transformation, as the narrator comments: "[Cuttle] was repeatedly heard to say in an undertone, as he looked with ineffable delight at Walter and Florence, 'Ed'ard Cuttle, my lad, you never shaped a better course in your life, than when you made that there little property over, jintly!'" (772). In giving Florence away, acting without wish for personal reward, his legacy is communicated to the future. But who or what Cuttle passes her on *to* remains unclear. In part because both Walter and Florence remain his surrogate children, Florence is not released from the confines of Cuttle's "family" at all. Within this phantasmic family unit, the loss of "that little property," Florence, can be contained in a recuperative union to the surrogate son, thereby becoming a principle of continuing social growth. For Dombey, the dispersion of family marks its demise; for Cuttle, the family line deepens precisely as a result of letting the daughter go. To be "almost a son" or daughter, from this vantage, is still to be bound as communal kin, since no absolute distinction can be made between real sons like little Paul and his doubles: surrogate sons

Walter Gay and Rob the Grinder, both "false Dombey[s]" in idiosyncratic respects, like Florence Dombey herself (265, 702).

With the union of Florence and Walter, the patriarchal plot of father and son—the plot of little Paul's compromise with an adult world of "competition, competition"—has opened out to a different tale of communal growth, rooted in invigorated habits of friendship and fellow feeling. It leads to the revelation of a *sensus communis,* a community of feeling arising among the novel's main characters and extending to the shared sentiments that the novel aims to prompt in readers. The finale suggests that fellow feeling isn't bad for business either. What had hindered Cuttle and Gills beforehand—their tendencies to selflessly distribute their "little property" among others—is reconceived as a profitable foundation for inheritance (772). We see this shift set up when Dombey's disgraced second wife, Edith, reappears to speak with Florence and her infant child. Resigned to spinsterhood, Edith has foresworn family and children. But she still notes the indirect effect of her actions on Florence's life. Looking at Florence's baby, she explains, "I said that I would die and make no sign. I could have done so, and I would, if we had never met, Florence" (937). Despite disclaiming a role in advancing the Dombeyan lineage, and having failed to "make a sign," it turns out that a sign has been made after all, albeit by supporting her stepdaughter Florence. Like Cuttle and Gills, Edith has no children or fortune of her own; instead, she prompts more roundabout routes of generation through her very self-denials.

In fact, the two figures that "make a sign" most emphatically are those who are not wedded at all, Cuttle and Gills. The narrator comments: "And how goes the wooden Midshipman in these changed days? Why, here he still is . . . and more on the alert than ever, being newly painted from his cocked hat to his buckled shoes and up above him, in golden characters, these names shine refulgent, GILLS AND CUTTLE" (943). It turns out that the Gills and Cuttle are not "behind the time" but have serendipitously anticipated the expanding empire's need for nautical instruments. Just as Florence is refashioned from "base coin" to the "golden link" in her father's lineage (13, 224), the Midshipman moves from a site without "substance" to one inscribed in "golden characters" (53, 943). The sign touts the condition of the two unmarried men as partners, having become "golden" through their very refusals of personal gain. As the narrator notes, "There is a fiction of a business in the Captain's mind which is better than any reality. . . . His delight in his own name over the door, is inexhaustible" (944). Business becomes reconstituted as a form of play; just as Cuttle's "pantomime" of family leads to actual attachments, the "fiction" of business remakes the marketplace over in an image of friendship, cooperation, and community. In this, Cuttle and Gills's partnership bears out Holly Furneaux's point that the Dickensian bachelor suggests "alternative presentations of kinship" that "displace the biological family as natural given" (22). Just as Paul Dombey's estate dries up, Gills's "fragment" reemerges as an all the more lucrative family fortune, the bequest for a lineage that they have helped indirectly to generate.

In imposing this resolution, the novel stops short of imagining a more fundamental transformation within the structure of capitalism; Dickens's fantasy of moral reform leaves intact the conditions that had engendered the mass immiseration and anomie of the hungry 1840s. But while the story never delivers readers to a more fundamentally transfigured world, its dimmer intimations of possibility continued to take hold in Victorian culture. With Darwin's eventual observations on moral life, readers found an account of past and present socialities situated within a curve of "other possible worlds" (Freeman, 16). This was a social Darwinism irreducible to Herbert Spencer's proclamations on the survival of the fittest and that more closely coincided with T. H. Huxley's observation that natural selection "repudiates the gladiatorial theory of existence."[51] Toward the *fin de siècle*, interest in the evolution of mutuality matured into a significant line of writings including Richard Holt Hutton's 1879 "The 'Sociology' of Ants" and Leslie Stephen's 1882 *The Science of Ethics* alongside more radical contributions from Jane Hume Clapperton, Patrick Geddes and J. Arthur Thomson, Henry Drummond, and Peter Kropotkin, which variously argued that fellow feeling is a supreme biological fact.[52]

Dickens's novel evokes what Kropotkin called "the feeling of human solidarity" through its antidevelopmental form (292). It does so by vindicating the inclusion of surplus figures such as Gills and Cuttle, who seem at first tangential to the plot of individual formation. Their presence is motivated, formally and thematically, by shifting from a "gladiatorial" tale of competition to a more encompassing ethos of organic bonds. That shift becomes most manifest in the resolution, which subordinates the novel's expected emphasis on Walter and Florence's marriage to a wider litany of unions, in which the "golden characters" of Cuttle and Gills stand paramount (943). These include the weddings of Susan Nipper and Toots, Harriet Carker and Mr. Morfin, Mrs. Macstinger and Captain Bunsby, and Dr. Feeder and Cordelia Blimber. The partnership between Gills and Cuttle is implicated in this succession of bonds (underscored, in no small part, by Cuttle's vehement refusals of a wife: the "shadowy terror that he might be married by violence," and the felicitous prospect of escaping it [926]). Their final connection calls to mind the Cheeryble brothers in *Nicholas Nickleby* (1839), the merchants with whom the penniless Nicholas finds work and benevolent bonds. And like Master Humphrey, who dreams of having "sons and daughters and grandchildren" while remaining a bachelor, Gills finds himself surrounded by descendants that he has not fathered.[53] Individuals like David Copperfield and Pip become more or less conventional representatives of their milieu, with reproductive futures that mark them as adults; Gills and Cuttle remain anomalous beings who, through their very lack of offspring, help to engender an ameliorated moral world.

Writing on the novel's "essentially autobiographical" form, Georg Lukács noted the genre's predilection for unexceptional individuals. Unlike the grandiose subjects of epic, who walk among the gods, the protagonists of fiction lack an immanence of meaning; they are consigned to think and feel about how things "should be" otherwise.[54] The world should be more meaningful—more stable, enduring, and integrated—than it is in fact. Mired in this condition, youths like Wilhelm Meister must learn to moderate their unique desires and aspirations, resigning themselves to a "community among men" that could offer some semblance of life's meaning, even as those youths wind up "more or less mediocre" in the process.[55] But *Dombey and Son* swerves from the plot of individual moral compromise set up in little Paul. Disrupting the tale of his growth, it shifts attention to satellite figures like Gills and Cuttle and to a more encompassing communal vision of what "should be."

So while critics often observe that the ending augurs a renewal of the Dombey lineage, with Walter and Florence ensuring its future, I wish to observe that it more radically installs the infertile figures of Gills and Cuttle as embodiments of organic regeneration. Ultimately, the "golden characters" that recompose Cuttle and Gills correspond to the "golden characters" that constitute the novel itself. From Dombey's goal of direct descent—the perfect replication of oneself in one's "issue"—Dickens's story enshrines the more wayward issues of its bachelors, who become vital to the novel's nineteen serial issues, the last of which appeared as Darwin was working to resolve his "one special difficulty."[56] Those characters have fostered the bonds between individuals and groups in multiplot fiction. Against the injunction to "competition, competition," *Dombey and Son* represents the productive outcomes of sexual failure and discovers, through nonreproduction, the possibilities for endless social growth: in Gills's words, "new invention, new invention—alteration, alteration!" (52).

CHAPTER 4

George Eliot's "Fine Excess"

Middlemarch, Energy, and Incalculable Diffusion

Her finely-touched spirit had still its fine issues, though they were
not widely visible. Her full nature . . . spent itself in channels which
had no great name on the earth. But the effect of her being on those
around her was incalculably diffusive.

—George Eliot, *Middlemarch*

The culmination of *Middlemarch: A Study of Provincial Life* returns to the
promise of its title in surprising form. Linking the terms of incompletion and
progress—the conjunction of "middle" and "march"—it projects a vision
of achievement in the midst of defeat. Dorothea Brooke's good intentions
have been squandered: her ambitions are "spent" in transience, lost rather
than transformed into an enduring social institution. But that failure leads
to a general vision of the social good, as her impulses exert an "incalculably diffusive" influence on the population. Like Tertius Lydgate's "wasted
energy" (825, 635), Dorothea's desires extend in unpredictable directions to
shape the lives of others. Such is the promise of the novel's name: a promise
that mere irresolution, the mere failure of individual accomplishment, might
reemerge as a higher sign of fulfillment. How might we understand such an
ambivalent ending? Or rather, how might we understand its resistance to a
conventionally bounded denouement in lieu of something more nebulous
and open: what goes by the name, in the finale, of incalculable diffusion?

This chapter takes up the questions raised in the finale by locating Eliot's understanding of incalculable diffusion within her vast scientific and
philosophical reading through the late 1860s and 1870s. For many educated
Victorians, the term "diffusion" articulated a set of newly perceived phenomena about energy. Far from a limitless resource, scientists proclaimed,
energy was constantly lost into indefinite channels, never again to perform
measurable work. But writers at midcentury tended to cast diffusion in op-

timistic terms, in contrast to more pessimistic perspectives at the century's close. *Middlemarch*, I show, represents diffusion as a mode of eternal fulfillment—of the incalculable increase of fellow feeling over the *longue durée*. I situate this ideal in treatises that defined diffusion in terms of the relation between the individual and the group, concentrating on new statistical studies among Eliot's contemporaries. These studies argued that the effects of "wasted energy" could be approximated through the calculus of probabilities, even when a total account of individuals remained elusive. Building on those insights, Eliot expressed diffusion in terms of the open possibilities for social improvement, so as to align the fact of individual defeat with longer-run prospects for moral amelioration.

By critical consensus, *Middlemarch* bears the impress of Eliot's interest in physical science more than any of her other writings.[1] What has remained unnoted, however, is the novel's acute ties to theories of diffusion. Eliot cultivated concepts of diffusion in two ways. First, she used them to reimagine her mature ethics of sympathy. The bonds of sympathetic feeling, Eliot conceded in her later lifetime, could not help but be inhibited in nineteenth-century Britain. Both Dorothea and Lydgate reflect this state of affairs: their experiences both reflect the erosion of social sentiments in a period of mass anomie, when youthful ambitions and attachments seemed scarcely possible to maintain. And yet one person's failed impulses could be mediated by another, and another after that, typifying the often-unobserved relations at the core of the realist novel. Certainly, Dorothea's lost "Puritan energy" (9) and Lydgate's "wasted energy" remain "unhistoric" (825) and are said to be ultimately unobservable. But the effects of their impulses accrue within the novel's total system of relations, so that their shortcomings have an immeasurable influence on the totality. When criticism casts the defeat of individuals in purely symptomatic terms, as a sign that Eliot's novels foreclose resistance to provincial social arrangements, it threatens to neglect her concern with the *post*subjective outcomes of failed feelings, desires, and actions within the social medium. Theories of diffusion informed Eliot's understanding of the individual as not just a self-contained being—bounded, stable, and securely located within an adult milieu—but an ensemble of developmental potentials conceived in relational terms.

Second, and in conjunction with Eliot's ethical aims, theories of diffusion shaped Eliot's brand of aesthetic formalism. Following her conviction that literature should remove itself from "petty politics," she found in diffusion a singular law of art's purposive purposelessness (178). For Eliot, the influence of a novel could hardly be tallied in individual acts of reading, though it could be inferred indirectly through the "curious little links of effect" that follow from them (412). Novels could contribute to the project of ethical revitalization through their lower-level, incalculable effects on the group, or what I term the outcomes of *diffusive reading*. Diffusive reading names Eliot's understanding of how books accrue ethical influence through their ongoing cultural circulation. Even as a novel becomes mediated by historical and cartographical distance, losing its initial relevance, readers can discover implications in it that transcend any prescriptive political content. Reading a text may not bring one nearer to achieving an immediate social goal; but many acts of reading can spiral in directions that, little by little, have larger outcomes unforeseen in their creation. As a foundation for this ideal, energy science led Eliot to reconcile conventional claims about the novel's social purpose with new notions of art's autonomy from politics.[2] Reading her work in dialogue with mathematicians, scientists, and philosophers reveals a distinctive vision of literature's unproductive powers, which wedded concepts of formal appreciation with the novel's long-standing social aims.

Middlemarch: A Study of Provincial Life presents itself both in its ethical and aesthetic registers as an actual contribution to scientific learning: a "study" in its own right, as J. Hillis Miller formatively observed.[3] With its attention to "the varying experiments of Time," in particular, it joins James Clerk Maxwell's statistical studies of diffusion through the 1870s, which were later hailed as culminating three decades of research into physical probabilities in Britain: as marking a turn to what Maxwell called "large numbers of variable events" in 1873.[4] *Middlemarch* and energy science conclude my book because they signal an apotheosis in this Victorian history of probabilistic thinking. With the 1874 opening of the Cavendish Laboratory under Maxwell's direction, soon after *Middlemarch*'s publication in 1871–72, and with the opening of Oxford's Clarendon Laboratory in 1872, physics had begun to assume several signs of professionalization. Those laboratories functioned as dedicated sites for physics training, research, and labor, with common methods of inquiry into topics that had been associated with astronomy, geology, and adjacent arenas. A parallel process of specialization was occurring in literature, fueled in part by Eliot's call to disengage fiction from politics. Avatars of the culture concept including Matthew Arnold, Walter Pater, and Oscar Wilde saw literature's inutility as its cardinal virtue, delivering Victorian readers to an aesthetic realm released from what J. S. Mill called the "art of getting on."[5] Literature could suspend the deadening ills of instrumental reason that Arnold aligned with the vocation of the scientist, in contrast to T. H. Huxley's proposals "to introduce physical science into ordinary education."[6]

But to emphasize the competitive cultural authority of scientists and humanists alone risks minimizing the shared sensibility I have identified throughout the period. Intellectuals like Eliot and Maxwell mutually elaborated forms of conditional historical thinking that had come to seem second nature in their lifetimes. This sensibility shaped the writing of fiction no less than investigations into celestial mechanics, optics, electricity, chemistry, and physiology; it informed contributions to mathematics, philosophical logic, and historiography, linking natural philosophers and mathematicians with writers for the general press, including novelists. Departing from classical conventions of maturation, those novelists accentuated a larger ensemble of developmental possibilities: the negated potentials that suffuse *The Ordeal of Richard Feverel* (chapter 1); the alternative relations between the past, present, and future in *Armadale* (chapter 2); and the prospects for moral and social variation in *Dombey and Son* (chapter 3). Contributing to this sensibility, Eliot returned attention to the novel's primitive meaning: its identification with what was new or unusual in an arresting fashion, as in the tales of Enlightenment-era progenitors such as Henry Fielding, Laurence Sterne, and Daniel Defoe, which established British conventions of self-formation. Framed as an extended examination of unpredictability, *Middlemarch* imagines collective chains of transformation that escape a holistic vantage. Thus departing from critical tendencies to read energy science as an artifact of *fin-de-siècle* ennui, this chapter reveals its salutary origins at midcentury, when theories of diffusion inspired attempts to imagine mass improvement.[7]

IMPOSSIBLE ECONOMIES: ELIOT, ENERGY, AND LOST POTENTIAL

I begin with an undated notebook entry composed by Eliot soon after the completion of *Middlemarch*. Entitled "A Fine Excess: Feeling Is Energy," the passage marks the movement of Eliot's mind over a range of topics: contemporary religion, recent political debates, and (not least) the "languor" of reformist impulses that only simulate sympathy. Taking up the latter point, it proceeds to the ethics underlying her art, with attention to *The Spanish Gypsy* (1868), Eliot's extended blank-verse poem. She quotes her narrator: "'Tis the grandest death! To die in vain / For greater love than sways the forces of the world." Eliot's later skepticism toward the dynamics of sympathetic exchange is evident. But skepticism leads to a more capacious conception of sympathy's aftermath. Bringing together a tone of disarming candor and cool scientific detachment, she explains: "I really believe and mean this,—not as a rule of general action, but as a possible grand instance of determining energy in human sympathy, which even in particular cases, where it has only a magnificent futility, is more adorable, or as we say divine, than unpitying force, or than a prudent calculation of results."[8] Eliot first remarks that "energy" can appear as waste or "futility" but then goes on to suggest that this resemblance is real. Futile feelings—personal sentiments that do not rise to the threshold of social utility—can continue to influence society at large. In fact, ardor can become "more adorable" when it fails to find direct recognition in another. Within Eliot's general economy of feeling, exhaustion and excess constitute a single standard of influence. Contradicting the logic of declining use value and diminishing returns—"a prudent calculation of results"—Eliot articulates a more primary logic of *unproductive* expenditure. Even as "excess" energy accumulates, it imparts ever-increasing possibilities for further growth. To be sure, eighteenth-century novelists like Samuel Richardson and Sarah Fielding had featured scenes of sympathetic recognition and response as a foundation for morals, in which the subject saw herself in another's suffering.[9] But for Eliot, the key event is the act of mediation: the "energy" of sympathy that, while not "calcul[able]," continues to circulate in society. Futile feeling has ancillary effects on the population.

One of the most familiar topoi of nineteenth-century culture, the connection between excessive emotion and self-loss served overwhelmingly to affirm the Victorian values of duty, restraint, and self-control. As *Middlemarch*'s narrator writes, the "roar on the other side of silence" could stifle the fragile sensorium, leaving the self susceptible to outward forces (194). In "A Fine Excess," however, Eliot conceives of another affective economy. Counterintuitively, the value of futile feeling lies in its power to transcend the boundaries of the individual.[10] Wasted feeling has an afterlife: unconstrained by both personal agencies and political forces ("worldly force"), it "sways the larger forces of the world." To represent futile feeling is to turn from the casuistry of "particular cases" to a more expansive evocation of possibilities for how individuals might influence the world.

Such impossible economies of feeling—collapsing loss into gain, death into life—represent a decisive shift in Eliot's creative maturity. Yet traditional historicist readings of subjugation have tended to yield partial perspectives on them. No novelist of the age appears to return with greater insistence to the point that individuals cannot transcend their insular social medium, as critics such as D. A. Miller and Nancy Armstrong argued influentially. The central lesson of her novels, it seems, is to moderate one's youthful desires and ambitions through what Miller termed the "surrender of desire or its reductive rescaling" and what Armstrong called "the operations of division and self-containment."[11] Such accounts have helped to divulge the mechanisms of ideological constraint buried beneath the surface of much Victorian fiction, including Eliot's, though at times inflating the coercive outcomes of her novels. As an influential line of feminist criticism pointed out, the subversion of Eliot's heroines might often be understood as a product of Victorian social arrangements rather than a fault of the fiction: the parochial institutions of education, work, and marriage that her novels critique as lacking. Against the drives toward terminal self-mastery, those critics charted less linear plots of emotional and spiritual experience.[12] "What looks like a disastrous *Bildung* by male standards," Susan Fraiman comments, "may actually looks something like a success within a renovated paradigm," defined through the cultivation of a luxurious interiority (123).

These sanguine accounts of arrested development can help us understand Eliot's ongoing formal experimentation with the bildungsroman in the late 1860s and afterward. In particular, "A Fine Excess" marks Eliot's turn toward a *post*subjective logic of development, in which individual influence could circulate throughout the social web. Undoing the antimonies between personal restriction and release, she suggested that the failed desires of one individual could have many minor aftereffects, limitlessly distributed through time and place. In Gilles Deleuze and Félix Guattari's terms, the small-scale "molecular" level of relations reveals phenomena that remain hidden at the more massive, "molar" scale of the population.[13] What initially looks like a sign of determination from the larger level— merely wasted energy—can be observed to have "unhistoric" consequences at the molecular level (825). In fact, the language of lost energy, in Eliot's journal, reflects an engagement with the many important scientific texts that she absorbed at this time. Besides encountering a litany of articles and reviews dealing with energy in the periodical press from the mid-1850s onward, Eliot read and owned influential works by William Grove and Hermann von Helmholtz (whom she met in her 1850s travels to Germany). Eliot's reading list for the years 1868 to 1871, the time of *Middlemarch*'s inception, reflects a focused interest in thermodynamics. Helmholtz features prominently, and Eliot describes rereading Grove "with renewed interest, after the lapse of years" in a diary entry from May of 1870.[14] The list also includes the scientist Fleeming Jenkin's influential essay on Lucretius's atomism, Bence Jones's *The Life and Letters of Faraday* (1870), and John Tyndall's *Fragments of Science for Unscientific People* (1871).[15] These were carefully selected works that located energy science within a field of ontological and epistemological concerns. "All I wish to point out," as Michael Faraday insisted, "is, by a reference to light, heat, electricity, &c., and the opinions formed on them, the necessity of cautious and slow decision on philosophical points . . . and the continual guard against philosophical prejudices."[16] Scientific subjects call for a "philosophical" approach in keeping with any other social subject and train the reader to suspend personal "prejudices" in favor of slow, deliberative habits of judgment.

These readings extended Eliot's lifelong interest in natural philosophical discourse with new attention to the rise of thermodynamics. Victorian energy science, or thermodynamics, consisted of two separate and seemingly antithetical laws. The first law of thermodynamics stated that the amount of energy in a system is always the same: in the case of a simple steam engine just as much as the cosmos in general, energy is neither gained nor lost (this was the law of *conservation*). The first law stipulated that energy remained constant through its individual states; manifesting variously as heat, light, electricity, or electromagnetism, energy itself is immutable. In any of these states, energy could be measured quantifiably in terms of physical "work." With the concept of work, Victorian scientists could calculate energy across its sundry manifestations. The second law of thermodynamics stated that entropy tends toward a maximum (this was the law of universal *diffusion*, also known as the entropy law). Demonstrating that the energy always declines in its potential to do work, scientists also showed that the cosmic mechanism as a whole was running down. The second law was formalized by the German scientist and mathematician Rudolf Clausius in 1850, building on speculations from earlier engineers, natural philosophers, and physiologists. Clausius showed that although energy is never destroyed, it becomes incapable of being measured and manipulated for work. Energy is constantly lost or "dissipated" as radiant heat and cannot be rechanneled into productive action without the use of external resources.

Taken together, the two laws of thermodynamics suggested a new natural economy in which "waste" and "energy" were aligned. Whereas classical Newtonian mechanics had ascribed to Providence an ongoing replenishment of resources, mid-nineteenth-century scientists argued that "unproductive" energy accumulates without end. It is true that the calamitous implications of the second law were well recognized by Victorians. One thinks of H. G. Wells's Time Traveler, who finds himself compelled to "watch with a strange fascination the sun grow larger and duller in the westward sky, and the life of the old earth ebb away" in the distant future of *The Time Machine* (1895).[17] Still, such *fin-de-siècle* observations on cosmic heat death remained relatively muted in the 1850s and 1860s. While noting the ultimate apotheosis of life over the *longue durée,* writers at midcentury tended to latch on to diffusion's more salutary outcomes. It is not so much that the effects of entropy were unintelligible but that their meanings were shaped by a prevailing liberal optimism in the aftermath of the hungry forties, the defeat of Chartist radicalism, and a new celebration of incremental progress.

For many British thinkers—including natural philosophers and popularizers such as Grove and Tyndall, more mathematically disposed scientists such as Peter Guthrie Tait, and novelists like Eliot—energy science suggested that life was unconfined to bounded bodies and that indeterminate traces of vitality suffused the world. Even as energy was lost to productive work—in the fading powers of a galvanic battery, a heat engine, a plant, or a human body—it continued to persist in incalculable forms of influence. "The effort we have made pervades and shakes the universe; nor can we present to the mind any exercise of force, which is thus not permanent in its dynamical effects," Grove explained in 1844, stating in the English lingua franca what would be codified into thermodynamic law: the total energy in existence is constant ("permanent in its dynamical effects"), though it is diffused into less calculable channels.[18] Like others in the late 1840s, Grove did not discriminate "force" from "energy"; only in the next decade did scientists begin to insist upon the distinction, as force came to designate a particular manifestation of energy expressed in terms of work. Still, Grove's language articulates an increasingly prevalent Victorian conviction: any particular "exercise of force" is indicative of a more enduring, "permanent" reservoir of influence in the universe.

It seems clear that Eliot incorporates ideas of this sort into *Middlemarch*, having read and reread Grove in the years leading up to its composition. But her research also included more recent theories that had yet to be accepted as good science. Specifically, "A Fine Excess" attests to her interest in statistical studies of energy that remained much debated in Britain: studies of energy in terms of individual deviations (what Eliot called "a *possible* grand instance") from the norm (the "rule of general action"). James Clerk Maxwell had developed this approach through the 1860s, laying the groundwork for what would later be seen as an epochal contribution to knowledge. But because his investigations were contested through the early 1870s, it is worth pausing to understand the relation between Maxwell's and Eliot's respective representational projects.

In a series of articles and lectures between 1859 and 1866, Maxwell posited that the laws of energy could be best represented in probabilistic form. The position itself was not entirely unique. In 1856, the German scientist August Krönig theorized that gas molecules could be interpreted through "the laws of probability." While "the path of each gas atom is so irregular that it defies calculation," Krönig wrote, he added a further consolation: "In accordance with the laws of probability, however, one can suppose, in place of this absolute irregularity, complete regularity."[19] Clausius elaborated another version of the premise soon thereafter, in calculations of what he termed the "mean free path" of individual atoms. What distinguished Maxwell's research was his interest in establishing a rigorous mathematical foundation for these speculations. He began to present his work not long after the annual meeting of the British Association for the Advancement of Science in 1859, a meeting galvanized by arguments about Henry Buckle's probabilistic history (as addressed in chapter 1). By 1860, Maxwell's research resulted in a new formula used to calculate the average velocities of molecules, later called the "Maxwell speed distribution." This was the first statistical law of physics, which Maxwell continued to revise over the decade, with modifications in his 1865 paper "On the Dynamical Theory of Gases," culminating in his monumental 1871 *Theory of Heat*.[20]

Imagine a cup of warm water. The liquid in the cup contains millions of atoms, so miniscule and unevenly distributed that one could never know their individual condition at a given instant. "We cannot," Maxwell explained, "ascertain the actual motion of any one of these molecules; so that we are obliged to abandon the strict historical method, and to adopt the statistical method."[21] By positing the haphazard, unobservable condition of individual atoms and molecules, Maxwell was led to revise assumptions about the universe at large. He focused specifically on the second law of thermodynamics, the law of entropy. While the law decreed that all available energy in a system must be lost to productive ends, Maxwell remained unconvinced that this inevitably held true. Although a hot body of water tends to lose heat, Maxwell imagined that a few atoms and molecules *might* get hot again; those exceptions to the rule might spontaneously regain energy for a time. It was not that the law of entropy was wrong but that it held true only as a generalization about the likely path of most molecules. By reasoning in this manner, Maxwell speculated that the diffusion of energy could be more realistically represented in probabilistic terms. This thesis had far-reaching ramifications, for Maxwell imagined the unpredictable nature of atoms at all scales of being, from the little system of a teacup to the grand megasystem of the cosmos.

Steeped in the rigorously reformed Mathematical Tripos curriculum at Cambridge, in addition to a general curriculum of logic, metaphysics, and natural philosophy at the University of Edinburgh, Maxwell also drew significant inspiration from the periodical press. As Theodore Porter notes, his statistical formulas were inspired directly by John Herschel's 1850 "Quetelet on Probabilities," the essay that also informed Charles Darwin's development. Maxwell read that article at least twice, first remarking that "the true Logic for this world is the Calculus of Probabilities," and praising it again in 1857, when it was reprinted.[22] When he reread Herschel, he began to conceive of an analogue between the astronomer's error law, glossed in Herschel's article, and the physics of diffusion. But Maxwell's labors were also informed by J. S. Mill's *System of Logic* (1843), George Boole's writings on logic and probability, and other texts that Eliot read, including Henry Buckle's *History of Civilization in England*. ("A bumptious book," Maxwell said.)[23] Buckle's *History* used the astronomer's error law to theorize a fatalistic "doctrine of averages" in social history, a premise that Victorian commentators pilloried, as discussed in chapter 1.[24] Maxwell read Buckle's work about a year before his first statistical inquiries and afterward cited Buckle when disparaging the notion that statistical regularities were prescriptive. These texts formed a common matrix of writings that Maxwell drew upon as he began to advance a more conditional historical sensibility.[25]

Maxwell's contribution to statistical mechanics now goes without saying in intellectual histories of science, though the specific cultural processes that led to its acceptance remain less understood. Porter credits him with "first introducing . . . probability distributions into physics" and with being "the first to use distribution formulas in a significant and productive way in any science."[26] But the acceptance of Maxwell's work cannot be explained by its innate merits. While his publications on statistical diffusion date to 1860, it was well over a decade and a half before they gained approval within the scientific mainstream—and even then, not in Britain but in Germany. First in 1872, and again with greater precision in 1877, the German scientist Ludwig Boltzmann developed more convincing restatements of Maxwell's work by translating it into concrete mechanical terms, as opposed to Maxwell's abstract mathematics. Boltzmann's 1877 elaboration of Maxwell's mathematics is now understood as marking the first full unification of thermodynamics and statistics; the Maxwell-Boltzmann distribution, as it became known, was soon hailed as a triumph, and described as "one of the most profound, most beautiful theorems of physics, indeed of all science" by Boltzmann's successor at the University of Vienna, Friedrich Hasenöhrl.[27] But between 1860 and the late 1870s, Maxwell's work occupied a less secure position within the British establishment. Experimentalists balked at the esoteric nature of his theorems, which were expressed in algebraic derivations that were (and remain to this day) daunting. Scientists like Clausius published significant critiques as well, "despairing that there was too little information to permit quantitative estimates," as the historian of science Robert D. Purrington writes.[28] In addition to those technical impasses, there also stood a troubling epistemological hurdle. The ultimate realities of our world could only be inferred in statistical terms, Maxwell claimed. As a negative hypothesis about the limits of knowledge, it was not a truth claim subject to traditional tests of verification but an assertion about the shortcomings of what could be objectively known.

Thus Eliot's Middlemarch notebooks advance a statistical conception of energy, rooted in the individual's "possible" but "incalculable" effects, at a time when its salience remained much in doubt. In what sense did Maxwell and Eliot coincide in their representational labors? To speak of Eliot as appropriating scientific insights is inexact, given the tenuous position of Maxwell's work. This is science being born. A new idea is issued in a culture and then invested with meanings, as writers affirm, complicate, critique, or ignore it, variously helping it succeed or fail. As a statistical "study" of energy, Eliot's novel joined a Victorian culture of letters in which the physical sciences and mathematics were widely and diversely deliberated. *Middlemarch*'s account of "unhistoric acts" (825) makes diffusion into an element of fictional realism *before* Maxwell's own challenge to the "strict historical method" was enshrined as sound scientific doctrine.[29]

REDEMPTIVE DIFFUSION: THE POETICS OF ENERGY IN VICTORIAN CULTURE

In part, the ties that bound Maxwell and Eliot can be traced to the biographical record: the two knew one another and interacted throughout the 1860s and afterward. Eliot encountered Maxwell's work directly—from his publications, public lectures, and private conversations—and indirectly, from her partner George Henry Lewes and from friends in London like William Clifford and John Tyndall.[30] Eliot demonstrated familiarity with Maxwell in the notes she culled from his work on vortex atoms, for example: "If a whirling ring be once generated . . . it will go on forever . . . and could never be divided or destroyed," Maxwell argued in an 1870 passage that Eliot copied directly.[31] Lewes's monumental *Problems of Life and Mind* (1874–79), undertaken concurrently with *Middlemarch,* devoted significant space to Maxwell. For his part, Maxwell styled himself as an amateur poet and voracious reader of novels including *Middlemarch,* having penned a letter that interpreted it as a scientific mythos: "I think Middlemarch is not a mere unconscious myth, as the Odyssey was to its author, but an elaborately conscious one, in which all the characters are intended to be astronomical or meteorological," he wrote.[32]

In addition to these biographical connections, Eliot and Maxwell drew on the same lay writings about probabilities in Britain, including those from Herschel, Augustus De Morgan, and James Fitzjames Stephen. Both encountered the iconoclastic reactions to Buckle's historicism in the late 1850s and 1860s, among which was Lewes's fiery "Mr. Buckle's Scientific Errors."[33] It was clear to Eliot and Maxwell, as to most Victorian intellectuals, that Buckle's "average man" was a chimera and that no universalist history could follow from his faith in the Platonic truth of the average (as discussed in chapter 1). Eliot wrote to Charles Bray that Buckle's work was a "suggestive book" with "strangely unphilosophical opinions mixed with its hard philosophy"; her skepticism continued in a droll comment to John Blackwood that "I am very far behind Mr. Buckle's millennial prospect, which is, that . . . superstition will vanish, and statistics will reign for ever and ever."[34] Still, she was attracted to the "great promise" of probabilistic outlooks on history, as was Maxwell. It seemed clear that Buckle's account was written on faulty foundations, but the prospect remained for a historical sensibility that questioned the iron rule of the average.

Maxwell developed this prospect in a range of contributions for specialist and nonspecialist audiences: not only full-length treatises but also articles, encyclopedia entries, lectures, letters, and poems. These include the paper with which I began this book, when in 1873 Maxwell spoke before the remaining members of the Cambridge Apostles, the intellectual club of his youth. There, he deliberated on the conditional nature of historical understanding, echoing ideas on which he had spoken several years beforehand. Upon his 1871 appointment to head the Cavendish Laboratory, he delivered an inaugural university address on the "statistical method . . . which in the present state of our knowledge is the only available method of studying the properties of real bodies."[35] From this platform he argued that "an adoption of the mathematical methods belonging to the theory of probability" (*Scientific Papers* 2:253) should structure future investigations of matter, energy, and force, and accentuated the philosophical value of that theory: "It is probable that important results will be obtained by the application of this method, which is as yet little known and is not familiar to our minds. If the actual history of Science had been different, and if the scientific doctrines most familiar to us had been those which must be expressed in this way, it is possible that we might have considered the existence of a certain kind of contingency a self-evident truth, and treated the doctrine of philosophical necessity as a mere sophism" (2:253). Of what do historical possibilities consist? What defines "a certain kind of contingency"? While raising these questions, the passage withholds an axiomatic answer and moves from an account of probabilistic principles *in* science to what seems "probable" and "possible" *about* science. Just where we might expect an assertion about the inevitable advancement of learning Maxwell conjures up variations from the "actual history of Science": what is "*possible* that we *might* have considered" in a counterfactual history of knowledge. With these strategies, Maxwell distinguishes his focus from the tradition of Joseph Priestley's *The Doctrine of Philosophical Necessity Illustrated* (1777). Priestley's work, which had long been associated with the Cambridge curriculum, defended determinism on the grounds that "all things, past, present, and to come, are precisely what the Author of nature really intended them to be, and has made provision for."[36] Instead imagining a nonhomogeneous account of the past, present, and future, Maxwell invited listeners to join in a shared thought experiment: an alternative history of ideas, a world where Priestley's ideas of "philosophical necessity" never gained traction at all.

No "strict historical method," then, but a metahistory: a narrative of alternative possibilities with a "generally poetic" structure, as Hayden White defines it, in the basic sense that the narrative arranges a continuum of events through time.[37] Maxwell's narrative is an optative one—a narrative of what might have been in a world without the doctrine of philosophical necessity. In fact, the poetics implicit in his historical ideasl feature throughout his actual verse of the 1870s, including "A Paradoxical Ode (After Shelley),", sent privately to Peter Guthrie Tait in 1878. In the final lines, the speaker's attention extends from the causal chain of God's design to an intimation of possible worlds:

> Still may thy causal chain, ascending,
> Appear unbroken and unending,
> . . . .
> And where that chain is lost to sight
> Let viewless fancies guide my darkling flight,
> Through atom-haunted worlds in series infinite.[38]

Maxwell's speaker posits a "chain" governing all physical phenomena, while granting that there can be no direct observation of it. That recognition sets up the salutary turn of the final couplet: if it is impossible to observe the total sequence of causes and consequences in history, then an infinite series of possible worlds might supplement obeservational knowledge. With this point, the poem opens out from what Stella Pratt-Smith calls the "limitations of empiricism" to "a sphere of multiple possibilities where the material of the physical world itself is spectral."[39] This physics of other worlds is a distinctively literary-aesthetic one, framed in a Romantic register of the infinite sublime and advanced through the lyricism of the closing couplet. The final slant rhyme resists the drive toward tightly bounded closure, as the poem registers potentials that exceed exact perceptual enumeration.

To take one other poetic example, consider Maxwell's 1876 poem, also shared with Tait, playfully titled "Report on Tait's Lecture on Force." The poem develops what Barri Gold calls an "antiforce sentiment" in keeping with the terms of "A Fine Excess":

> For, then, is Force, but mark you! Not a thing,
>   Only a Vector;
> Thy barbed arrows now have lost their sting,
>   Impotent spectre!
> Thy reign, O force! Is over. Now no more
>   Heed we thine action.[40]

The language of Maxwell's poem is culled from Tait's lecture at a meeting of the British Association for the Advancement of Science that year, as Gold and Daniel Brown have noted. "Thus it appears that *force* is a mere name," Tait commented: "merely a convenient term . . . not to be regarded as a *thing*."[41] Scientists like Tait and Maxwell conceived of force as a mathematical representation rather than an irreducible "thing," though the general premise was shared. Most influentially, Faraday had developed a relational understanding of force vectors, which he called "lines of force" in the years leading up to his 1852 paper "On the Physical Character of the Lines of Magnetic Force." Understanding force as the "source or sources of all possible actions of the particles or materials of the universe" (as he explained in an 1857 letter to Maxwell), Faraday declined to experimentally explain the physical constitution of isolated forces; instead, he became interested in representing the distribution of forces within a shared spatial "field."[42] These speculations provided the foundations for Maxwell's quantitative approach to the field concept in his *Treatise on Electricity and Magnetism* (1873), in which he translated Faraday's ideas into more complete mathematical form. Maxwell's poem affirms that the regime of force has ended in an epoch liberated from experimental examinations of isolated sequences of "action" and reaction, as investigations of mass molecular phenomena burgeoned. The excitement of this transition is underscored through the double caesura and enjambment of the penultimate line, which announce a shift from the preceding metrical regularities no less than a shift from older ontologies of "force."

But the literary orientation of Maxwell's ideas, as instanced in these speeches and poems, gained its most monumental inflections in his discussions of the *clinamen*. That word originated in the Roman poet Titus Lucretius Carus's *On the Nature of Things,* which Maxwell read both in Latin and in his acquaintance Hugh Andrew Johnstone Munro's English translation (which Eliot reread in the late 1860s). Lucretius used the term to denote the eternal whirl of matter: the chance recombination of primordial atoms in the void, resulting in provisional but beautiful forms. "No limit has been set on the dissolution of bodies," Lucretius wrote, and the "possibility of alteration" also remained limitless.[43] It was this vision of the swerve to which Victorians like Maxwell were returning again, investing Lucretius's understanding of the "possibility of alteration" with a precision and clarity never before imagined.[44] "I am afraid to say anything of Lucretius," Maxwell confessed in an 1866 letter to Munro, "because his words sometimes seem so appropriate."[45] He nevertheless conscripted Lucretius often and elaborately when theorizing the unpredictable motion of atoms. "Lucretius," Maxwell explained in his 1873 "Molecules" lecture, building on an article devoted to Lucretius by Fleeming Jenkin (which Eliot also read), "attempted to burst the bonds of Fate by making his atoms deviate from their courses and quite uncertain times and places."[46] Maxwell's professional publications allude to Lucretius with equal enthusiasm. He introduced "On the Dynamical Theory of Gases," for example, by accentuating the influence of Lucretius's atomism. "The opinion that the observed properties of visible bodies apparently at rest are due to the action of invisible molecules in rapid motion is to be found in Lucretius," he wrote, "[who] describes the invisible atoms as all moving downwards with equal velocities, which, at quite uncertain times and places, suffer an imperceptible change, just enough to allow of occasional collisions taking place between the atoms."[47] Uncertain times and places: in keeping with the "atom-haunted worlds" of his verse, Maxwell anchors his atomic account in literary terms. Classical culture makes new ideas intuitively familiar and acceptable, while older legacies of thought assume modern scientific relevance.

This is not to say that Victorian scientists embraced Maxwell's mythmaking ambitions whole cloth. His focus departed notably from investigators such as Tyndall, whose 1874 Belfast Address cultivated an aggressively antimetaphysical posture, critiquing Maxwell's mathematical inductions and stating that "all our philosophy, all our poetry, all our science, and all our art—Plato, Shakespeare, Newton, and Raphael—are potential in the fires of the sun."[48] While Tyndall stopped short of fatalism, preferring to characterize his position as a "higher materialism" that allowed for "latent powers" in the universe, as noted in chapter 2, his "potential" contrasts with the potential worlds of Maxwell's verse (*Fragments* 2:191–92). For whatever qualifications Tyndall made elsewhere in the address, the image of an ultimate solar source of vitality leads to the implication that individuals are predetermined manifestations of its energy. To strengthen his claims, Tyndall located his work within a lineage of classical atomists including Democritus, Epicurus, and Lucretius. But unlike Maxwell, as Daniel Brown notes, Tyndall deemphasized Lucretius's understanding of atoms' erratic combinations and recombinations.[49] This was precisely the understanding that Maxwell reaffirmed as an alternative to ontological materialism. Maxwell wrote an anonymous 1874 poem for *Blackwood's Magazine* entitled "Notes of the President's Address," parodying Tyndall's conviction that "the swift whirl of the atoms has hurried us, ruthless, along" and that "there is nothing but atoms and void, all else is mere whims out of date!"[50] Maxwell continued to underscore the alternatives to "ruthless" law in an early version of his *Encyclopedia Britannica* "Atom" article of 1874, which considered Lucretius in detail. "At quite uncertain times and places," he wrote, "atoms are deflected . . . and from their fortuitous concourse they form visible bodies."[51] Vying for cultural control over the meaning of the atom, Maxwell drew on Lucretius to render his philosophical premises accessible to the scientist and layperson alike, celebrating "the existence of a certain kind of contingency" against a reductive ontological determinism.[52]

And so, amid the specialization of physics through the 1860s and 1870s, a common mythmaking project linked intellectuals like Maxwell and Eliot. Casaubon's catalog of fixed, enduring mythemes stands as a foil to the theory of illimitable transformations that they and other Victorians discovered in Lucretius. But perhaps nowhere were the conceptual circuits between Eliot and Maxwell more suggestive than in the latter's well-known "demon" paradox. It has been said that Maxwell's demon represents "one of the most famous conundrums in the history of science," entering into contemporary culture through the postmodern novel.[53] But it is debatable whether the demon ever existed outside of popular letters. Its origins can be traced to one of the iconic thought experiments of the nineteenth century, found in Laplace's *Philosophical Essay on Probabilities* (1801), which began by asking readers to imagine a supernatural being able to observe the total forces behind all events in the past, present, and future (see chapter 1). No one could hope to match the demon's historical acumen, Laplace wrote. Even so, he added that one could approximate it through the calculus of probabilities.

Maxwell's thought experiment reinforced this point, although his demon occupied the lowest levels of the microcosmos. It controlled a doorway between warmer (fast-moving) and colder (slower) molecules; from this location, the demon could observe individual molecular motions, selectively choosing them so that colder ones could pass back into the warmer system. As a result of this sorting process, Maxwell wrote to William Thomson in 1868, "the hot system has got hotter and the cold colder and yet no work has been done, only the intelligence of a very observant and neat fingered being has been employed."[54] This was the counterintuitive lesson of Maxwell's thought experiment: the "law" of diffusion could be contravened, for it operated only as a probabilistic conjecture, a law of large numbers that did not encompass each individual.[55]

Maxwell's demon paradox is itself a theory of realism, rooted in the tension between empirical observation and mass molecular tendencies. It dovetails with Eliot's later realism in several respects. It posits a detached observer of multiple individuals and interactions who follows unpredictable sequences of action. "There are so many of us, and our lots are so different," as Eliot's narrator wrote in *Adam Bede* (1859).[56] But Eliot departed from Maxwell's model as well. Distinctively, Maxwell's demon suggested a resplendent figure of intellectual labor, which consumed no energy in its sorting action: the work of mental sifting was freed from the ordinary laws of physical expenditure. ("These beings should do no work," as Stewart and Tait observed [125].) But in *Middlemarch,* entropy is ineluctably bound up with the narrator and the limitations of her work. While the narrator notes "exceptional" instances that resist the general rule of entropic decline, she also affirms the value of energy that is not reconverted—and, moreover, underscores its incalculable nature in the end.

While critics have noticed Eliot's interest in Maxwell's work, its integral importance to *Middlemarch* has remained unobserved. Jesse Rosenthal has shown that in *Daniel Deronda* (1876) Eliot drew on statistical ideas, including

Maxwell's, to suggest an alternative to organic social relations. For Rosenthal, however, *Deronda*'s interest in "statistics and probability" (also indicated in references to gambling and racial demographics) breaks from *Middlemarch*'s focus on individuals. "The traditional *Bildungsroman*, as exemplified by *Middlemarch*," he writes, "shows an implicit reliance on the ability to represent society as compiled inductively from individual units," nowhere more manifestly than in Dorothea's "incalculably diffusive" influence.[57] But although the rhetoric of diffusion may seem self-evident in *Middlemarch*, it in fact marks a sophisticated turn from the classical bildungsroman both in the finale and in the novel's core conceptions of individual and social formation throughout. Indeed, we can see Eliot's interest in thermodynamics registered as early as *Adam Bede*. Her narrator reflects on Adam's labor at the forge: "What was a moment before joy, vexation, or ambition, begins its change into energy. All passion becomes strength when it has an outlet from the narrow limits of our personal lot in the labor of our right arm" (17). Personal potential can transform into useful work, forming a closed circuit between feeling, bodies, and an encompassing environment. Here, the invocation of energy sets up the vision of a functional social system: an organic whole in which each element contributes to the meaningful life of the collective. But embarking on a new stage of her career in the late 1860s, Eliot expressed growing dissatisfaction with the virtues of community. Long attuned to the incommensurable wants and needs of individuals, her novels increasingly exhibit the tensions, antagonisms, and general unpleasantries of communal living. The powers of fellow feeling, once hailed as auguring an ethically revitalized world, appeared ephemeral and fugitive. Acts of sympathetic exchange seemed to be grounded in the egoism of the perceiving self. Passion could turn into strength "*when* it has an outlet," but in *Middlemarch*, that fact leads to a further dilemma: passionate impulses that cannot find an outlet at all.

So, then, there were urgent reasons for Eliot's interest in diffusion at this juncture and urgent reasons for accentuating its incalculable effects. How could mass improvement take place in a world of individual limitation? And how could the fact of thwarted desire—of youths who lose their ardor and fail to inspire institutional change—suggest something other than the fatalistic rule of the norm? In *Middlemarch*, Eliot turned to thermodynamics for a solution to these impasses. As Eliot's friend Tyndall wrote in 1865, "The mode of motion changes, but the motion continues."[58]

DIFFUSION AS DEVELOPMENT IN *MIDDLEMARCH*

Nearly all major characters in *Middlemarch* lose personal potential, in the sense of an increasing disproportion between their actions and the results they achieve. In the slippage between inspiration and accomplishment, Eliot's characters enact the order of an inefficient universe: a world moving toward total decline. It seems self-evident why this is the case for Eliot's egoists (Edward Casaubon, Peter Featherstone, Rosamond Vincy, and Nicholas Bulstrode). Whether squandered in jealousy, revenge, or scrupulous isolation, the self-directed impulses of these characters cannot endure in perpetuity. But it is less obvious why the narrative imparts a shared logic of depletion to its more celebrated characters, Dorothea Brooke and Tertius Lydgate, who undergo analogous experiences of wasted effort. Conventionally, this can be explained in light of the novel's need to punish and rebuke their desire for transcendence: in their efforts to exceed the limitations of their world, Dorothea and Lydgate are enslaved to them. But in another sense, the fact of emotional attenuation appears as a precondition for subjectivity itself. Personal powers are circumscribed in nineteenth-century culture, so that the nature of the self is defined by the particular forms of expenditure that one's impulses assume.

The downward direction of energy, dissipation, emerges as an organizing problem in the prelude. In particular, it is underscored through the example of St. Theresa, whose vitality is associated with an older ideal of "fuel" (that is, "material for burning, combustible matter as used in fires" (*OED*). Observing the distinction between Theresa's social circumstances and those of nineteenth-century Britain, the narrator articulates that distinction in terms of their respective natural economies—namely, the new ideal of limitation that the nineteenth century has produced. Theresa's "flame quickly burned up that light fuel; and, fed from within, soared after some illimitable satisfaction, some object which would never justify weariness, which would reconcile self-despair with the rapturous consciousness of life beyond self" (3). The long sequence of clauses condenses the epic that *Middlemarch* is not: Theresa's "flame" spent its early sources of fuel; this flame "feeds" from her own self-generated resources; finally, it conquers "weariness" itself. In St. Theresa's development, energy provides its own magical solution to the problem of enervation. Her "fuel" can be used to overcome its very exhaustion. But the nineteenth century will not facilitate such strategies for Dorothea, whose powers cannot be replenished from within. In the language of energy science, diffusion cannot be reversed without the addition of external resources. As the narrator comments, "Here and there is born a Saint Theresa, foundress of nothing, whose loving heart-beats and sobs after an unattained goodness tremble off and are dispersed among hindrances, instead of centering in some long-recognizable deed" (4). Whereas her precursor's "passionate, ideal nature demanded an epic life," the conditions of Dorothea's world will not allow a "constant unfolding of far-resonant action" (3).

Pitting an ideal of "constant unfolding" action against one of endless dispersion, the prelude sets up a defining issue in Dorothea's narrative: will her potential lead to an epic achievement, resulting in a "life beyond self," or scatter into evanescence? The issue is all the more poignant since readers know from the beginning that an epic life is impossible. Instead shifting the terms of the question, Eliot's novel reconciles its two implications. In keeping with new thermodynamic concepts, *Middlemarch* aligns "constant unfolding" with the constant increase of wasted energy. And in this sense, it finds a new standard of influence in the limitations of nineteenth-century life. The novel marks this shift in the movement from "dispersion" in the prelude to "incalculably diffusive" influence in the finale (4, 825). First, Dorothea is singled out as an embodiment of lost potential; she then briefly regains energy; and finally, she loses energy again in the turn to her "diffusive" effect.

The open secret of Dorothea's marriage—what everyone *except* Dorothea knows—is her husband's enervation. In her new connubial life with Casaubon, Dorothea believes that she "was going to have room for the energies which stirred uneasily under the dimness and pressure of her own ignorance. . . . Now she would be able to devote herself to large yet definite duties" (44). These duties promise to focus her aspirations into an active channel: "To Dorothea Mr. Casaubon had been the occasion which had set alight the fine inflammable material of her youthful illusions" (82). But far from being "the book which," Dorothea believes, "will make your vast knowledge useful to the world" (194), Casaubon's *Key to all Mythologies* is an emblem of futility. His search for fixed, master meanings corresponds to Lydgate's search for the ultimate rudiments of matter, although the latter escapes the novel's severest judgment in the end. Whereas Lydgate becomes an unexceptional adult—a husband, parent, and London professional who has learned to temper his youthful ambitions—Casaubon's childless death reinforces his absence of vitality all along. His enervation contrasts with the salutary embodiments of nonreproduction in Collins's *Armadale* and Dickens's *Dombey and Son*. For Midwinter, Sol Gills, and Ned Cuttle, an avoidance of reproductive manhood is a desirable alternative to life as an *homme moyen;* in Eliot's novel, Casaubon inhibits Dorothea's desire to become anything but a *femme moyen:* a woman who is "shapen after the average" (142). As a novelist attuned to the dynamics of female formation, Eliot examines nonnormative routes of male maturation, while also disclosing how stunted men might thwart similar prospects for women. And after observing Dorothea's desultory marriage, the novel raises a further prospect in turn: How might Dorothea's lost ardor continue to shape the world in less "definite" form (44)?

An answer begins to emerge through the rhetoric of diffusion. The narrator writes of Casaubon's "surprise that though he had won [Dorothea], he had not won delight" (83). She explains, "It is true that he knew all the classical passages implying the contrary; but knowing classical passages, we find, is a mode of motion, which explains why they leave so little extra force for their personal application" (84). The passage may allude to the subtitle of Tyndall's *Heat: A Mode of Motion* (1868), though the conceit was widespread in thermodynamics discourse. Natural philosophers had made the point that energy consists of a finite quantity of matter in motion (appearing as heat, light, electricity, or electromagnetism): energy can be employed in active work or diffused as radiant heat but cannot be maintained indefinitely. "The fact is," the British scientist William Thomson observed, "the work is lost to man irrecoverably; but not lost in the material world."[59] In keeping with this assertion, the narrator quips that Casaubon's knowledge has "little extra force for . . . personal application." He cannot feed from internal sources in the manner of St. Theresa either. The narrator comments: "Mr. Casaubon had never had a strong bodily frame, and his soul was sensitive without being enthusiastic: it was too languid to thrill out of self-consciousness into passionate delight; it went on fluttering in the swampy ground where it was hatched. . . . His experience was of that profound narrow sensitiveness which has not mass enough to spare for transformation into sympathy, and quivers thread-like in small currents of self-preoccupation or at best of an egoistic scrupulosity" (279). Casaubon lacks the requisite "mass" to convert languor into "passionate delight." Conceived as so much expended energy, his feeling quivers "thread-like in small currents." Eliot's prose appears at the edge of analogy; it draws on the rhetoric of science to imagine the enervation of feeling that cannot "thrill out" and merely moves to less perceptible channels. As it turns out, Casaubon's energies do continue after his death— both in his codicil's prohibition of Dorothea and Will Ladislaw's marriage and in his demand that she should continue his research. These injunctions further dilute Dorothea's idealism while also becoming an indirect impetus for the welfare of others, when she uses Casaubon's money to alleviate Lydgate's difficulties.

Instead of concentrating her passion into a single productive action, then, Dorothea experiences marriage as a mode of self-attenuation. She learns that her passion is finite and subject to decline. After Lydgate diagnoses her husband's fatal condition, in chapter 42, the narrator comments, "She hesitated, fearing to offend him by obtruding herself; for her ardor, continually repulsed, served, with her intense memory, to heighten her dread, as thwarted energy subsides into a shudder" (415). The image of obstruction neatly encapsulates the deadening nature of her marriage: "thwarted" energy is energy that fails to do productive work. It is "dispersed among hindrances," like the "small currents" into which Casaubon's own efforts fall (4). Since it cannot be maintained, such energy "subsides into a shudder" and cannot be rechanneled. The language of energy indicates a sense of implacable distance despite the close proximity of her characters; Eliot has turned the second law of thermodynamics into a means of figuring failed sympathies. "Friction," as Balfour Stewart wrote in 1873, "will prove itself to be, not the destroyer of energy, but merely the converter of it into some less apparent and perhaps less useful form."[60] Likewise, Dorothea's "Puritan energy" is not negated but becomes "less apparent" and "less useful" than she first imagined.

What structures the logic of Dorothea's development, then, is not the question of whether passionate feeling can be sustained but rather of what happens after it is lost in individuals and how the afterlife of individual impulses might be represented in realistic terms. For while Dorothea's energies are squandered, they continue to have lower-level effects: "Dorothea's ideas and resolves seemed like melting ice floating lost in the warm flood of which they had been but another form. She was humiliated to find herself a mere victim of feeling, as if she could know nothing except through that medium: all her strength was scattered in fits of agitation . . . and then again in visions of complete renunciation, transforming all hard conditions into duty" (192). Rather than resolving into a focused action, Dorothea's ambitions are "scattered" in the manner of ice after heat is applied. The image is one of irreversible motion. Melting ice is what physicists call a "time-asymmetric" phenomenon, meaning that the diffusion of molecules cannot conceivably be reversed in the exact order.[61] This suggestion of irreversibility runs through Dorothea's final moments with Casaubon: "She sat listening . . . with a dumb inward cry for help to bear this nightmare of a life in which every energy was arrested by dread" (367). Her energy is "arrested" and cannot be restored; even so, it is all the more palpable as a generalized anxiety. "The excessive feeling manifested would alone have been highly disturbing to Mr. Casaubon" (194). Despite the fact that Dorothea's "excess" feeling is lost ("arrested by dread"), it persists in an imperceptible form that has a powerful effect on her husband.

Such signs of lost energy extend to other characters whose ambitions are also blocked. The logic of productive diffusion features prominently, for instance, in the aftermath of old Peter Featherstone's death, which turns upon the two versions of his will. Featherstone's will is literally thwarted when Mary Garth refuses to burn the revised version, an act that prevents Fred Vincy from securing the inheritance he has sought. Fred's struggle to cultivate Featherstone's good graces, and Featherstone's own deathbed decision to reward him, are set up without issuing in a generative outcome. Instead of leading to Fred's ascension into the upper echelon of Middlemarch and his long-awaited betrothal to Mary, the ordeal of Featherstone's inheritance has an altogether less definite result: the romantic triangle between Fred, Mary, and Mr. Farebrother, the latter of whom emerges as a new rival for Mary's affections.

The digressive force of the narrative is illuminated in the smoldering "movement of the flame" at Featherstone's death. While confined to the fireplace, its radiant heat "communicat[es] itself to all objects" beyond (318). For the triangular relationship between Fred, Mary, and Farebrother extends the leitmotif of lost potential until it appears as a salutary ideal in its own right. Both Fred and Farebrother are defined through their prodigal expenditures, namely in Farebrother's gambling and Fred's dilettantism. Neither individual can consolidate his interests in isolation; even so, their respective losses translate into a form of collective benefit when Farebrother abnegates his immediate interests. In a moment of ethical revelation, he elects to aid his romantic rival at his own expense. Rather than pursuing his un-requited love for Mary, Farebrother allows his personal failure to ensure Middlemarch's continuation into the next generation (through the marriage of Fred and Mary), while Fred's own unrecuperated inheritance forces him to learn the newly ascendant Victorian virtues of duty, work, and self-help. Ultimately, the marriage of Fred and Mary signals a new future for the Mid-dlemarch community, though their marriage is enabled precisely by Fare-brother's failed passions, which find no expression in his immediate affairs.

The power of the dying flame suggests a lesson that the novel every-where explores: even when potential is lost to the individual, it is never annihilated. Such losses give rise to a form of limitless circulation: influence that "comunicat[es] itself to all" (318). This ideal marks a limit to the goal of representing knowable communities in fiction, while still sustaining the ethical rationale for doing so. In Raymond Williams's well-known account, the Victorian novel could serve as an anodyne to the fragmentation of industrial-era culture by "offer[ing] to show people and their relationships in essentially knowable and communicable ways."[62] But *Middlemarch* moves in a slightly different direction, toward what C. S. Pierce later called "indefinite community" and what Grove, in an earlier but related vein, had described as "indefinitely" communicated influence.[63] While delineating knowable char-acters and connections, the novel sets up a higher, complementary scale of relations articulated through the language of energy and entropy.[64] But the goal is the same: to register, in an age of unprecedented disaggregation, the potential for wider and more meaningful connections.

This understanding finds full articulation in the finale, although it runs throughout the narrative leading up to it—for instance, in the Raffles sub-plot. In his very name, Raffles conjures up the world of betting and lottery draws that marked the earliest elaborations of probabilistic thinking.[65] As a figure of ethical transgression, he disrupts the well-ordered affairs of the Bulstrodes and those connected with them in order to maintain his habits of gambling and drinking. When Bulstrode begins to weigh the odds of Raffles's premature death, not long after his appearance, it is through the discourse of "probabilities": "It seemed to him a sort of earnest that Provi-dence intended his rescue from worse consequences; the way being thus left open for the hope of secrecy. That Raffles should be afflicted with illness, that he should have been led to Stone Court rather than elsewhere, Bulstrode's heart fluttered at the vision of probabilities that these events conjured up.

If it should turn out that he was freed from all danger of disgrace . . . his life should be more consecrated than it had ever been before" (697). Bulstrode's "vision of probabilities" is indulged in bad faith: fixating on the best of possible worlds, he neglects to imagine the full range of outcomes that might follow from Raffles's demise. As it turns out, Raffles's death does not close off the threat of scandal but ignites the uncontrolled outbreak of rumor and gossip that surrounds its circumstances. The scandal will implicate Lydgate and Rosamond Vincy in the later chapters, driving their expulsion from the neighborhood, but not without advancing a central characteristic of *Middlemarch*'s own probabilistic vision: the power of dead hands like Raffles, Casaubon, and Featherstone, whose unpredictable influence increases all the more when their vitality is lost.

Eventually, the disgrace that hangs over Lydgate's and Rosamond's affairs will have happy outcomes in the lives of others. But one finds an anticipation of redemptive diffusion even earlier, when the narrator first introduces Raffles in chapter 41. Here, the probabilistic logic of "raffles" is shown to coincide with the nature of writing itself:

> Who shall tell what may be the effect of writing? If it happens to have been cut in stone, though it lie face downmost for ages on a forsaken beach . . . it may end by letting us into the secret of usurpations and other scandals gossiped about long empires ago. . . . As the stone which has been kicked by generations of clowns may come by curious little links of effect under the eyes of a scholar . . . so a bit of ink and paper which has long been an innocent wrapping or stop-gap may at last be laid open under the one pair of eyes which have knowledge enough to turn it into the opening of a catastrophe. (412)

What defines "the effect of writing" is a law of unintended consequences. Whether "cut in stone" or printed on "ink and paper," its impact accrues from many unplanned peregrinations. There is no end to the iterative effects of language, even when writing appears as a "stop-gap," in Eliot's ludic illustration. The modulation of metaphors—from the cut stone to the kicked rock to the crumpled page—demonstrates that there can be no clinching conclusion to the movement of literary reference. So the opening question—what may writing do?—turns out to have no definite response so much as a "vision" of ramifying future potentials, of diffusive reading acts across time and place. We can hardly know for certain what writing is and might mean. "To Uriel watching the progress of planetary history from the sun," the narrator concludes, "the one result would be just as much of a coincidence as the other" (412). The slapdash crumpling of a page and a well-wrought tragedy, the outcomes of "the sun" and a dying man's fire: these form paired demonstrations of unpredictability. Writing follows the same diffusive logic as the universe itself.

The narrator's recursive "vision of probabilities" invites an additional implication, posed less as an assertion than as a problem of fictional form. What if narratives aimed not to diminish the play of alternative possibilities? Good fiction, classically conceived—fiction exhibiting what E. M. Forster called a "final sense (if the plot has been a fine one)"—admits of no aberrations and aims to pull its indications of contingency back into a superintending structure of meanings.[66] If such stories do occasionally let accidents creep in, then they are mostly incorporated into the final design; the conclusion is set up all along. Might there exist a poetic of fiction that courts surplus developmental possibilities that remain foreclosed or otherwise unincorporated into the plot? Narrative theorists like Peter Brooks think not. Plot, Brooks writes, is "what shapes a story and gives it a certain direction or intent of meaning," that which "demarcates, encloses, establishes limits, orders" (xi, 4). When we open the pages of a novel, it is in a state of ever-present anticipation about "the structuring power of . . . endings" (94). Even *peripeteia*—the sudden reversal of fortunes in tragedy—should confirm the integrity of the narrative, attesting to a purposive logic that motivates each incident in its fabric.

Middlemarch complicates these conventions with its focus on the dynamics of lost potential. Its developing "vision of probabilities" aligns a massive field of individual lives and, in the end, evokes possibilities that cannot be represented in individualistic terms at all. Henry James used another term to describe the novel: "diffuseness." *Middlemarch* "sets a limit, we think, to the development of the old-fashioned English novel," he wrote in 1873. "Its diffuseness, on which we have touched, makes it too copious a dose of pure fiction."[67] James's observation speaks less and more than he intends. For him, the novel's branching narrative is a sign of creative hyperabundance, a surplus that stretches the economy of plot to a maximum and that troubles the very meaning of fiction. "Pure fiction," properly devoted to the lives of select individuals, cannot tolerate too much diffuseness, lest it become an account of population trends. With this point, however, he also suggests how

Eliot enlisted the science of diffusion to challenge conventions of fictional representation on those very terms. In *Middlemarch*'s study of "excessive" or "scattered energies" (194, 192), we see the mechanics of statistical diffusion issuing in a new narrative mimesis: a model of unaccountably ramifying relations between and across individuals, leading to an account of *possible* relations through time in the end.

Increasingly, the problem of dispersion in Dorothea's experience extends to the total structure of the novel—a problem of content that *Middlemarch* addresses through the logic of its form. In the gradual broadening of perspectives beyond Dorothea after chapter 11, the story envisages a developing dissemination of narrative energy. And as it turns out, the narrator's perspective does finally move outside the web of Middlemarch (and *Middlemarch*). Except for Farebrother, Fred, and Mary, every main character leaves the community. But the novel recasts the fear of dispersion itself en route to the finale, so that it becomes consistent with a more valedictory "vision" of diffusive social relations (697). In particular, to resolve the issues of diffusion introduced in Dorothea's narrative, the novel traces the "determining energy" of its other main protagonist, Tertius Lydgate.[68]

"ETHEREAL ATOMS" AND THE VICTORIAN SOCIAL IMAGINARY

As Eliot's only major character concerned with experimental discovery, Lydgate appears as a touchstone in literature and science studies, which often situate him within the rise of Victorian medical and biological discourses.[69] But while Lydgate's vocational ambitions are associated with medical reform, they also suggest the *limits* of bodily knowledge and locate the body within a general field of energy conversions. From the start, *Middlemarch* aligns Lydgate with an intuitive insight into "ethereal atoms"—a line of investigation not wholly opposed to medical science but beyond its immediate concerns (162). To what end? Significantly, both Lydgate's scientific intuitions and actual social relationships are figured through the terms of energy science (145). In the turn from Lydgate's early theoretical machinations to his subsequent conditions of living, we shall see, his circumstances come to illustrate the discovery of diffusion that he fails to make.

As in its depiction of Dorothea, the novel identifies Lydgate with an ardor that exceeds the "average" in Middlemarch and shows how his energies strain against the "hampering threadlike pressures" of its inhabitants (142, 180). Introducing Lydgate in chapter 11, the narrator comments: "Among our valued friends is there not someone or other who is a little too self-confident and disdainful; whose distinguished mind is a little spotted with commonness; who is a little pinched here and protuberant there with native prejudices; or whose better energies are liable to lapse down the wrong channel under the influence of transient solicitations? All these things might be alleged against Lydgate" (147). Like Dorothea's "Puritan energy" (9), Lydgate's "better energies" are threatened by the prospect of finitude: of "laps[ing] down the wrong channel." But whereas that tendency appears at the levels of theme and language in Dorothea's narrative, it also organizes Lydgate's actual scientific quest. The misfortune of Lydgate's development follows from this point: his intimations about the energy of "ethereal atoms" are exhibited in his social surroundings but exceed his horizons of understanding. Lydgate's diffusive circumstances—the lapsing of his "energies," brought by a premature marriage to the wrong person—illustrate the very breakthrough he had hoped to find. Unable to scrutinize his affairs, he also becomes incapable of observing "the last refinement of energy" (161).

Middlemarch associates Lydgate with "the limit of anatomical analysis" from his earliest scenes in the novel (146). Reflecting upon his scientific hero Marie François Xavier Bichat, Lydgate muses: "That great Frenchman first carried out the conception that living bodies, fundamentally considered, are not associations of organs . . . but must be regarded as consisting of certain primary webs or tissues, out of which the various organs . . . are compacted, as the various accommodations of a house are built up in various proportion of wood, iron, stone, brick, zinc, and the rest, each material having its peculiar composition and properties" (145). Bichat, contemporaries believed, was on the verge of discovering an atomic substratum linking all matter.[70] Like many forerunners of energy conservation (foremost among them Helmholtz, Tyndall, and James Joule), he understood his work as an attempt to trace the forces that animate organic bodies. And like those forerunners, Lydgate aims to rethink the boundaries between organic and inorganic forms through an analysis of foundational physical phenomena.[71] "The more he became interested in special questions of disease," the narrator notes, "the more keenly he felt the need for that fundamental knowledge of structure which just at the beginning of the century had been illuminated by [Bichat]" (145).

Just as the novel aligns Lydgate's work with subsequent insights into energy, it introduces his habits of mind in those terms. In Lydgate's often-quoted study scene, the narrator rehearses his ambitions:

> [He possessed] the imagination that reveals subtle actions inaccessible by any sort of lens, but tracked in that outer darkness through long pathways of necessary sequence by the inward light which is the last refinement of Energy, capable of bathing even the ethereal atoms in its ideally illuminated space. . . . [H]e wanted to pierce the obscurity of those minute processes which prepare human misery and joy, those invisible thoroughfares which are the first lurking places of anguish, mania, and crime, that delicate poise and transition which determine the growth of a happy or unhappy consciousness. (161–62)

As Selma B. Brody has observed, "This is a physicist's reverie, not a physician's."[72] The imagery of thermodynamics abounds in the passage, with reference in particular to Tyndall's *Fragments,* which Eliot had been reading at this time.[73] The "ethereal atoms" indicate the ultimate objects of scientific knowledge. Lydgate's concerns are not with the infinitely hard, destructible atoms of eighteenth-century science but with *ethereal* matter. As Victorian scientists argued, the world is constituted by a total vacuum of energy, or ether, and all action transpires within it. "We on the earth's surface live night and day in the midst of ethereal commotion," as Tyndall wrote. "The medium is never still."[74] The ether principle substantiated the notion of a universal medium of energy relations, in which energy could assume measurable manifestations but could also be dissipated as radiant heat.

The goal of Lydgate's research is not a particular material substance, then, but energy's "last refinement"—the "minute processes," and "invisible thoroughfares" of atoms. And in this sense, his research in the late 1820s anticipates cutting-edge investigations at the time of *Middlemarch's* publication: Maxwell's statistics of diffusion in the 1860s and 1870s, which addressed *possible* movements of atoms and molecules that could never be seen in isolation. The mistake of Lydgate's vision lies in this fact: instead of imagining a spectrum of molecular possibilities, he subscribes to the notion of "necessary sequence." That error emerges as a reflexive failing when he begins to see his own life as determined. His conditions come to seem unalterable to him, even as the novel's readers are invited to entertain other possibilities through the language of diffusion.

More and more, what Lydgate fails to comprehend as a scientific principle is worked out through the *social* medium of *Middlemarch*. Society is imagined as a continuum of energy and forces, and Eliot's characters become legible through the play of small-scale interactions that shape the total unit. Most notably, Lydgate's downfall is conceived in terms of his scattered energies; in his disintegrating marriage, Rosamond Vincy absorbs his "best energies" and demonstrates their "laps[ing]" down the wrong channel. Here Eliot highlights how social life and scientific knowledge are dialectically linked: mundane human structures (including common concepts, analogies, metaphors, and images) may aid investigators in explaining nonhuman phenomena, leading in turn to sharpened structures of representation. But Lydgate fails to observe these associations as his prospects diminish. The narrator comments: "The terribly inflexible relation of marriage had lost its charm of encouraging delightful dreams. . . . The Lydgate with whom she had been in love had been a group of airy conditions for her, most of which had disappeared, while their place had been taken by everyday details which must be lived through slowly from hour to hour, not floated through with a rapid selection of favorable aspects" (649). The "airy conditions" of Rosamond's attraction recasts Lydgate's "ethereal" intimations about the natural medium: "He had no longer free energy enough for spontaneous research and speculative thinking" (656). In place of the early excitement of their courtship, defined by a "rapid selection of favorable aspects," their marriage resolves into the slow grind of the mundane. Emotionally depleted, Lydgate cannot contemplate the nature of energy. With this fact, however, his "scattered energies" actually *exemplify* the discovery that eludes him (194). The further point is that the rhetoric of diffusion is expressed through Rosamond's indirect discourse. She suggests precisely the ideas that her husband has failed to discover, so as to further ironize the distance between them.

But Lydgate's lost potential still inspires the union between Dorothea and Ladislaw; as it turns out, his defeated desires have a more mediated influence on others. The chain of action is notoriously circuitous. First, Dorothea asks Lydgate to call at Lowick, her fascination piqued by "an awakening conjecture as to what Lydgate's marriage might be to him" (761). Then learning of his despondent condition, Dorothea offers to intercede on his behalf; what impels her is precisely Lydgate's "wasted energy." This leads in turn to her discovery of Rosamond and Ladislaw together; to her resolve to act on Lydgate's behalf in spite of her own desires; and, finally, to Rosamond's confession of Ladislaw's love for Dorothea. The narrator comments: "All the active thought with which she had before been representing to herself the trials of Lydgate's lot, and this marriage union which, like her own, seemed to have its hidden as well as evident troubles—all this vivid sympathetic experience returned to her now as a power. . . . She said to her own irremediable grief, that it should make her more helpful, instead of driving her back from effort" (776). Through Rosamond's mediations, Lydgate's stifled energies become the condition for Dorothea's new "power" and "vivid sympathetic experience." It is not that Dorothea directly assimilates Lydgate's energies; her "irremediable grief" has not been reversed by his influence. Rather, that influence indirectly compels her selfless "effort" with Rosamond. And although framed as a scene of sympathetic recognition, the characters' connection does not resolve into an act of mutual exchange per se. Dorothea and Rosamond's bond is inherently ephemeral; the two are speaking at cross-purposes, so that their scene stages an absence of perfect sympathy. But despite the slippage between them—indeed, because of it— their feeling has ancillary effects in the movement of "life beyond self" (3).

As an *indirect* result of Rosamond and Lydgate's lives, then, Dorothea does regain "energy" and lends aid to those around her. While Saint Theresa's "fuel" had been replenished from within, Dorothea's "energy" can contravene the law of decline for only a moment: diffusion, Dorothea's experience indicates, is a general trend rather than an absolute injunction. In Maxwell's language, "There is nothing inconsistent with the laws of motion in supposing that in a particular case a very different event might occur."[75] Both of Eliot's main protagonists had hoped to resist the trend toward exhaustion, although Dorothea alone recovers some of her youthful passion, while Lydgate is "shapen after the average" (142).

Yet to interpret the scene in purely individualist terms is to miss its *post*individualist inflections. For Dorothea's renewal stems from the influence of others not present at all: not only from Rosamond, that is, but also from the "scattered energies" of Lydgate, whose failures had driven Rosamond to Ladislaw. So while Lydgate's ardor remains unrecuperated, it continues to shape the lives of those apart from him. Here we see the novel setting up an understanding of influence that the finale bears out as a "vision of probabilities" (697). It seems clear, whatever Dorothea's interaction with Rosamond, that passionate feeling is finite and cannot be endlessly conserved. The meaning of a life lies not in its recuperation of energy but in the diffusive effects of one's actions on the population. Eliot thus troubles the absolute antithesis between her two protagonists; they are linked through a larger narrative pattern whereby "wasted energy" becomes the condition for incalculable influence in the future. Commenting on the later history of Dorothea's life, the narrator observes:

> Certainly those determining acts of her life were not ideally beautiful. They were the mixed result of a young and noble impulse struggling amidst the conditions of an imperfect social state, in which great feelings will often take the aspect of error, and great faith the aspect of illusion. For there is no creature whose inward being is so strong that it is not greatly determined by what lies outside it. A new Theresa will hardly have the opportunity of reforming a conventual life: . . . the medium in which [her] ardent needs took shape is for ever gone. (824–25)

Whereas a now-antiquated medium had enabled modes of epic transcendence, the ethereal "medium" of the nineteenth century presumes the inevitability of defeat. In a mixed and modernizing "social state," "great feelings will often take the aspect of error" and "lapse down the wrong channel" (147). True to this new milieu, what defines passionate feeling is its ineluctable lapsing. So much does the narrator conclude: Dorothea's "finely-touched spirit had still its fine issues, though they were not widely visible. Her full nature . . . spent itself in channels which had no great name on the earth" (839). Her spirit is *"finely*-touched" and has *"fine"* consequences. Suggesting "a *fine* excess," the enduring effect of Dorothea's ardor is incalculable.[76] Impulses that are lost to "effective action," as the narrator puts it, have a posthumous life within the group (648).

The cosmological orientations of this vision were all the more manifest in the novel's first edition. In that version, the narrator draws directly on Maxwell: "While this is the social air in which we mortals begin to breathe, there will be collisions such as those in Dorothea's life, when great feelings will often take the aspect of error" (852). The phrase "social air" extends the narrator's earlier evocation of Lydgate and Rosamond's relationship as a "group of airy conditions" (649). Namely, the figure of "collisions" in the "social air" refers to Maxwell's statistical thermodynamics. Individual molecules in a closed system, Maxwell argued, are incapable of being observed except as a distribution of probabilities, or what was called the "error curve" and "astronomer's error law" (chapter 1). Error assumes a double meaning from this vantage. For feelings to "take the aspect of error" is not only to take the appearance of failure. For Eliot's educated readers, it would also mean something like to "take the aspect of *the error curve*": to take on an appearance of large-level possibilities, whose ramifications can be neither observed nor anticipated in full.

Building on Maxwell's metahistorical vision—his alternative to the "strict historical method"—Eliot's novel represents the diffusion of "unhistoric acts" in the end (825).[77] This shared ideal resonates through the last lines: "But the effect of her being on those around her was incalculably diffusive: for the growing good of the world is partly dependent on unhistoric acts; and that things are not so ill with you and me as they might have been, is half owing to the number who lived faithfully a hidden life, and rest in unvisited tombs" (825). The celebratory tone of this passage, as D. A. Miller points out, is rife with qualification. *"Partly* dependent," *"so* ill": the phrases seem to undermine the progressive vision that the sentence invites.[78] But the passage's goal is in fact to stress the aftereffects of Dorothea's actions: her "diffusive" influence stems from its collateral power and inheres in the unpredictable effects of futile feeling. This estimate of Dorothea's life is partial but still sanguine, as the novel imagines individuals like her ("many Dorotheas") who could continue to transform "the social air" (839). As an intimation of possible relations between individuals, actions, and locations, the moment extends the ensemble effects we have seen in previous novels of formation. Like Sir Austin Feverel's glance through the windowpane, Ozias Midwinter's departures from the temporal present, and Sol Gills's ruminations on a lost life, wife, and son, Dorothea is situated within a matrix of potentials in excess of one place and time.

This turn to Dorothea's incalculable influence has metafictional significance as well: it recasts an anxiety of diffusive form in the telling of *Middlemarch*. Like the "dispersion" indicated in the prelude, the narrator's powers are threatened by transience; instead of resolving into an epic achievement, "an ardent outset may be followed by declension" (4, 818). As the narrator explains, "I at least have so much to do in unraveling certain human lots, and seeing how they were woven and interwoven, that all the light I can command must be concentrated on this particular web, and not dispersed over that tempting range of relevancies called the universe" (139). Throughout the novel, the narrator's efforts had appeared as a second-level narrative that looked uncannily like that of her characters: can the writer of realist fiction "concentrate" her energies into an epic achievement, or will they scatter into obscurity? The problem of narrative dispersal would have weighed acutely upon the novel's initial readership. In its initial serial publication (in eight numbers appearing every two months between December 1871 and October 1872, with the last two volumes appearing in November and December of that year), the fictional problem of dispersion *was* unresolved, making its interest in diffusive energy a recursive concern.[79]

Like Lydgate and Dorothea, most of the major figures are gone by the finale. The narrator's perspective is, in the end, "dispersed over that tempting range of relevancies" outside the community. It offers a distribution of possible outcomes (a "range"), and not a punctuated conclusion. Yet this dispersive ending, like the dispersion indicated in the prelude, has been reconceived as "diffusive influence" (825). Providing its own solution to the terror of a dissipating form, the novel embraces that prospect as an actual developmental ideal. Dorothea's and Lydgate's impeded development issues in a higher "vision of probabilities" within the totality.

The finale accentuates fiction's own unending power as well. For readers are also implicated in its diffusive vision, as the perspective shifts from the characters and conditions within the novel (set in the late 1820s and early 1830s) to "the imperfect social state" of the present. The audience's milieu may be even more diffusive than the "ethereal" medium of the past. ("In the past," as Richard Feynman puts it, "the universe was more ordered, in the technical sense, than it is today," since the cosmic process of diffusion has had more time to play out.)[80] Within this state of affairs, improved conditions of living may not result from a single, transcendent contribution to the social good but from impulses that never find visible realization. This holds true in the act of reading, in the bond between "you and me" (825), reader and writer, which is conceived as at once personal and inherently incomplete. Because one cannot account fully for the intentions of the text—because of the very slippage between "you and me"—the reader ensures its vitality in the future. Imperfect though they are, one's reactions to *Middlemarch*'s "diffusive influence" guarantee its continuing circulation in the future.

In this sense, Eliot's ideal of redemptive diffusion finds its ultimate expression through the act of reading *Middlemarch* itself. For Eliot, it is not that reading is socially productive rather than unproductive, useful and not unuseful. The very unproductive process of novel reading becomes a condition for generating additional affective capital and for fostering a sense of interconnections in the larger population. The idea runs through the final sentences: Dorothea's feeling *"spent* itself" in diffusive channels; in its very unremunerative nature, such feeling adds to the total reservoir of "invisible conditions" in the social medium (839). By consenting to "learn what everything costs," Dorothea is not only aligned with the norms of a middle-class culture but also associated with a more general economy of expenditure that continues in the act of reading the novel at hand (801). Dorothea's excessive energies persist through the lives of *Middlemarch*'s audience as the novel's indeterminacies issue in wider, less "definite" modes of influence in the future (44).

The counterfactual shape of the finale looks in two directions, both backward and forward, turning from retrojection about what might have been in Eliot's novel to projected futures outside the covers of the book. Lydgate's final years were haunted by the suspicion that he "had not done what he once meant to do," we learn, just as Dorothea endures a "feeling that there was always something better which she might have done" (835). But the recognition of failure is balanced by an awareness that their lost potentials have imperceptible social benefits. As Avrom Fleishman puts it, *"Middlemarch* . . . is, not a novel about what England was in the first third of the nineteenth century but a novel about how that society showed the marks of coming to an end and opening itself to become something else."[81] From the vantage of the 1870s, Eliot's defeated heroes can be seen as anticipating the intellectual legacies of thermodynamics, the condition of England after the Second Reform Bill, and the as-yet unknown afterlives of the Victorians themselves, in the future condition of "you and me."

So the shortcomings of *Bildung* within the novel are allayed by Eliot's depiction of them, as a now-completed "study" that adds to statistical studies of diffusion in the 1870s. Eliot does what Lydgate had not. His vocational failure, like Dorothea's, has become a precondition for Eliot to join contributions on energy's "last refinement" (161). At the historical moment when the occupation of the professional physicist was emerging in Britain, Eliot positioned herself as continuing her heroes' developmental goals and contributing to a rich network of ideas about incalculable diffusion. That ideal, which remained debated among physical scientists, becomes an intuitive foundation for *Middlemarch*'s realism. At the same time, Eliot does not cede cultural prestige to science. In the process of representing diffusion, she identifies it as something more than a sui generis scientific concept. The term exists within what Maxwell called "the general stream of thought," as a node within a larger lineage of writings including—perhaps above all—those that have failed to make a measurable contribution.[82]

For a generation of earlier British thinkers like Charles Babbage and Augustus De Morgan, probabilities were understood as an illusion of the mind. They were a reflection of our own ignorance about the determining chain of historical causes. For Maxwell and a new wave of intellectuals in the 1860s and 1870s, however, norms and deviations had become more than the metric of one's "internal feeling" of possibilities.[83] They represented the true position of an object in space or the ultimate nature of sensation (chapters 1 and 2); they referred to a new biological lineage or trait (chapter 3); they pointed to a molecule that spontaneously recovered energy. In each of these respects, British thinkers were moving toward what Ian Hacking calls "ultimate indeterminism," though it would be several decades before the thought of an acausal, truly stochastic universe could be put into words.[84] The possible worlds of Maxwell and Eliot were not quite modernist ones. Did Maxwell's probabilities function as artificial constructions, or did they suggest the operation of irreducible randomness? This was an issue that his writings raise but never fully confront; "chance" remained a black box to be seen from multiple angles but never opened once and for all.

We can detect this indistinction in *Middlemarch*'s homiletic last paragraphs as well, but to more generative effect. In keeping with Maxwell's own ambivalence, Eliot straddles the line between possibilities that are imaginary and real. Her narrator cultivates a hybrid position between the lives inside the text and the extradiegetic level of "you and me," so that the representation of fictional, subjective possibilities can be thought to have nonfictional outcomes. "We insignificant people," the narrator writes, "with our daily words and acts, are preparing the lives of many Dorotheas" (835). What was and remained an indistinction, in the work of scientists and mathematicians, emerges as a means of affirming the novel's phantasmagorical power: its capacity to imagine alternative historical conditions of experience that might become realized.

"What may be the effect of writing?" Eliot's narrator had asked. In the end, Eliot abstains from defining the empirical effects of a novel and instead imagines its more circuitous, transtemporal influence: an ideal of diffusive reading rooted in the narrator's "vision of probabilities" (697). In the history of the nineteenth-century novel, *Middlemarch* thus stands between conventional claims about the social purpose of fiction (which defined its role as intervening in political realities) and an Arnoldian ideology of culture (which defined it in opposition to "petty politics" [178]). Working with ideas about energy's incalculable influence, Eliot developed an aesthetic practice that renounced interventionist goals and that defined art as suffusing social life in more mediated form. Wayward, prodigal, and devoid of purpose, the futility of fiction could have incalculable influences on the totality.

To be sure, Eliot's appeals to redemptive diffusion continued both within her novels and beyond them after *Middlemarch*. The notebooks in preparation for her next novel, *Daniel Deronda,* contain several entries on Maxwell, with special attention to what he called "finely divided matter."[85] The novel's published version extends this theme, as its characters' "inborn energy of egoistic desire" find an apotheosis in the dispersion of such sentiments—in Daniel Deronda's commitment to the ego-depleting crusade of Jews and Gwendolen Harleth's quest for moral improvement after the wasted wreck of her marriage.[86] There, Eliot took special care to mention Maxwell, as Jesse Rosenthal notes, when an unnamed minor character suggests that ideas can circulate "by changing the distribution of gases" (525).[87] And in the sketch entitled "The Political Molecule" in Eliot's last work of fiction, *Impressions of Theophrastus Such* (1879), she returned to her interest in the physics of social relations. But *Middlemarch*'s study on the diffusive powers of fiction stands as a culminating moment in Eliot's engagement with the physical sciences and mathematics and as an important turning point in British cultural formation. In subsequent years, formalist doctrines of art proposed that literature should withdraw from the trivializing task of political change. Yet *Middlemarch: A Study of Provincial Life* advances a more ludic understanding of art. In it, Eliot imagines how the very powerlessness of the novel—its distance from the problems of the present and its lack of a stable referential relation to the world—could also appear as a source of agency, allowing it to confer alternative trajectories of growth. Eliot's "fine excess" attempts to produce, in the form of the realist novel, a singular solution to the problems of an increasingly disaggregated society, one that sees the potential for growth in its dispersive conditions and realizes in its excesses the possibilities for refinement.

Conclusion
"The Varying Experiments of Time"

History is not merely what happened: it is what happened in the context of what might have happened. Therefore it must incorporate, as a necessary element, the might-have-beens.
> —Hugh Trevor-Roper, "History and Imagination" (1971)

If science must at the present stage perforce be content with a *belief* in the immediate permanency of the universe (based on a probability, which in practical life we should term certainty), we must at the same time remember that because a proposition has not yet been proved, we have no right to infer that its converse must be true.
> —Karl Pearson, *The Grammar of Science* (1892)

The preceding chapters have traced the advent of a distinctively Victorian idea: the notion that alternatives to the register of history had a physics, an ontology that could be represented and even experienced in the pages of novels. This book has examined the development of that physics and articulated its surprising formal, affective, and psychological life in British culture circa 1850 to 1880, concentrating on a handful of organizing questions. How were its ideals elicited? What cultural mechanisms influenced its growth, the forms it assumed, and the ethical commitments it fostered? The historian Theodore Porter offers one starting point. In Porter's account, disenchantment with the iron rule of averages spanned a profusion of fields from the late 1850s onward, when scientists turned from an awed attention to mass regularities—the golden mean that Adolphe Quetelet and Henry Buckle believed to animate all historical change—to the larger share of outliers. They shifted focus to "the role of variation," or deviations from standard values.[1] This shift, Porter writes, began with "critics of the idea of statistical law put forward by Quetelet and the historian Henry Thomas Buckle," before infusing more specialized studies that transformed "the various sciences of observation and measurement" (8, 3). But while my account confirms the significance of Buckle's critics, I have shown that innovations in the physical sciences converged with trends in historiographical thinking throughout this era. Far from arising as an insulated discourse, modern mathematical physics shared origins with a collective legacy of writings in the conditional or subjunctive mood. Fiction, in particular, played an instrumental hand in this intellectual sojourn. At a zenith in the Victorian novel's fame, its representational repertoire for imagining alternative possibilities grew in tandem with the hard sciences; across the three decades that preceded "physics," the physics of possibility took hold as an influential physics of fiction.

In this sense, the story of my book has been a tale of how Victorian novelists joined scientists in the slow migration of the possible from Enlightenment-era theology and mathematics to the burgeoning fields of matter, energy, and force. Once investigators began to view probabilities as something other than an abstraction, a mental crutch to compensate for our ignorance of God's clockwork design, a gray area appeared around their phenomenological nature. Whether defined as "chances," "frequencies," or "probabilities," the realm of the possible moved into contested terrain between the imaginary and real. Eventually, the cross-pollination between British imaginative writers and scientists helped to eclipse the theological mantra that probabilities were mere mental figments and animated a brief but important interlude in the political life of the novel. For the referential indistinction of probabilities, among physical scientists and mathematicians, had uniquely expansive import in fiction—particularly in novels that questioned the persistence of Victorian assumptions about gender, economics, and law. Proceeding through the looking glass of other pasts and futures, these novels conjure up lifeworlds less violent and emotionally pulverizing, less competitive, patriarchal, and atomizing than the world in which Victorians lived. Indeed it was not just that fiction joined scientific studies of what T. H. Huxley called "nebulous potentiality"; again and again, novelists highlighted how their counterworlds could be activated and made real through the experience of reading.[2] Their narratives aim at something more than a moment's reprieve from the now. They represent something like a cosmopoiesis: an actual practice of world making meant to transform Victorian conventions of living. To read these texts is to find that the conventions of the past and present are limned with alternative vectors of becoming, potentials that one could learn to sense, feel, and enter en route to altered futures.

In resuscitating this tradition, I have devoted significant space to the aesthetics of fiction: the thematic, formal, psychological, and affective organization of four novels that I found relentlessly ironic in their reformulations of the classical bildungsroman. Yet it should be clear that my goal has not been to provide an exhaustive consideration of physics and fiction. Rather, I have articulated a powerful and neglected field of writings spanning physical science, mathematics, and one dominant fictional subgenre before the disciplining of "science" and "literature" as autonomous arenas. My premise has been that literature does distinctive work in the onset of scientific doctrines and hence rewards rigorous attention to form. Through their formal organization, novels do not merely mimic scientific truth claims. They anticipate, complicate, critique, and negotiate between ideas in nonpropositional terms, sometimes all within a single text. To be clear: I have demonstrated that experiments in novel writing contributed to theories incipient in science and *as* science. I have focused on experiments in the novel of formation for this reason. Conceived as fables of arrested development, the novels I have studied by George Meredith, Wilkie Collins, Charles Dickens, and George Eliot each suspend the linear logic of *Bildung* from juvenile irresolution to an adult world of labor, marriage, and productive social bonds. Thwarting the route to middle-class manhood (the "average man," in Quetelet's and Buckle's idiom), they advance an ensemble of less reified prospects for formation and attend to what *Middlemarch*'s narrator calls "the varying experiments of Time" (3).

Scientific concepts can serve disparate ideological ends. Like symbolic economies in general, they gain differential inflections through acts of writing and reinscription that can continue along new paths and congeal into altered habits of mind. When I say that the ontological location of the "possible" was in flux, I do not ignore its instrumentalization in the service of competing political goals; the indistinction I have studied was articulated diversely, again and again, in diverse cultural sites. For Quetelet and Buckle, the normal curve did not suggest that the "norm" was an illusion or sustain an egalitarian politics. In their accounts, isolated individual beings appeared as "errors" or mistakes in nature's design, each deviating more or less from a transcendent racial average that fueled historical progress; for them, individuals in the flesh had no more significance than the errors of observation that astronomers had tried to average out.[3] And although Buckle's dream of a prescriptive social average died down amid fiery criticism in the late 1850s, the probabilistic calculus continued to underwrite the prospect of a racially uniform utopia for Francis Galton and his intellectual successor, Karl Pearson, in the 1870s and afterward. Galton's and Pearson's major contributions to the statistics of variation, including Galton's correlation and regression methods and Pearson's concept of the "standard deviation," were first formulated as aspects of their eugenicist creeds. ("In comparing the worth of different races," as Galton wrote in his 1869 *Hereditary Genius*, "I shall make frequent use of the law of deviation from an average.")[4] The medical treatises of Henry Maudsley capture the first flavor of this outlook in the 1860s, when Maudsley defined effeminacy and hysteria as an abnormal "deviation from the normal state" of British character (377). Generally speaking, however, the novelists I have studied turned the physics of variation toward progressive social agendas, affirming fiction's power to trouble foundationalist hierarchies of character through the phantasmic, provisional, and anticlosural play of forking paths. Even Pearson himself, notwithstanding his confidence in the "immediate permanency" of the way that things are, admitted that this faith amounted to no more than a "belief . . . based on a probability," and not an absolute "certainty" (as he writes in the second epigraph to this conclusion).[5]

In short, a dominant vogue for physical probabilities—spanning professional scientists, mathematicians, and lay commentators—tended, in its very focus on the existence of what John Herschel called "nonhappenings," to travel through the cultural vicinities of novel writing, where the ambiguities between what was empirical and nonempirical gained unique moral and mimetic ballast ("Quetelet" 4). But the traffic between writers of fiction and science rarely followed linear lines of interaction, despite my occasional wish to isolate instances of connection as proof of a larger intellectual habitus. To understand the formation of ideas, I have reassembled what sociologists of science call a network of actors, following Bruno Latour's emphasis on how concepts develop, converge, and come apart in different directions and intensities of affiliation at once. Instead of observing the traffic between social and scientific "contexts," my readings have accentuated a more inclusive "process of assembling": "an on-going process made up of uncertain, fragile, controversial, and ever-shifting ties," in Latour's terms (1, 28). In practice, this has meant mapping a wider range of mechanisms for knowledge production, inflected by different objects (including telescopes, microscopes, and chronometers) and practices of representation (including mathematical formulas, graphs, and lectures alongside fiction and lyric poetry). So while I have occasionally identified local lines of appropriation, zeroing in on the transmission of ideas from one text to another text, I have sought to foreground the dialogical interaction between British scientists and novelists alongside less local patterns of formal and conceptual connection across a multiplicity of artifacts. Without flattening all texts into indices of a superintending spirit of the age, this approach has the benefit of teasing out the matrix of affinities, asymmetries, and tensions that can coalesce through time and shape the life of scientific concepts.

The dynamic configuration of these ties comes into fuller focus across individual chapters, in topics ranging from the orbit of stars to the meandering movement of atoms. Critiques of Buckle's statistical determinism, among philosophers and historians in the late 1850s, informed Meredith's *Richard Feverel,* while explicitly shaping James Clerk Maxwell's early research program (respectively discussed in chapters 1 and 4). Buckle's inspiration, Quetelet, drew on the astronomer's error law and Gaussian "normal curve" in his doctrines of the average man, but in introducing Quetelet to British readers, the astronomer John Herschel ironically focused on the role of deviations from typical values (chapters 1 and 2). In turn, Herschel's account was read by Charles Darwin at a formative moment in his development and actively informed Maxwell's mathematical formulas (chapters 3 and 4).[6] The connections between scientists and novelists proved no less varied. Wilkie Collins's fiction mediated between "statistical" and "sensorial" explanations of a nonunified present in the 1860s; Dickens's self-abnegating bachelors and intimate friends in *Dombey and Son* suggest, avant la lettre, the theories of moral variation that Darwin was still struggling to articulate. And as a "study" of incalculable diffusion, *Middlemarch* gave familiar form to Maxwell's statistical thermodynamics, which had yet to find full scientific acceptance at the time.

As this brief recapitulation suggests, I have charted a heterogeneous set of relations rather than a fixed doctrine or gestalt. Their further elaboration is an undertaking that I have left to others. But I hope that this book's close attention to the nuances of fictional texts will not distract from its insights about a certain prevailing form of historical thinking in Victorian Britain—what I have described as a generative, misunderstood set of techniques for representing alterities leading up to the two cultures of science and literature. To be sure, we can find their presence throughout Victorian culture. What I have said about the counterfactual form of *Richard Feverel* remains applicable to other subversions of the compassionate marriage plot, including Meredith's own *The Egoist* (1879), with its Darwinian focus on natural variation and competition. Over the course of Sir Willoughby Patterne's failed engagement with Constantia Durham and subsequent oscillations between Laetitia Dale and Clara Middleton, the drive toward marriage is itself shown to be vacant, so that Middleton and Patterne's final union underscores all that might have led to a more felicitous ending. Likewise, the evocation of a nonhomogenous present in Collins's fiction resonates throughout the sensation novels of Mary Elizabeth Braddon and Ellen Wood and in antibildungsromans that challenged middle-class conventionalism in associated respects. One thinks of Lucy Snowe, the acutely elusive, hesitating heroine of Charlotte Brontë's *Villette* (1853), whose avoidances of self-disclosure function to "transform Lucy's silence and refusal into a statement of alternative plausibility and action," as Brenda Silver puts it.[7] Lucy's famously recessive characterization culminates in her languorous, drug-induced stroll through the fête in Haute-Ville, which is untethered to the experiential immediacies of others and anticipates her final silence about a prospective marriage to M. Paul Emmanuel. And in a significant lineage of British naturalism, novelists joined Eliot's interest in the relation between physical law and different possible trajectories for character. *The Return of the Native*, for instance, begins with the description of an indistinct "single atom" in the "obscurity" of Egdon Heath, which is revealed to be Diggory Venn, whose name evokes the mathematician and philosopher John Venn.[8] That opening signals the conditional orientation of the narrative as a whole, which spins out a series of missed opportunities in the lives of Clym Yeobright, Tamsin Yeobright, and Eustacia Vye, consistent with what Gillian Beer calls the novel's "vertiginous loosing of hazard."[9] Hardy's practice in this vein continued in novels with an explicit scientific subtext, including *Two on a Tower* (1882), where "two infinitesimal lives [appear] against the stupendous background of the stellar universe," as Hardy put it.[10] And in Olive Schreiner's *Story of an African Farm* (1883), the ruined life of Lyndall is set within a more massive, undirected scale of temporal changes conceived through the rhetoric of "energy," "force," and variation.[11]

What became of these ideas after the disciplining of physics? In 1902, the American scientist Josiah Willard Gibbs introduced the term statistical "ensemble," a kindred concept to the ensemble effects we have encountered in fiction. As Gibbs defined it, a statistical ensemble expressed a variety of possible states that a molecular system might incarnate at a given instant; each possibility represented a different virtual version of the actual system, which could never be observed firsthand.[12] Norbert Weiner, the pioneering theorist of cybernetics, hailed the concept as a cornerstone of modern physics: "It is . . . Gibbs rather than Einstein or Heisenberg or Planck to whom we must attribute the first great revolution of twentieth century physics," Wiener wrote, an assessment that N. Katherine Hayles and others have taken seriously.[13] Like Maxwell, who introduced an early version of the ensemble concept in 1881, Gibbs understood the ensemble as a model of "possible outside worlds," as Wiener put it; the concept was meant as a useful abstraction—a tool to approximate single molecular realities that escaped observation (21).[14] It was precisely this understanding that subsequent scientists revised. With the onset of quantum mechanics, physicists explored the notion that each of the molecular possibilities had a sui generis character: they could *all* be real, and all at the same time. As Niels Bohr, Werner Heisenberg, Max Planck, Howard Percy Robertson, and Erwin Schrödinger variously proposed, each particle in a system existed in all possible states simultaneously. Their blow to traditional causality came in the midst of Albert Einstein's proofs that time is relative to specific systems of reference; the theory of general relativity, which Einstein was working toward between 1905 and 1915, "had the effect, figuratively, of placing a clock in every gravitational field in the universe," writes Stephen Kern.[15] Or as Ernst Cassirer put it, "The 'here' gains its meaning only with reference to a 'there,' the 'now' only with reference to an earlier or later contrasted with it. . . . They are and remain systems of relations."[16]

Certainly, signs of the coming revolutions in relativity and quantum mechanics can be discerned in nineteenth-century culture. What J. S. Mill called the "doctrine of the Relativity of our knowledge," in 1865, became a common refrain in mid-Victorian thought.[17] As Christopher Herbert has shown, writers as diverse as William Hamilton, J. S. Mill, Herbert Spencer, J. M. Stallo, and Pearson himself affirmed the relative and relational underpinnings of human understanding.[18] In 1880, the mathematician C. H. Hinton theorized the existence of non-Euclidean dimensions of space (dramatized in the second section of Edwin Abbott's 1884 *Flatland*, "Other Worlds," which investigates worlds with different dimensions). And in international settings, writers like Henri Bergson, Hippolyte Taine, E. R. Clay, and William James variously theorized the modular nature of temporal experience. Assumptions of absolute space and time continued to fray in important contributions like Ernst Mach's 1883 textbook, *The Science of Mechanics,* widely read in English translation, which critiqued Newtonian space-time as an "idle metaphysical conception." These kinds of critiques found increasing experimental validation—for example, when the physicists Albert Michelson and Edward Morley published the results of an important 1887 experiment on the ether and announced that time might decelerate as light was propagated through the ethereal medium.[19]

And so the road to relativity and quantum mechanics was fairly wide and well traveled. Yet scholars have downplayed the specificity of mid-Victorian thought when narrating the onset of modernist physics, which is too often conceived as a sharp shift from Enlightenment cosmologies. Timothy Morton, for example, writes that pre-twentieth-century investigators subscribed to "the view of space and time as flat, universal containers," whereas "quantum theory blew a huge hole in the idea of particles as little Ping-Pong balls."[20] Similarly, Diana Coole and Samantha Frost call attention to the transformation from "substantialist Cartesian or mechanistic Newtonian accounts of matter" to twentieth-century "particle physics" and "chaos and complexity theory" by omitting the mid-Victorian interregnum.[21] That juncture has remained an enabling absence in scholarship that thus heightens a narrative of modern epistemic rupture. But it was precisely as artifacts from a moment of cultural intensification, when Newtonian assumptions were crumbling but still salient, that the physics of variation took hold.

Still, the Victorians' "varying experiments" in time *do* persist within contemporary cultural analysis, as recent philosophical, sociological, and historiographical trends make clear. Influential contributions from Stuart Hampshire, Geoffrey Hawthorn, Niall Ferguson, and others have turned the study of counterfactuals (what the historian Hugh Trevor-Roper called "the might-have-beens") into a rigorous research topic, correcting an antediluvian disregard for them as an amateur's "parlor game," in E. H. Carr's words.[22] Ferguson, for example, writes that "the counterfactual scenarios" that animate modern historiography "are not mere fantasy: they are simulations based on calculations about the relative probability of plausible outcomes" (85). The rhetoric of probabilistic calculation is heuristic here, used to lend scientific seriousness to the goal of weighing canceled futures. Yet the terms indicate a more ample province of ideas in high Victorian Britain: the buried life of thought that I have assembled across the literature and culture of the age. Calculations of alterity, now in vogue among humanists and social scientists, first emerged within the conditional timescapes of Victorian fiction, physical science, and mathematics. This attests to the period's rich and often-overlooked resources for historical thinking and indicates further work to be done in their retrieval.

It remains a founding paradox of the novel that it imagines possible worlds with a provisional claim to exist. Reading fiction seems to demand some suspension of disbelief, a willful blurring between what is or is not actual. That paradox gained new teeth in conjunction with the Victorian physics of variation, as novelists explored the moral and emotional force of nonhappenings in their pages. For even as studies on the "internal feeling" of possibilities traveled into more material realms of investigation, it never ceased to be a practice of the passions.[23] It maintained ties to states of expectation, uncertainty, ambivalence, and retrospection, which also fundamentally inform the experience of novel reading. Looking back to this cultural moment reveals a unique understanding of alterity—the understanding of a history that is never quite itself, never quite singular and self-standing, and that remains replete with trajectories that we might learn to imagine, feel, and finally live.

Notes

INTRODUCTION

1. Henry James, preface to *The Tragic Muse,* in *The Novels and Tales of Henry James,* New York ed., 24 vols. (New York: Scribner's, 1908), 7:vii.

2. I. B. Cohen, "Scientific Revolutions, Revolutions in Science, and a Probabilistic Revolution, 1800–1930," in *The Probabilistic Revolution, Ideas in History,* ed. Lorenz Krüger et al., 2 vols. (Cambridge, MA: MIT Press, 1987), 1: 35–52; Ian Hacking, "Was There a Probabilistic Revolution, 1800–1930?" in *Probability since 1800: Interdisciplinary Studies of Scientific Development,* ed. Michael Heidelberger, Lorenz Krüger, and Rosemarie Rheinward (Bielefeld: B. Kleine Verlag, 1987), 45–58; Theodore Porter, "Statistics and Physical Theories," in *The Cambridge History of Science,* vol. 5, *The Modern Physical and Mathematical Sciences,* ed. Mary Jo Nye (Cambridge: Cambridge University Press, 2002), 488–504.

3. On probability and the novel, see Rüdiger Campe, *The Game of Probability: Literature and Calculation from Pascal to Kleist,* trans. Ellwood Wiggins (Stanford, CA: Stanford University Press, 2012); Ross Hamilton, *Accident: A Philosophical and Literary History* (Chicago: University of Chicago Press, 2007); Paul Fyfe, *By Accident or Design: Writing the Victorian Metropolis* (New York: Oxford University Press, 2015); Leland Monk, *Standard Deviations: Chance and the Modern British Novel* (Stanford, CA: Stanford University Press, 1993); Sandra Macpherson, *Harm's Way: Tragic Responsibility and the Novel Form* (Baltimore: Johns Hopkins University Press, 2009); Jesse Molesworth, *Chance and the Eighteenth-Century Novel: Realism, Probability, Magic* (Cambridge: Cambridge University Press, 2010); Douglas Patey, *Probability and Literary Form: Philosophic Theory and Literary Practice in the Augustan Age* (Cambridge: Cambridge University Press, 1984).

4. James Clerk Maxwell, "Does the Progress of Physical Science Tend to Give Any Advantage to the Opinion of Necessity (or Determinism) over That of the Contingency of Events and the Freedom of the Will?" in Lewis Campbell and William Garnett, *The Life of James Clerk Maxwell, with a Selection from His Correspondence and Occasional Writings* (London: Macmillan, 1882), 435. The group was a club composed of former members of the Cambridge Apostles and named Eranus.

5. Maxwell, "Does the Progress of Physical Science Tend to Give Any Advantage," in Campbell and Garnett, *The Life of James Clerk Maxwell*, 434, 438, 444.

6. Eric Hayot, *On Literary Worlds* (New York: Oxford University Press, 2012), 71.

7. George Meredith, *The Ordeal of Richard Feverel: A History of Father and Son*, ed. Edward Mendelson (New York: Penguin), 23.

8. Susan Fraiman, *Unbecoming Women: British Women Writers and the Novel of Development* (New York: Columbia University Press, 1983), 10.

9. Peter Brooks, *Reading for the Plot: Design and Intention in Narrative* (Cambridge, MA: Harvard University Press, 1992), 108.

10. Jane Bennett, *Vibrant Matter: A Political Ecology of Things* (Durham, NC: Duke University Press, 2010), 96.

11. Elizabeth Barrett Browning, *Aurora Leigh*, ed. Kerry McSweeney (New York: Oxford University Press, 1993), 97.

12. Fredric Jameson, *The Political Unconscious: Narrative as Socially Symbolic Act* (Ithaca, NY: Cornell University Press, 1982), 145.

13. Franco Moretti, *The Way of the World: The Bildungsroman in European Culture* (London: Verso, 1987), 181–85.

14. Fraiman, *Unbecoming Women;* Rita Felski, *Beyond Feminist Aesthetics: Feminist Literature and Social Change* (Cambridge, MA: Harvard University Press, 1989); also see Elizabeth Abel, Marianne Hirsch, and Elizabeth Langland, introduction to *The Voyage In: Fictions of Female Development*, ed. Abel, Hirsch, and Langland (Hanover, NH: University Press of New England, 1983), 1–19; Lorna Ellis, *Appearing to Diminish: Female Development and the British Bildungsroman, 1750–1850* (Lewisburg, PA: Bucknell University Press, 1999). For recent accounts of the bildungsroman's fragmentation, see Gregory Castle, *Reading the Modernist Bildungsroman* (Gainesville: University Press of Florida, 2006); Elisha Cohn, *Still Life: Suspended Development in the Victorian Novel* (New York: Oxford University Press, 2015); Jed Esty, *Unseasonable Youth: Modernism, Colonialism, and the Fiction of Development* (New York: Oxford University Press, 2012); Douglas Mao, *Fateful Beauty: Aesthetic Environments, Juvenile Development, and Literature, 1860–1960* (Princeton, NJ: Princeton University Press, 2008); Joseph R. Slaughter, *Human Rights, Inc.: The World Novel, Narrative Form, and International Law* (New York: Fordham University Press, 2007).

15. George Eliot, *Middlemarch*, ed. David Carroll (Oxford: Clarendon, 1986), 825.

16. Cohn, *Still Life*, 3.

17. Niall Ferguson, "Virtual History: Towards a 'Chaotic' Theory of the Past," in *Virtual History: Alternatives and Counterfactuals*, ed. Ferguson (New York: Basic Books, 2000), 1–90, 71.

18. Evelyn Fox Keller, *Reflections on Gender and Science* (New Haven, CT: Yale University Press, 1995), 133–34; Donna Haraway, "A Cyborg Manifesto: Science, Technology, and Socialist-Feminism in the Late Twentieth Century," in *Simians, Cyborgs and Women: The Reinvention of Nature* (New York: Routledge, 1991), 149–81, esp. 153; N. Katherine Hayles, *How We Became Posthuman: Virtual Bodies in Cybernetics, Literature, and Informatics* (Chicago: University of Chicago Press, 1999), 84–90.

19. Karen Barad, *Meeting the Universe Halfway: Quantum Physics and the Entanglement of Matter and Meaning* (Durham, NC: Duke University Press, 2007), 67.

20. Transformations in Victorian demography, insurance, and risk management have been brilliantly studied by scholars such as Elaine Freedgood, *Victorian Writing about Risk* (Cambridge: Cambridge University Press, 2001), 13–41; Timothy Alborn, *Regulated Lives: Life Insurance and British Society, 1800–1914* (Toronto: University of Toronto Press, 2009); Mary Poovey, *A History of the Modern Fact* (Chicago: University of Chicago Press, 1998); Audrey Jaffe, *The Affective Life of the Average Man* (Columbus: Ohio State University Press, 2010).

21. Michel Foucault, *Abnormal: Lectures at the Collège de France, 1974–1975,* trans. Graham Burchell, ed. Valerio Marchetti and Antonella Salomoni (New York: Picador, 2003), 42; Foucault, *Security, Territory, Population: Lectures at the Collège de France 1977–1978,* trans. Graham Burchell, ed. Michel Senellart (New York: Picador, 2007), 62.

22. Reinhart Koselleck, *Futures Past: On the Semantics of Historical Time,* trans. Keith Tribe (Cambridge, MA: MIT Press, 1985), 23.

23. Tyndall, "Scientific Materialism," in *Fragments of Science,* 2 vols. (London: Longmans, Green, 1871), 2:82–98. On scientific materialism, see Frank Turner, *Contesting Cultural Authority: Essays in Victorian Intellectual Life* (Cambridge: Cambridge University Press, 1993), 264–67; Bernard Lightman, *The Origins of Agnosticism* (Baltimore: Johns Hopkins University Press, 1987), 4–32; Gowan Dawson, *Darwin, Literature, and Victorian Respectability* (Cambridge: Cambridge University Press, 2007), 82–97; Gowan Dawson and Bernard Lightman, introduction to *Victorian Scientific Naturalism: Community, Identity, Continuity,* ed. Dawson and Lightman (Chicago: University of Chicago Press, 2014), 1–26.

24. Adrian Desmond and James Moore, *Darwin: The Life of a Tormented Evolutionist* (New York: Warner Books, 1991), 568.

25. T. H. Huxley, "On the Physical Basis of Life," in *Lay Sermons, Addresses, and Reviews* (London: Macmillan, 1870), 132–61, 132. See, for example, Clifford's redefinition of "exact" science as an ideal incommensurate with the fallible nature of observation in "On the Aims and Instruments of Scientific Thought," in Clifford, *Lectures and Essays,* ed. Leslie Stephen and Frederick Pollock, 2 vols. (London: Macmillan, 1879). Alluding to new statistical studies of gases, Clifford explains that "accuracy depends on the enormous numbers involved; and so . . . exactness cannot be theoretical or absolute" (2:139). He extends this point to biological, chemical, and geological developments before concluding that mechanical objectivity is impossible "however early the children of the future begin to read their Newton" (2:149).

26. Charles Babbage, *The Ninth Bridgewater Treatise* (London: Murray, 1838), 194.

27. John Herschel, "Quetelet on Probabilities," *Edinburgh Review* 92 (July 1850): 1–57; Herschel, "Probabilities," in *Essays from the Edinburgh and Quarterly Reviews, with Addresses and Other Pieces* (London: Longman, Brown, Green, Longmans, and Roberts, 1857). The subjects in the July 1850 *Edinburgh Review* number typify the age's promiscuous packaging of essential scientific writings with those devoted to literature, history, politics, general education, and religion. In addition to Herschel's

essay, which opened the number, the contents include titles such as "Merivale's *Rome under the Empire*," "Church and State Education," "Mérimée's *History of Pedro the Cruel*," "Blackie's *Æschylus*," "Göthe's Festival," "Guizot on the English Revolution," "The African Squadron" (on the slave trade), and "The Gorham Controversy" (on the relation between secular law and the Church of England).

28. Theodore Porter, "A Statistical Survey of Gases: Maxwell's Social Physics," *Historical Studies in the Physical Sciences* 12 (1981): 77–116; C. C. Gillespie, "Intellectual Factors in the Background of Analysis by Probabilities," in *Scientific Change: Historical Studies in the Intellectual, Social, and Technical Conditions for Scientific Discovery and Technical Invention*, ed. A. C. Crombie (New York: Basic Books, 1963), 431–53.

29. Roland Barthes, "An Introduction to the Structural Analysis of Narrative," trans. Lionel Duisit, *New Literary History* 6 (1975): 241.

30. Ruth Ronen, *Possible Worlds in Literary Theory* (Cambridge: Cambridge University Press, 1994), 41.

31. P. M. Harman, *Energy, Force, and Matter: The Conceptual Development of Nineteenth-Century Physics* (Cambridge: Cambridge University Press, 1982), 148.

32. Andrew H. Miller, *The Burdens of Perfection: On Ethics and Reading in Nineteenth-Century British Literature* (Ithaca, NY: Cornell University Press, 2008), 191; Catherine Gallagher, "What Would Napoleon Do? Historical, Fictional, and Counterfactual Characters," *New Literary History* 42 (2011): 321.

33. For example, see Harman, *Energy, Force, and Matter*, 1–12.

34. See Iwan Morus, *When Physics Became King* (Chicago: University of Chicago Press, 2005), 227–45.

35. Caroline Levine, *Forms: Whole, Rhythm, Hierarchy, Network* (Princeton, NJ: Princeton University Press, 2015), 17.

36. Koselleck, *Futures Past*, 239.

37. Anne-Lise François, *Open Secrets: The Literature of Uncounted Experience* (Stanford, CA: Stanford University Press, 2007), 64.

38. Wilkie Collins, *Armadale*, ed. Catherine Peters, 2nd ed. (New York: Oxford University Press, 1999), 157.

39. Elizabeth Grosz, "Darwin and Feminism: Preliminary Investigations into a Possible Alliance," in *Time Travels: Feminism, Nature, Power* (Durham, NC: Duke University Press, 2005), 38.

40. Charles Dickens, *Dombey and Son*, ed. Andrew Sanders (New York: Penguin, 2002), 52.

41. Levine, *Forms*, xii–xiii.

42. Marianne Hirsch, "Spiritual *Bildung*: The Beautiful Soul as Paradigm," in Abel, Hirsch, and Langland, *The Voyage In*, 23–48, 27.

43. Claire Colebrook, "Queer Vitalism," *New Formations* 68 (2009): 77.

44. T. H. Huxley, "Evolution and Ethics," in *Collected Essays*, 9 vols. (London: Macmillan, 1893–95), 9:47–116, 50.

45. Elizabeth Freeman, *Time Bends: Queer Temporalities, Queer Histories* (Durham, NC: Duke University Press, 2010), xv.

46. See Richard Yeo, *Defining Science: William Whewell, Natural Knowledge and Public Debate in Early Victorian Britain* (Cambridge: Cambridge University Press, 1993), 12.

47. Gerd Gigerenzer et al., *The Empire of Chance: How Probability Changed Science and Everyday Life* (Cambridge: Cambridge University Press, 1989), xiii.

48. The North British appellation was first introduced by Crosbie Smith to name a circle of engineers and physical scientists from Glasgow and Cambridge (including Maxwell, Tait, Joule, William and James Thomson, and Fleeming Jenkin) who disputed the bellicose materialism attributed to London-based naturalists like T. H. Huxley and Tyndall in favor of an approach more harmonious with Christian doctrine. See Crosbie Smith, *The Science of Energy: A Cultural History of Energy Physics in Victorian Britain* (Chicago: University of Chicago Press, 1998), 170–91; also see Lightman and Dawson, introduction to *Victorian Scientific Naturalism.*

49. "In place of a worldview defined by doctrines of matter," the historian of science P. M. Harman observes, "Maxwell suggests a more elevated vision of scientific knowledge which would transcend Tyndall's reductionism," where "fact" and "thought" could converge. Harman, *The Natural Philosophy of James Clerk Maxwell* (Cambridge: Cambridge University Press, 2001), 199.

50. See Thomas Kuhn, "Energy Conservation as an Example of Simultaneous Discovery," in *Critical Problems in the History of Science: Proceedings of the Institute for the History of Science,* ed. Marshall Clagett (Madison: University of Wisconsin Press, 1959), 321–56.

51. See Smith, *The Science of Energy,* 192–210.

52. On these developments, see Andrew Warwick, *Masters of Theory: Cambridge and the Rise of Mathematical Physics* (Chicago: University of Chicago Press, 2003); also see Alice Jenkins, *Space and the "March of Mind," 1815–1850* (New York: Oxford University Press, 2007), 92–93; Theodore Porter, *The Rise of Statistical Thinking, 1820–1900* (Princeton, NJ: Princeton University Press, 1986), 31–39; Robert D. Purrington, *Physics in the Nineteenth Century* (New Brunswick, NJ: Rutgers University Press, 1997), 9–32; Yeo, *Defining Science,* 29–32. Jenkins's study, which ends in 1850, provides a historical complement to my account (leading up to a perceived "shift away from the mechanical, material explanations of the forces that operate in the universe," as Jenkins writes [126–27]).

53. F. R. Leavis, *Two Cultures? The Significance of C. P. Snow* (Cambridge: Cambridge University Press, 2013), 4.

54. See Lynn L. Merrill, *The Romance of Victorian Natural History* (Oxford: Oxford University Press, 1989).

55. Isaac Newton, "General Scholium," in *The Principia: Mathematical Principles of Natural Philosophy,* trans. I. Bernard Cohen, Anne Whitman, and Julia Budenz (Berkeley: University of California Press, 1999), 943.

56. For an overview of Newton's materialism, see P. M. Harman, *Metaphysics and Natural Philosophy: The Problem of Substance in Classical Physics* (New York: Barnes and Noble Books, 1982), 3–38.

57. Pierre Simon Laplace, *Philosophical Essay on Probabilities,* trans. F. W. Truscott and F. L. Emory (New York: Wiley, 1902), 3.

58. Morus, *When Physics Became King*, 80–81. For Faraday's status in nineteenth-century literary culture, see Jenkins, *Space and the "March of Mind,"* 199–207; also see Barri Gold, *ThermoPoetics* (Cambridge, MA: MIT Press, 2011), 95–97.

59. See Harman, *Energy, Force, and Matter*, 130–32.

60. Mary Somerville, *On the Connexion of the Physical Sciences* (London: Murray, 1834), 1.

61. W. R. Grove, "On the Correlation of Physical Forces," in *The Correlation and Conservation of Forces: A Series of Expositions by Prof. Grove, Prof. Helmholtz, Dr. Mayer, Dr. Faraday, Prof. Liebig and Dr. Carpenter*, ed. Edward L. Youmans (New York: Appleton, 1865), 14.

62. See Porter, *The Rise of Statistical Thinking*, 194–208.

63. James Clerk Maxwell, "Drafts of Lecture on 'Molecules,'" in *The Scientific Papers of James Clerk Maxwell*, ed. W. D. Niven, 2 vols. (New York: Dover, 1890), 2:932. Maxwell was responding directly to Buckle's positivist method of history in this paragraph.

64. For representative accounts, see Harman, *Energy, Force, and Matter*, 133–55, and Porter, *The Rise of Statistical Thinking*, 194–219.

65. Maxwell, "Does the Progress of Physical Science Tend to Give Any Advantage," in Campbell and Garnett, *The Life of James Clerk Maxwell*, 444. Galton writes in a similar vein, "It is difficult to understand why statisticians commonly limit their inquiries to averages, and do not reveal more comprehensive views" of deviations. Galton, *Natural Inheritance* (New York: Macmillan, 1889), 62–63.

66. Bernard Lightman, *Victorian Popularizers of Science: Designing Nature for New Audiences* (Chicago: University of Chicago Press, 2010), 12–28.

67. Katherine Pandora, "Knowledge Held in Common: Tales of Luther Burbank and Science in the American Vernacular," *Isis* 92 (2001): 484–516, 491, 492.

68. My account of these interrelations stands largely in agreement with Barri Gold's cultural history of thermodynamics. As Gold writes, "Literature has often, perhaps always, influenced science, especially in the delicate, early stages of a scientific development, before a phenomenon has been named or a hypothesis adequately articulated. Literature participates in creating as well as expressing the cultural milieu in which science happens." Gold, *ThermoPoetics*, 15.

69. Eve Sedgwick, "Paranoid Reading and Reparative Reading, or, You're So Paranoid, You Probably Think This Essay Is about You," in *Touching Feeling: Affect, Pedagogy, Performativity* (Durham, NC: Duke University Press, 2003), 123–51; Sharon Marcus, *Between Women: Friendship, Desire, and Marriage in Victorian England* (Princeton, NJ: Princeton University Press, 2007), Rita Felski, *The Limits of Critique* (Chicago: University of Chicago Press, 2015), 157; Levine, *Forms*, 19.

70. Sedgwick, "Paranoid Reading," 130, 149. Elisha Cohn observes Sedgwick's usefulness in her account of blocked bildungsromans; though I encountered Cohn's study at a late stage in this book's completion, her focus is cognate with my own. "Reparative criticism suggests that nineteenth-century literature has already unsettled the notion of the autonomous subject," Cohn writes, "and thus the critique of the

novel's normativity produces an unnecessarily narrow view not only of the novel's exploration of affective life but also of the possible range of critical projects" (24).

71. The aesthetics of possible worlds were considered formatively by Thomas Pavel, Ruth Ronen, Marie-Laure Ryan, and others who used fiction to explore enigmas of logical possibility. These critics found inspiration in Saul Kripke's statement that "[Sherlock] Holmes does not exist, but in other states of affairs, he would have existed." Saul A. Kripke, *Naming and Necessity* (Cambridge, MA: Harvard University Press, 1980), 158. At what diegetic levels do the operations of "worlding" happen: a sentence, a chapter, or an entire text? What defines the internal logic of fictional worlds, and how do those worlds correspond to the extratextual realities that novels are said to index? In treating these questions, studies of possible worlds suggested a new interdisciplinary formalism that avoided an "atomistic approach" to literature while holding fast to the essential workings of textuality. Lubomír Doležel, *Heterocosmica: Fiction and Possible Worlds* (Baltimore: Johns Hopkins University Press, 2000), 2. By linking linguistic and philosophical conundrums to the methods of literary studies, it seemed conceivable to treat significant issues in each field. Yet it now seems clear that, in practice, formalist criticism was best suited to theorizing the many different possible worlds evoked in novels, not to advancing a systematic, transhistorical account of them. In elaborating a fresh history of possible literary worlds, then, I extend formalist observations on narrative's ramifying possibilities while locating what Eric Hayot calls "the 'physics' of aesthetic worldedness" within high Victorian culture (7). See Catherine Gallagher, "The Rise of Fictionality," in *The Novel*, ed. Franco Moretti, 2 vols. (Princeton, NJ: Princeton University Press, 2006), 1:354–55; Thomas G. Pavel, *Fictional Worlds* (Cambridge, MA: Harvard University Press, 1989); Ronen, *Possible Worlds in Literary Theory*; Marie-Laure Ryan, *Possible Worlds, Artificial Intelligence, and Narrative Theory* (Bloomington: University of Indiana Press, 1994).

72. Karl Marx and Friedrich Engels, *The German Ideology*, ed. C. J. Arthur (New York: International, 1970), 57 (emphasis in original).

73. Ernst Bloch, *The Principle of Hope*, trans. Neville Plaice, Stephen Plaice, and Paul Knight, 2 vols. (Cambridge, MA: MIT Press, 1983), 1:7. On potentiality, see Giorgio Agamben, *Potentialities: Collected Essays in Philosophy*, trans. Daniel Heller-Roazen (Stanford, CA: Stanford University Press, 2000).

74. Huxley, "Evolution and Ethics," in *Collected Essays*, 9:50.

1. THE LOST FUTURES OF THE NOVEL

1. Samuel Lucas, "Richard Feverel," review of *The Ordeal of Richard Feverel*, by George Meredith, *Times*, 14 October 1859, in Ioan Williams, ed., *Meredith: The Critical Heritage* (New York: Barnes and Noble, 1973), 83.

2. For readings of organic holism in *Richard Feverel*, see John W. Morris, "Inherent Principles of Order in *The Ordeal of Richard Feverel*," PMLA 78 (1963): 333–40; William R. Mueller, "Theological Dualism and the 'System' in *Richard Feverel*," ELH 18 (1951): 138–54; Donald D. Stone, *Novelists in a Changing World* (Cambridge, MA:

Harvard University Press, 1972); Walter Wright, *Art and Substance in George Meredith* (New York: Greenwood, 1980). For a counterpoint to these tendencies, see Cohn, *Still Life*, which argues that *"Richard Feverel* fiercely criticizes both Sir Austin's program of education and his draconian strategies for pursuing it" through the novel's lyrical scenes of "passionate passivity" (120).

3. On Meredith and the Obscene Publications Act, see Sally Shuttleworth, *The Mind of the Child: Child Development in Literature, Science, and Medicine, 1840–1900* (New York: Oxford University Press, 2011), 162–69; also see Dawson, *Darwin, Literature and Victorian Respectability,* 135–38.

4. For example, see Georges Canquilhem, *The Normal and the Pathological,* trans. Carolyn R. Fawcett (New York: Zone Books, 1991); Waltraud Ernst, "The Normal and the Abnormal: Reflections on Norms and Normativity," in *Histories of the Normal and the Abnormal: Social and Cultural Histories of Norms and Normativity,* ed. Ernst (New York: Routledge, 2007), 1–25.

5. Porter, *The Rise of Statistical Thinking,* 11.

6. Porter, *The Rise of Statistical Thinking,* 10; Ian Hacking, *The Taming of Chance* (Cambridge: Cambridge University Press, 1990), 4–5.

7. On these developments, see Lorraine J. Daston, *Classical Probability in the Enlightenment* (Princeton, NJ: Princeton University Press, 1995), esp. 32–33, 253–57; Hacking, *The Taming of Chance,* esp. 101–3; Porter, *The Rise of Statistical Thinking,* 91–96; for Pearson and Galton, see George Levine, *Dying to Know: Scientific Epistemology and Narrative in Victorian England* (Chicago: University of Chicago Press, 2002), 220–444; Nicholas Gillham, *A Life of Sir Francis Galton* (New York: Oxford University Press, 2001), esp. 241–68.

8. Abraham de Moivre, *The Doctrine of Chances* (London: Pearson, 1738), 241.

9. Porter, *The Rise of Statistical Thinking,* 72–73.

10. Audrey Jaffe and Christopher Kent have examined Quetelet's influence in Britain. Kent traces to Quetelet's "average man" a growing fascination with normal social subjects, while Jaffe concentrates on emergent anxieties about being average. Christopher Kent, "The Average Victorian: Constructing and Contesting Reality," *Browning Institute Studies* 17 (1989): 41–52; Jaffe, *The Affective Life of the Average Man,* 10–14, 26–31.

11. Porter notes the existence of this British tradition, but regards it as a minor adjunct to innovations on the continent. See Porter, *The Rise of Statistical Thinking,* 149–51.

12. Porter, *The Rise of Statistical Thinking,* 74.

13. Elaine Hadley, *Living Liberalism: Practical Citizenship in Mid-Victorian Britain* (Chicago: University of Chicago Press, 2010), 9.

14. Adolphe Quetelet, *A Treatise on Man and His Faculties* (Edinburgh: Chambers, 1842), x.

15. As Porter notes, "De Morgan was one of the first thinkers to examine at length the pertinent philosophical issues, and helped to establish the logic of probability as a worthy philosophical problem." Porter, *The Rise of Statistical Thinking,* 74.

16. On the study of judiciary probabilities, see Hacking, *The Taming of Chance,* 87–94, and Porter, *The Rise of Statistical Thinking,* 75–76.

17. Henry Thomas Buckle, *History of Civilization in England,* 2 vols. (London: Parker, Son and Bourn, 1857–61), 1:24.

18. Mark Pattison, *"The History of Civilization in England,"* review of *History of Civilization in England,* by Henry Thomas Buckle, *Westminster Review* 68 (1857): 375.

19. For an overview of these reactions, see Helen Small, "Chances Are: Henry Buckle, Thomas Hardy, and the Individual at Risk," in *Literature, Science, Psychoanalysis, 1830–1970,* ed. Helen Small and Trudi Tate (New York: Oxford University Press, 2003), 67–68.

20. Acton developed the articles in close collaboration with his friend the *Rambler*'s coeditor Richard Simpson, who urged him to use the space to outline his own alternative historical vision. See Ian Hesketh, *The Science of History in Victorian Britain* (London: Pickering and Chatto, 2011), 37–41.

21. John Acton, "Mr. Buckle's Thesis and Method," *Rambler* 22 (July 1858): 31; see also Acton, "Mr. Buckle's Philosophy of History," *Rambler* 22 (August 1858): 88–104.

22. James Fitzjames Stephen, "Buckle's History of Civilization in England," review of *History of Civilization in England,* by Henry Thomas Buckle, *Blackwood's Edinburgh Review* 107 (1858): 465–512; Stephen, "The Study of History," *Cornhill Magazine* 3 (1861): 666–80.

23. John Stuart Mill, *Collected Works of John Stuart Mill,* ed. J. M. Robson, 19 vols. (Toronto: University of Toronto Press, 1963), 7:iv.

24. Bruno Latour, *Reassembling the Social: An Introduction to Actor-Network-Theory* (Oxford: Oxford University Press, 2005), 5.

25. Porter, *The Rise of Statistical Thinking,* 164.

26. Hayden White, *Metahistory: The Historical Imagination in Nineteenth-Century Europe* (Baltimore: Johns Hopkins University Press, 1973). In his introduction, "The Poetics of History," White argues for the narrative organization of historiographical works, which he describes as "a verbal structure in the form of a narrative prose discourse that purports to be a model, or icon, of past structures and processes in the interest of explaining what they were by representing them" (2).

27. Ferguson, *Virtual History,* 67.

28. Paul Ricoeur, *Time and Narrative,* trans. Kathleen McLaughlin and David Pellauer, 2 vols. (Chicago: University of Chicago Press, 1984), 1:91, x.

29. See J. W. Cross, *George Eliot's Life: As Related in Her Letters and Journals* (Edinburgh: Blackwood, 1885), 235; George Henry Lewes, "Mr. Buckle's Scientific Errors," *Blackwood's Edinburgh Magazine* 90 (1861): 582–96.

30. George Eliot, *"The Shaving of Shagpat,"* review of *The Shaving of Shagpat,* by George Meredith, *Leader* 7 (1856): 13–17; George Eliot, "Belles Lettres and Art," *Westminster Review* 67 (1856): 638–39; Pattison, *"The History of Civilization in England."* On Meredith's periodical contributions, see Maurice Forman, *A Bibliography of the Writings in Prose and Verse of George Meredith* (Edinburgh: Dundin, 1922), 191–232.

31. Augustus De Morgan, *An Essay on Probabilities* (London: Longman, 1838), 7.

32. For discussions of the "system" and Victorian child-rearing, see Terry Grabar, "'Scientific' Education and *Richard Feverel*," *Victorian Studies* 14 (1970): 129–41; Shuttleworth, *The Mind of the Child*, 151–80; Sven-Johan Spanberg, "The Theme of Sexuality in *The Ordeal of Richard Feverel*," *Studia Neophilologica* 46 (1974): 202–24.

33. De Morgan, *An Essay on Probabilities*, 3.

34. J. C. D. Clark, "What If There Had Been No American Revolution?" in Ferguson, *Virtual History*, 125–75, 173.

35. Herschel, "Quetelet on Probabilities," 5.

36. See David E. Foster, "Rhetorical Strategy in *Richard Feverel*," *Nineteenth-Century Fiction* 26 (1971): 188–89.

37. U. C. Knoepflmacher, *Laughter and Despair: Readings in Ten Novels of the Victorian Era* (Berkeley: University of California Press, 1973), 124.

38. William Acton, *The Functions and Disorders of the Reproductive Organs in Childhood, Youth, Adult Age, and Advanced Life*, 3rd ed. (London: John Churchill, 1865), 3; Shuttleworth, *The Mind of the Child*, 151–80; Spanberg, "The Theme of Sexuality in *The Ordeal of Richard Feverel*," 202–12.

39. Miller, *The Burdens of Perfection;* Hillary P. Dannenberg, *Coincidence and Counterfactuality: Plotting Time and Space in Narrative Fiction* (Lincoln: University of Nebraska Press, 2008); William Galperin, "Describing What Never Happened: Jane Austen and the History of Missed Opportunities," *ELH* 73 (2006): 355–82.

40. Lucas, "*Richard Feverel*," in Williams, *Meredith: The Critical Heritage*, 83.

41. I borrow the term "retrodiction" from Meir Hemmo and Orly R. Shenker, who use it in reference to probabilistic calculations about the past. See Hemmo and Shenker, *The Road to Maxwell's Demon: Conceptual Foundations of Statistical Mechanics* (Cambridge: Cambridge University Press, 2012), 84.

42. John Lubbock and John Drinkwater, *On Probability* (London: Baldwin and Cradock, 1830), 1. Although Drinkwater later changed his legal name with the addition of the "Bethune" surname, I retain the name he used to publish the volume when referring to its authorship.

43. On Smollett's interest in probabilistic doctrines, see Patey, *Probability and Literary Form*, 182–86, and Molesworth, *Chance and the Eighteenth-Century Novel*, 132–33.

44. *Hansard Parliamentary Debates*, 3rd series, vol. 146 (25 June 1857), c. 329, quoted in M. J. D. Roberts, "Morals, Art, and the Law: The Passing of the Obscene Publications Act, 1857," *Victorian Studies* 28 (1985): 613. By making the sale of obscene material a state offense rather than a violation of common law, the Obscene Publications Act gave the courts power to seize and destroy offending works.

45. See Emily Allen, "A Shock to the System," *Victorian Literature and Culture* 35 (2007): 92.

46. Judith Butler, *Gender Trouble: Feminism and the Subversion of Identity* (New York: Routledge, 1990), 179 (emphasis in original).

47. As Richard C. Stevenson writes, "Meredith is bent on bringing traditional notions of the 'heroic' into question," in which "what we see is a wholly artificial

standard of conduct." Stevenson, *The Experimental Impulse in the Novels of George Meredith* (Lewisburg, PA: Bucknell University Press, 2004), 57.

48. Aristotle, *Poetics,* trans. Anthony Kenny (New York: Oxford University Press, 2013), 27.

49. Lucas, *"Richard Feverel,"* in Williams, *Meredith: The Critical Heritage,* 83.

2. "THE INTERVAL OF EXPECTATION"

1. Nicholas Daly, "Railway Novels: Sensation Fiction and the Modernization of the Senses," *ELH* 66 (1999): 464.

2. Jenny Bourne Taylor explains that sensation novels "worked directly on the body of the reader" in a way that "encapsulated the experience of modernity itself— the sense of continuous and rapid change, of shocks, thrills, intensity, excitement." Taylor, *In the Secret Theatre of Home* (New York: Oxford University Press, 1987), 3–4. In Alison Winter's words, "The route from page to nerves was direct." Winter, *Mesmerized: Powers of Mind in Victorian Britain* (Chicago: University of Chicago Press, 1998), 324. Like these critics, D. A. Miller aims to uncover the historical construction of sensation in the 1860s so as to trace "the social significance of nervousness." But while questioning the "natural immediacy of sensation" in contemporary criticism, Miller remains unable to avoid the assumption that the novels naturally see sensation as immediate. Miller, *The Novel and the Police* (Berkeley: University of California Press, 1988), 149. On similar responses to sensation novels in the nineteenth century, see Taylor, *In the Secret Theatre of Home,* 7–10, and Winter, *Mesmerized,* 321–24. My emphasis extends Nicholas Dames's account of Victorian physiological accounts of the temporality of reading in *The Physiology of the Novel: Reading, Neural Science, and the Form of Victorian Fiction* (New York: Oxford University Press, 2007), 207–46.

3. Edward Boring's formative study cast the relation between statistical and psychological studies as a triumphal shift from the former to the latter, in which physio-psychological thinkers revealed what former probabilistic accounts had merely missed. Delay, he writes, was "obviously the sort of physiological problem that, along with sensation, was destined to become the property of the new physiological psychology." Boring, *A History of Experimental Psychology* (New York: Appleton, 1950), 133. More recent revisionist historians like Jimena Canales have shown that the astronomer's statistical studies continued to flourish through the mid-nineteenth century. Canales, *A Tenth of a Second: A History* (Chicago: University of Chicago Press, 2011), esp. 21–58.

4. *Armadale's* superimposed temporalities have been interpreted through the optics of race, empire, and associationist theories, and I join these accounts by focusing on the science of the present. See Lauren Goodlad, *The Victorian Geopolitical Aesthetic: Realism, Sovereignty, and Transnational Experience* (New York: Oxford University Press, 2015), 110–33; Taylor, *In the Secret Theatre of Home,* 171–90.

5. Quoted in Winifred Hughes, *Maniac in the Cellar: Sensation Novels of the 1860s* (Princeton, NJ: Princeton University Press, 1980), 47.

6. Michel Foucault, *Discipline and Punish: The Birth of the Prison*, trans. Alan Sheridan (New York: Pantheon, 1977), 31.

7. Lauren Berlant, *Cruel Optimism* (Durham, NC: Duke University Press, 2011); Carolyn Dinshaw, *How Soon Is Now? Medieval Texts, Amateur Readers, and the Queerness of Time* (Durham, NC: Duke University Press, 2012), 5, 4 (emphasis in original); Freeman, *Time Bends*, 16.

8. Michel Foucault, "Nietzsche, Genealogy, History," in *Language, Counter-Memory, Practice: Selected Essays and Interviews*, ed. D. F. Bouchard (Ithaca, NY: Cornell University Press, 1977), 90.

9. John Venn, *The Logic of Chance: An Essay on the Foundations and Province of the Theory of Probability* (London: Macmillan, 1866), 224.

10. De Morgan, *An Essay on Probabilities*, 7.

11. Freeman, *Time Bends*, 16.

12. Boring, *A History of Experimental Psychology*, 147–49; Simon Schaffer, "Astronomers Mark Time: Discipline and the Personal Equation," *Science in Context* 2 (1988): 116–19.

13. F. W. Bessel to C. F. Gauss, 15 June 1818, in *Briefwechsel zwischen Gauss und Bessel* (Leipzig: Veranlassung der Koniglich Preussischen Akademie der Wissenschaften, 1880), 272, trans. and quoted in Christof Hoffman, "Constant Differences," *British Journal for the History of Science* 40 (2007): 344. On Gauss's relationship with Bessel, see Canales, *A Tenth of a Second*, 34, and Hoffman, "Constant Differences," 341–45.

14. See, for example, Z. G. Swijtink, "The Objectification of Observation: Measurement and Statistical Methods in the Nineteenth Century," in Krüger et al., *The Probabilistic Revolution*, 1:261–85; Canales, *A Tenth of a Second*, 34–35; Hoffman, "Constant Differences," 341–42.

15. Porter, *The Rise of Statistical Thinking*, 96; Canales, *A Tenth of a Second*, 63–65; also see Hoffman, "Constant Differences," 344.

16. John Pond, *Astronomical Observations Made at the Royal Observatory at Greenwich in the Year 1832*, part 5, *Supplement* (London: T. Bensley, Carne Court, Fleet Street, 1833), iv.

17. Schaffer, "Astronomers Mark Time," 118; Jimena Canales, "Sensational Differences: Individuality in Observation, Experimentation, and Representation (France 1853–1895)" (Ph.D. diss., Harvard University, 2003), 9.

18. William Carpenter, *Mechanical Philosophy, Horology, and Astronomy* (London: W. S. Orr, 1844), 395.

19. Johannes Müller, *Elements of Physiology*, trans. William Baly, 2 vols. (London: Taylor and Walton, 1838), 1:638.

20. Boring, *A History of Experimental Psychology*, 54.

21. Alexander Bain, *The Senses and the Intellect* (London: Longmans, 1855), 64.

22. James Sully, *The Senses and Intuition: Studies in Psychology and Aesthetics* (London: H. S. King, 1874), 39.

23. Lorraine J. Daston and Peter Galison, *Objectivity* (London: Zone Books, 2007), 263–65. Also see Henning Schmidgen, *The Helmholtz Curves: Tracing Lost Time* (New

York: Fordham University Press, 2014). Schmidgen argues that Helmholtz's finding "marks the beginning of a new epoch in the quantitative study of organic life" (23).

24. Canales, *A Tenth of a Second*, 21–43; Hoffman, "Constant Differences," 363–65.

25. Billie Inman, *Walter Pater and His Reading, 1844–1847, with a Bibliography of His Library Borrowings, 1878–1894* (New York: Garland, 1981), 230.

26. Hippolyte Taine, *On Intelligence*, trans. T. D. Haye (London: Reeve, 1871), 284–85.

27. Henry Maudsley, *The Physiology and Psychology of the Mind* (London: Routledge, 1993), 370.

28. Caroline Levine observes that "Victorian culture consistently cast self-suspension as a quintessentially feminine virtue." Levine, *The Serious Pleasures of Suspense* (Charlottesville: University of Virginia Press, 2003), 85.

29. David K. Robinson, "Reaction-Time Experiments in Wundt's Institute and Beyond," in *Wilhelm Wundt in History*, ed. Robert Rieber and David K. Robinson (New York: Kluwer Academic, 2001), 164–67; Nicholas Gillham, *A Life of Sir Francis Galton* (New York: Oxford University Press, 2001), 211–14.

30. Robinson, "Reaction-Time Experiments," in *Wilhelm Wundt in History*, ed. Rieber and Robinson, 188.

31. Daston and Galison, *Objectivity*, 264.

32. Robinson, "Reaction-Time Experiments," 174–75, 189–90.

33. Joseph Jastrow, *The Time-Relations of Mental Phenomena* (New York: N. D. C. Hodges, 1890), 23.

34. Rick Rylance, *Victorian Psychology and British Culture, 1850–1880* (New York: Oxford University Press, 2000), 6–7.

35. George Levine, *Darwin and the Novelists: Patterns of Science in Victorian Fiction* (Chicago: University of Chicago Press, 1992), 56–83; see also Gold, *ThermoPoetics*, 33–68; Adelene Buckland, *Novel Science: Fiction and the Invention of Nineteenth-Century Geology* (Chicago: University of Chicago Press, 2013), 57–69.

36. Walter Pater, "The Poems of William Morris," *Westminster Review* 150 (1868): 302.

37. I develop this interpretation in "The Impassive Novel: 'Brain-Building' in Walter Pater's *Marius the Epicurean*," *PMLA* (forthcoming).

38. Huxley, "Evolution and Ethics," in *Collected Essays*, 9:49.

39. John Tyndall, *Fragments of Science for Unscientific People: A Series of Detached Essays, Lectures, and Reviews*, 2 vols. (London: Longmans, Green, 1898), 2:191–92; Huxley, "Materialism and Idealism," in *Collected Essays*, 9 vols. (London: Macmillan, 1893–4), 1:131. On Tyndall's address and its reception, see Bernard Lightman, "Scientists and Materialists in the Periodical Press: Tyndall's Belfast Address," in *Science Serialized: Representations of the Sciences in Nineteenth-Century Periodicals*, ed. Geoffrey Cantor and Sally Shuttleworth (Cambridge, MA: MIT Press, 2004), 199–238.

40. Cohn, *Still Life*, 16.

41. Wilkie Collins, *The Dead Secret*, ed. Ira B. Nadel (New York: Oxford University Press, 1997), 5. On the turn to an aesthetics of slowness in Victorian print culture, see Elizabeth Miller, *Slow Print: Literary Radicalism and Late-Victorian Print Culture* (Stanford, CA: Stanford University Press, 2013).

42. Wilkie Collins, *The Woman in White,* ed. John Sutherland (New York: Oxford University Press, 2008), 334.

43. Peter K. Garrett, "Sensations: Gothic, Horror, Crime Fiction, Detective Fiction," in *The Cambridge History of the English Novel,* ed. Robert L. Caserio and Clement Hawes (Cambridge: Cambridge University Press, 2012): 469–84; also see Goodlad, *The Victorian Geopolitical Aesthetic,* 123. Anna Maria Jones observes that *Armadale* "reject[s] the narrative structure of the bildungsroman" in *Problem Novels: Victorian Fiction Theorizes the Sensational Self* (Columbus: Ohio State University Press, 2007), 48.

44. Nathan K. Hensley, "*Armadale* and the Logic of Liberalism," *Victorian Studies* 59 (2009): 617.

45. Quoted in Hughes, *Maniac in the Cellar,* 47.

46. Catherine Peters, introduction to *Armadale,* by Wilkie Collins, ed. Peters (New York: Oxford University Press, 1989), ix–x.

47. Wilkie Collins to Edward Pigott, quoted in Peters, introduction to *Armadale,* ix.

48. Taylor writes, "Midwinter's shiftiness and twitchiness are both cultural—the particular interpretation of a set of physical responses—and physiological" (164–65).

49. See Taylor, *In The Secret Theatre of Home,* 165.

50. Francis Baily, "Report on the New Standard Scale of this Society. Drawn Up at the Request of the Council, by F. Baily, and One of the Vice-Presidents of the Society. Presented December 11, 1835," *Memoirs of the Royal Astronomical Society* 9 (1836): 93.

51. Lisa M. Zeitz and Peter Thoms note that "the story of Major Milroy and his clock emphasizes Collins's perception of irregularity and confusion in the world." Zeitz and Thoms, "Collins's Use of the Strasbourg Clock in *Armadale,*" *Nineteenth-Century Literature* 45 (1991): 499.

52. Sue Zemka, *Time and the Moment in Victorian Literature and Society* (Cambridge: Cambridge University Press, 2012), 7.

53. As one reviewer wrote, "*Armadale,* from first to last, is a lurid labyrinth of improbabilities" in which events accrue in unaccountably "grotesque" and "*bizarre*" respects (emphasis in original). "*Armadale,*" unsigned review of *Armadale,* by Wilkie Collins, *Saturday Review* (16 June 1866): 726.

54. Georg Lukács, "Narrate or Describe?," in *Writer and Critic and Other Essays,* trans. and ed. Arthur Kahn (London: The Merlin Press, 1970): 110–48, 111, 116; Émile Zola to Henry Céard, 22 March 1885, in Zola, *Oeuvres Complètes,* ed. Menri Mitterand (Paris: Cercle du Livre Précieux, 1969), 14:1440. For a recent reappraisal of Lukács's argument, see Cannon Schmitt, "Interpret or Describe?," *Representations* 135 (2016): 102–18.

55. Foucault, "Nietzsche, Genealogy, History," in *Language, Counter-Memory, Practice,* 90.

56. Zemka, *Time and the Moment,* 7. I draw on Zemka's account of standard time developments on pp. 4–7.

57. I draw here on Lauren Berlant's account of her project, in *Cruel Optimism,* as an investigation of neoliberal-era constructions of the present: "a kind of proprioceptive history, a way of thinking about represented norms of bodily adjustment as key

to grasping the circulation of the present as a historical and affective sense." Berlant, *Cruel Optimism,* 20.

58. Levine, *The Serious Pleasures of Suspense,* 3.

59. "The dream disrupts the coherent order of narrative and is the means by which the past, in another register, exerts pressure on the future." Taylor, *In the Secret Theatre of Home,* 163.

60. Heather Love, *Feeling Backward: Loss and the Politics of Queer History* (Cambridge, MA: Harvard University Press, 2007), 63.

61. "*Armadale,*" 726.

62. Taylor, *In the Secret Theatre of Home,* 170.

63. Taylor, *In the Secret Theatre of Home,* 171.

64. Harry Harootunian, "Remembering the Historical Present," *Critical Inquiry* 33 (2007): 478.

65. See Hensley, "*Armadale* and the Logic of Liberalism," 617–28; Goodlad, *The Victorian Geopolitical Aesthetic,* 110–33.

66. Daston and Galison, *Objectivity,* 264.

67. Freeman, *Time Bends,* 16.

68. Baily, "Report on the New Standard Scale," 92.

69. Foucault, "Nietzsche, Genealogy, History," in *Language, Counter-Memory, Practice,* 90.

3. "A NAT'RAL BORN FRIEND"

1. Charles Darwin, *The Origin of Species: A Variorum Text,* ed. Morse Peckham (Philadelphia: University of Pennsylvania Press, 1959), 414.

2. Alfred Russel Wallace, *Letters and Reminiscences,* ed. James Marchant, 2 vols. (London: Cassell, 1916), 1:210. For an account of Wallace and Darwin's interaction on the topic, see Malcolm Jay Kottler, "Charles Darwin and Alfred Russel Wallace: Two Decades of Debate over Natural Selection," in *The Darwinian Heritage,* ed. David Kohn (Princeton, NJ: Princeton University Press, 1985), 367–434.

3. Robert J. Richards, *Darwin and the Emergence of Evolutionary Theories of Mind and Behavior* (Chicago: University of Chicago Press, 1987), 142–56; Helena Cronin, *The Ant and the Peacock: Altruism and Sexual Selection from Darwin to Today* (Cambridge: Cambridge University Press, 1993), 5; Thomas Dixon, *The Invention of Altruism: Making Moral Meanings in Victorian Britain* (New York: Oxford University Press, 2008), 130. A wealth of scholarship converges around Darwin's "difficulty" with altruism. Stephen Jay Gould characterizes altruism as "the greatest stumbling block" for a Darwinian model of social behavior, an assessment that Richards substantiates in detail. In contrast, Helena Cronin contends that "Darwin viewed altruistic behavior as relatively unproblematic in general" (307), while Dixon adds that "Darwin did not think that cooperative and self-sacrificing actions and feelings were especially difficult to explain on evolutionary principles" (142). Cronin and Dixon observe that Darwin had no trouble accepting several established explanations for altruism; neo-

Lamarckians, for example, had speculated that mutually beneficial actions could become innate over many generations, as could the effects of praise and punishment in cases where individuals are taught to act altruistically. But these two Lamarckian explanations were inadequate in explaining nonreproductive altruism, since the individuals in question neither reaped reciprocal rewards nor seemed socialized to act for others nor produced offspring at all. It was this problem within the larger umbrella of altruistic phenomena that captivated Darwin's attentions. S. J. Gould, "Sociobiology and the Theory of Natural Selection," in *Sociobiology: Beyond Nature/Nurture?*, ed. G. W. Barlow and J. Silverberg (Boulder, CO: Westview, 1980), 257–69, 260.

4. Dixon, *The Invention of Altruism*, 158–62; David Stack, *The First Darwinian Left: Socialism and Darwinism, 1859–1914* (Cheltenham: New Clarion, 2003).

5. On the history of friendship, see Alan Bray, *The Friend* (Chicago: University of Chicago Press, 2003); Richard Dellamora, *Friendship's Bonds: Democracy and the Novel in Victorian Britain* (Philadelphia: University of Pennsylvania Press, 2004); Marcus, *Between Women*; Martha Vicinus, *Intimate Friends: Women Who Loved Women, 1778–1928* (Chicago: University of Chicago Press, 2004). Scholarship on the bachelor in Victorian fiction begins with U. C. Knoepflmacher's description of the "avuncular view" in *Middlemarch*, in which unmarried uncles in the novel have more prominent familial roles than biological fathers. Knoepflmacher's emphasis on the "uniformly destructive" role of the bachelor, however, has been tempered by Snyder, leading in turn to Eileen Cleere's and Holly Furneaux's examinations of "avunculate care" in Dickens's novels. See U. C. Knoepflmacher, "*Middlemarch*: An Avuncular View," *Nineteenth-Century Fiction* 30 (1975), esp. 77; Eileen Cleere, *Avuncularism: Capitalism, Patriarchy, and Nineteenth-Century English Culture* (Stanford, CA: Stanford University Press, 2004); Katherine V. Snyder, *Bachelors, Manhood, and the Novel, 1850–1925* (Cambridge: Cambridge University Press, 1999); Holly Furneaux, *Queer Dickens: Erotics, Families, Masculinities* (New York: Oxford University Press, 2009).

6. Grosz, "Darwin and the Ontology of Life," in *Time Travels*, 35–42, 41.

7. Charles Darwin to Joseph Hooker, in *The Correspondence of Charles Darwin*, ed. Fredrick Burkhardt et al., 26 vols. (Cambridge: Cambridge University Press, 2012), 19:53.

8. Tina Choi, "Natural History's Hypothetical Moments: Narratives of Contingency in Victorian Culture," *Victorian Studies* 51 (2009): 275.

9. For example, see Gigerenzer et al., *The Empire of Chance*, 141–62; Porter, *The Rise of Statistical Thinking*, 134–35; Curtis Johnson, *Darwin's Dice: The Idea of Chance in the Thought of Charles Darwin* (Cambridge: Cambridge University Press, 2014), 1–27; M. J. S. Hodge, "Natural Selection as a Causal, Empirical, and Probabilistic Theory," in Krüger et al., *The Probabilistic Revolution*, 2:233–70.

10. Desmond and Moore, *Darwin*, 463–64.

11. Fred Somkin, "The Contributions of Sir John Lubbock, F.R.S. to the *Origin of Species*: Some Annotations to Darwin," *Notes and Records of the Royal Society of London* 17 (1962): 183–91. For Darwin's ties with Herschel, see S. S. Schweber, "John Herschel and Charles Darwin: A Study of Parallel Lives," *Journal of the History of Biology* 22 (1989): 40–43.

12. Charles Darwin to Charles Lyell, in *The Correspondence of Charles Darwin,* 8:260.

13. Devin Griffiths, *The Age of Analogy: Science and Literature between the Darwins* (Baltimore: Johns Hopkins University Press, 2016), 11.

14. Charles Darwin, *The Descent of Man, and Selection in Relation to Sex,* 2 vols. (London: Murray, 1871), 1:38.

15. Gigerenzer et al., *The Empire of Chance,* 66–67; also see Choi, "Natural History's Hypothetical Moments," 286–91.

16. Leonard Huxley, ed., *Life and Letters of Thomas H. Huxley,* 2 vols. (New York: Appleton, 1901), 1:245 (emphasis added).

17. Charles Darwin, *Charles Darwin's Notebooks, 1836–1844: Geology, Transmutation of Species, Metaphysical Enquiries,* ed. Paul H Barrett, Peter J. Gautrey, Sandra Herbert, David Kohn, and Sydney Smith (Cambridge: Cambridge University Press, 1987), 195.

18. Johnson, *Darwin's Dice,* 18–22.

19. Darwin, *Charles Darwin's Notebooks,* 428 (emphasis in original).

20. As Dov Ospovot writes, "By Early December, Darwin reversed his previous position on man, saying he was a 'chance' production. . . . Within a month or two of reading Malthus, Darwin concluded that the natural selection of accidental variations couldn't be reconciled with the idea of a plan of creation." Ospovot, *The Development of Darwin's Theory, 1838–1859* (Cambridge: Cambridge University Press, 1981), 72.

21. Ospovot, *The Development of Darwin's Theory,* 80–86; Johnson, *Darwin's Dice,* 48–60; Choi, "Natural History's Hypothetical Moments," 278.

22. William Paley, *Principles of Moral and Political Philosophy* (Indianapolis: Liberty Fund, 2012), 66.

23. Charles Darwin, *Charles Darwin's Notebooks,* 552 (emphasis in original).

24. William Kirby and William Spence, *An Introduction to Entomology: Or Elements of the Natural History of Insects,* 2 vols. (London: Longman, 1826), 1:491.

25. Darwin's annotation appears in his edition of Kirby and Spence, *Introduction to Entomology,* 2:455. Quoted in Richards, *Darwin and the Emergence of Evolutionary Theories of Mind and Behavior,* 44.

26. Charles Darwin, *Charles Darwin's Natural Selection, Being the Second Part of His Big Species Book Written from 1856–1858,* ed. R. Stauffer (Cambridge: Cambridge University Press, 1975), 466.

27. See Catherine Gallagher, *The Body Economic: Life, Death, and Sensation in Political Economy and the Victorian Novel* (Princeton, NJ: Princeton University Press, 2008), 159.

28. Charles Darwin, [Instincts in wasps and bees] in *The Complete Work of Charles Darwin Online,* ed. John van Wyhe, MS 73.21–22, accessed 10 October 2015, http://darwin-online.org.uk.

29. Darwin, *Charles Darwin's Natural Selection,* 510.

30. Kathleen Frederickson, *The Ploy of Instinct: Victorian Sciences of Nature and Sexuality in Liberal Governance* (New York: Fordham University Press, 2014), 19–22. Frederickson observes that "'neuter' instincts present Darwin with a problem because he cannot, first, accept the proposition that instinct does not carry some orientation

toward futurity," then noting the late-nineteenth-century elaboration of his account by anarchist socialists such as Peter Kropotkin and Edward Carpenter (85, 88).

31. Darwin, *The Descent of Man,* 1:38.

32. Desmond and Moore, *Darwin,* 275–76.

33. Darwin, *The Origin of Species,* 421.

34. Darwin, *Charles Darwin's Notebooks,* 232; see Buckland, *Novel Science,* 247–73.

35. Charles Dickens, *Martin Chuzzlewit,* ed. Margaret Caldwell (Oxford: Clarendon Press, 1982), 326.

36. Discussing Dickens's influence on Darwin, Gillian Beer examines how "the theme of hidden yet all-pervasive kinship is one which their narratives share." Beer, *Darwin's Plots: Evolutionary Narrative in Darwin, George Eliot and Nineteenth-Century Fiction* (Cambridge: Cambridge University Press, 1981), 21. Likewise, George Levine claims that "the attitudes implicit in the language and structure of Dickens's books are, like the attitudes essayed in his journals and a lot in scientific thought in the 1830s and 1870s, premonitory of the argument Darwin was constructing." Levine, *Darwin and the Novelists,* 123; see also 260–61.

37. Anne Lohrli, ed., *Household Words: A Weekly Journal, 1850–1859* (Toronto: University of Toronto Press, 1973), 24.

38. Darwin, *The Origin of Species,* 14.

39. Robert Clark, "Riddling the Family Firm: The Sexual Economy in *Dombey and Son,*" *ELH* 51 (1984): 70.

40. Alex Woloch, *The One vs. the Many: Minor Characters and the Space of the Protagonist in the Novel* (Princeton, NJ: Princeton University Press, 2004), 13.

41. Garrett Stewart, *Novel Violence: A Narratography of Victorian Fiction* (Chicago: University of Chicago Press, 2009), 25.

42. Lyn Pykett, "*Dombey and Son:* A Sentimental Family Romance," *Studies in the Novel* 19 (1986): 17; see also Paul D. Herring, "The Number Plans for *Dombey and Son:* Some Further Observations," *Modern Philology* 68 (1970): 152.

43. These bonds correspond to what Furneaux describes as "an alternative historical concept of kinship" associated with the bachelors in *Nicholas Nickleby* (1839) and *A Tale of Two Cities* (1859). In those novels, Furneaux argues that familial bonds advance "along lines that do not automatically instate marriage or biology as the central determinant" (27). I share Furneaux's interest in alternative models of kin relations but depart from her nonbiological account by tracing the mutual relations between Dickens and Darwin on nonreproduction.

44. For a related consideration of the Whittington narrative, see Amy Sadrin, *Parentage and Inheritance in the Novels of Charles Dickens* (Cambridge: Cambridge University Press, 1994), 51–52.

45. Levine, *Darwin and the Novelists,* 92.

46. Levine, *Darwin and the Novelists,* 145–52. I am indebted to Levine's language in describing Dickens's eroding spiritual convictions.

47. Working notes for *Dombey and Son,* quoted in Sadrin, *Parentage and Inheritance,* 55.

48. Catherine Gallagher, *The Industrial Reformation of English Fiction: Social Discourse and Narrative Form, 1832–1867* (Chicago: University of Chicago Press, 1988), 132–33; Andrew Sanders, introduction to *Dombey and Son*, xxii–xxv.

49. Diane Sadoff, *Monsters of Affection: Dickens, Eliot, and Bronte on Fatherhood* (Baltimore: Johns Hopkins University Press, 1982), 63.

50. Hilary Schor, *Dickens and the Daughter of the House* (Cambridge: Cambridge University Press, 1999), 53–54.

51. Huxley, "Evolution and Ethics," in *Collected Essays*, 9:82.

52. Richard Holt Hutton, "The 'Sociology' of Ants," in *Criticisms on Contemporary Thought and Thinkers: Selected from The Spectator*, 2 vols. (London: Macmillan, 1894). 2:322–30; Leslie Stephen, *The Science of Ethics* (London: Smith, Elder, 1882); Jane Hume Clapperton, *Scientific Meliorism and the Evolution of Happiness* (London: Kegan Paul, Trench, 1885); Patrick Geddes and J. Arthur Thomson, *The Evolution of Sex* (London: Walter Scott, 1889); Henry Drummond, *The Lowell Lectures on the Ascent of Man* (London: Hodder and Stoughton, 1894); Peter Kropotkin, *Mutual Aid: A Factor in Evolution* (Harmondsworth: Penguin, 1939).

53. Charles Dickens, *Master Humphrey's Clock*, 2 vols. (London: Chapman and Hall, 1840–41), 2:422.

54. Georg Lukács, *The Theory of the Novel: A Historico-Philosophical Essay on the Forms of Great Epic Literature*, trans. Anna Bostock (Cambridge, MA: MIT Press, 1971), 77, 47.

55. Lukács, *The Theory of the Novel*, 77; Georg Lukács, *The Historical Novel*, trans. Hannah Mitchell and Stanley Mitchell (Lincoln: University of Nebraska Press, 1962), 33.

56. Darwin, *The Origin of Species*, 414.

4. GEORGE ELIOT'S "FINE EXCESS"

1. For a representative sample, see S. Pearl Brilmyer, "Plasticity, Form, and the Matter of Character in *Middlemarch*," *Representations* 130 (2015): 60–83; Ian Duncan, "George Eliot's Science Fiction," *Representations* 125 (2014): 15–39; Robert A. Greenberg, "Plexuses and Ganglia: Scientific Allusion in *Middlemarch*," *Nineteenth-Century Fiction*, 30 (1975): 33–52; George Levine, "George Eliot's Hypothesis of Reality," *Nineteenth-Century Fiction* 35 (1980): 1–28; Michael York Mason, "*Middlemarch* and Science: Problems of Life and Mind," *Review of English Studies* 22 (1971): 151–69; Richard Menke, "Fiction as Vivisection: G. H. Lewes and George Eliot," *ELH* 67 (2000): 617–53; Lawrence Rothfield, *Vital Signs: Medical Realism in Nineteenth-Century Fiction* (Princeton, NJ: Princeton University Press, 1994); Sally Shuttleworth, *George Eliot and Nineteenth-Century Science: The Make-Believe of a Beginning* (Cambridge: Cambridge University Press, 1984); Jeremy Tambling, "*Middlemarch*, Realism, and the Birth of the Clinic," *ELH* 57 (1990): 939–69; Kay Young, *Imagining Minds: The Neuro-Aesthetics of Austen, Eliot, and Hardy* (Columbus: Ohio State University Press, 2010).

2. Following Crosbie Smith, I use the term "energy science" to describe investigations on energy from the early 1850s onward; "energy science" denotes a range of

topics that physicists would eventually claim as their own but that did not suggest a coherent program of research until the 1870s. Smith, *The Science of Energy.*

3. J. Hillis Miller, "Optic and Semiotic in *Middlemarch,*" in *The Worlds of Victorian Fiction,* ed. Jerome H. Buckley (Cambridge, MA: Harvard University Press, 1975), 135–45, 138.

4. James Clerk Maxwell, "Drafts of Lecture on 'Molecules,'" in *Scientific Letters and Papers,* 2:932. Maxwell was responding directly to Buckle's positivist method of history in this paragraph.

5. Mill, *Collected Works of John Stuart Mill,* 3:221. Eliot's links to aestheticism were first mapped by U. C. Knoepflmacher, who suggested how Eliot translated Arnold's culture concept into narrative form: "It was George Eliot's concrete novelistic conversion of ideas highly similar to [Arnold's] own," Knoepflmacher writes, "which stimulated the development of a next generation of novelists which included, among others, Mrs. Humphry Ward, Arnold's niece; Walter Pater, Arnold's successor as apostle of 'culture'; and Henry James, Arnold's steadfast admirer." Knoepflmacher, *Religious Humanism and the Victorian Novel* (Princeton, NJ: Princeton University Press, 1965), 69.

6. Huxley, "Science and Culture," in *Collected Essays,* 3:136. As a public intellectual battle, the terms of the debate between Arnold and Huxley were structured upon an antithesis between science and literature largely absent in 1850 and that began to anticipate Snow's distinction between those "two cultures." Arnold's "Literature and Science" (1882) railed against "the present movement for ousting letters from their old predominance in education, and for transferring the predominance in education to the natural sciences," in contrast to Huxley's defense of a practical scientific education in "Science and Culture." Arnold, *The Complete Prose Works of Matthew Arnold,* ed. R. H. Super, 12 vols. (Ann Arbor: University of Michigan Press, 1962), 10:53–73, 57; Huxley, *The Complete Prose Works of Matthew Arnold,* ed. R. H. Super, 12 vols. (Ann Arbor: University of Michigan Press, 1962), 10:53–73, 57.

7. On pessimistic attitudes to entropy in Victorian Britain, see Levine, *Darwin and the Novelists,* 153–70; Greg Myers, "Nineteenth-Century Popularizations of Thermodynamics and the Rhetoric of Social Prophecy," in *Energy and Entropy: Science and Culture in Victorian Britain: Essays from Victorian Studies,* ed. Patrick Brantlinger (Bloomington: Indiana University Press, 1989), 307–38. For a revisionist account of *fin-de-siècle* energy science, see Anna Maria Jones, "Conservation of Energy, Individual Agency, and Gothic Terror in Richard Marsh's *The Beetle,* or, What's Scarier Than an Ancient, Evil, Shape-Shifting Bug?" *Victorian Literature and Culture* 39 (2011): 65–85; also see Allan MacDuffie, *Victorian Literature, Energy, and the Ecological Imagination* (Cambridge: Cambridge University Press, 2014), 170–98.

8. George Eliot, "Leaves from a Note-Book," in *Essays of George Eliot,* ed. Thomas Pinney (New York: Columbia University Press, 1963), 451.

9. See Audrey Jaffe, *Scenes of Sympathy: Identity and Representation in Victorian Fiction* (Ithaca, NY: Cornell University Press, 2000); Rachel Ablow, *The Marriage of Minds: Reading Sympathy in the Victorian Marriage Plot* (Stanford, CA: Stanford University Press, 2007).

10. Leading scientists such as William Thomson, Peter Guthrie Tait, and Balfour Stewart all advanced spiritual perspectives on energy, often in the service of a reinvigorated Christian theodicy. Stewart and Tait, for example, explained entropy as the sign of spiritual progress and of the endless enlargement of otherworldly powers, paralleling Eliot's sanguine understanding of it. As they wrote in *The Unseen Universe* (1875), "By far the larger portion of the high-class energy of the present universe . . . is gradually transferred into an invisible order of things. May we not regard the ether or the medium as not merely a bridge between one portion of the visible universe and another, but also as a bridge between one order of things and another?" Balfour Stewart and Peter Guthrie Tait, *The Unseen Universe* (London: Macmillan, 1875), 199. On the spiritual implications of energy science, see Graeme Gooday, "Profit and Prophecy: Electricity in the Late-Victorian Periodical," in *Science in the Nineteenth-Century Periodical*, ed. Geoffrey Cantor et al. (Cambridge: Cambridge University Press, 2004); also see Meyers, "Nineteenth-Century Popularizations of Thermodynamics."

11. D. A. Miller, *Narrative and Its Discontents: Problems of Closure in the Traditional Novel* (Princeton, NJ: Princeton University Press, 1981), 149; Nancy Armstrong, *Desire and Domestic Fiction: A Political History of the Novel* (New York: Oxford University Press, 1987), 21.

12. See Abel, Hirsch, and Langdon, introduction to *The Voyage In.*

13. Gilles Deleuze and Félix Guattari, *Anti-Oedipus: Capitalism and Schizophrenia*, trans. Robert Hurley, Mark Seem, and Helen R. Lane (Minneapolis: University of Minnesota Press, 1983), 181.

14. George Eliot, diary entry for 30 May 1870, quoted in Shuttleworth, *George Eliot and Nineteenth-Century Science*, 159.

15. Selma B. Brody, "Physics in *Middlemarch*: Gas Molecules and Ethereal Atoms," *Modern Philology* 85 (1987): 43n13. Several scholars have noted the novel's language of energy science but interpret it in light of Eliot's general understanding of the scientific process. For still valuable readings, see Brody, "Physics in *Middlemarch*"; Peter Allen Dale, *In Pursuit of a Scientific Culture: Science, Art, and Society in the Victorian Age* (Madison: University of Wisconsin Press, 1989).

16. Michael Faraday, "On the Forms of Matter" (1819), quoted in Bence Jones, *The Life and Letters of Michael Faraday*, 2 vols. (London: Longmans, 1870), 1:311.

17. H. G. Wells, *"The Time Machine" and "The Island of Doctor Moreau,"* ed. Patrick Parrinder (New York: Oxford University Press, 1996), 87.

18. Grove, "On the Correlation of Physical Forces," in *The Correlation and Conservation of Forces*, 2–210, 22. Grove's writings also resonated with her partner George Henry Lewes's claims in *Problems of Life and Mind* (1874). As Lewes writes, "The universe to us is the universe in Feeling, and all its varieties are but varieties of Feeling. With the feeling of difference or otherness arises the judgment of not-this, which in turn evolves the distinction of Self and Not-self. These two aspects are abstractions; in Feeling they emerge simultaneously as correlations." Lewes, *Problems of Life and Mind*, 2 vols. (London: Trübner, 1874), 2:194.

19. Quoted in Porter, *The Rise of Statistical Thinking*, 115.

20. The maturation of Maxwell's ideas in this vein are well documented. See Harman, *The Natural Philosophy of James Clerk Maxwell,* 113–45; Purrington, *Physics in the Nineteenth Century,* 132–47; Porter, *The Rise of Statistical Thinking,* 193–208; Warwick, *Masters of Theory,* 286–306.

21. James Clerk Maxwell, "Molecules," in *The Scientific Papers of James Clerk Maxwell,* 2:374.

22. See Harman, *The Natural Philosophy of James Clerk Maxwell,* 143, 294.

23. James Clerk Maxwell to Lewis Campbell, 22 December 1857, in Campbell and Garnett, *The Life of James Clerk Maxwell,* 295.

24. Buckle, *History of Civilization,* 1:22.

25. See Porter, *The Rise of Statistical Thinking,* 194–208.

26. Porter, *The Rise of Statistical Thinking,* 125.

27. Quoted in Englebert Broda, *Ludwig Boltzmann: Man, Physicist, Philosopher* (Woodbridge, CT: Ox Bow, 1983), 83. Hasenöhrl in turn taught Erwin Schrödinger and others of future repute. On Boltzmann and Maxwell, see Porter, *The Rise of Statistical Thinking,* 126–27, 208–19.

28. Purrington, *Physics in the Nineteenth Century,* 140; on the skepticism surrounding Maxwell's ideas, see Porter, *The Rise of Statistical Thinking,* 115–17.

29. Maxwell, "Molecules," in *The Scientific Papers of James Clerk Maxwell,* 2:374.

30. This not to say that these thinkers were sympathetic with each other. Maxwell remained skeptical about Tyndall's mathematical abilities, for example, and castigated the latter's reductive materialism. Even so, Tyndall suggests a basic understanding of Maxwell's work, which Tyndall paraphrased in his 1874 Belfast Address and other writings, including *Heat: A Mode of Motion* (1868). For an assessment of Tyndall and Maxwell's relationship, see Daniel Brown, *The Poetry of Victorian Scientists* (Cambridge: Cambridge University Press, 2013), 164–83.

31. See Gillian Beer, "The Death of the Sun: Victorian Solar Physics and Solar Theory," in *Open Fields: Science in Cultural Encounter* (New York: Oxford University Press, 1996), 219–41, esp. 232–36.

32. James Clerk Maxwell to Lewis Campbell, 3 April 1873, in Campbell and Garnett, *The Life of James Clerk Maxwell,* 386.

33. For Maxwell's interest in Buckle and Quetelet, see Harman, *The Natural Philosophy of James Clerk Maxwell,* 125, 202; Porter, *The Rise of Statistical Thinking,* 123.

34. Quoted in Cross, *George Eliot's Life,* 232, 235.

35. Maxwell, "Introductory Lecture on Experimental Physics," in *The Scientific Papers of James Clerk Maxwell,* 2:253.

36. Joseph Priestley, *The Doctrine of Philosophical Necessity Illustrated* (London: J. Johnson, 1777), 8.

37. Maxwell, "Molecules," in *The Scientific Papers of James Clerk Maxwell,* 2:374; White, *Metahistory,* ix.

38. Quoted in Campbell and Garnett, *The Life of James Clerk Maxwell,* 651.

39. Stella Pratt-Smith, "Boundaries of Perception: James Clerk Maxwell's Poetry of Self, Senses and Science," in *James Clerk Maxwell: Perspectives on His Life and Work,*

ed. Raymond Flood, Mark McCartney, and Andrew Witaker (Oxford: Oxford University Press, 2014): 233–57, 256.

40. Gold, *ThermoPoetics,* 115; the Maxwell poem is quoted in Campbell and Garnett, *The Life of James Clerk Maxwell,* 647–48.

41. Gold, *ThermoPoetics,* 115–17; Brown, *The Poetry of Victorian Scientists,* 116–32; Peter Guthrie Tait, *Lectures on Some Recent Advances in Physical Science, with a Special Lecture on Force* (London: Macmillan, 1876), 357. "Faraday," Maxwell observed in an 1856 draft of his paper "On Faraday's Lines of Force," "treats the distribution of forces in space as the primary phenomenon, and does not insist on any theory as to [their] nature." Quoted in Harman, *The Natural Philosophy of James Clerk Maxwell,* 88.

42. Michael Faraday to James Clerk Maxwell, 13 November 1857, in Campbell and Garnett, *The Life of James Clerk Maxwell,* 288–89.

43. Lucretius, *On the Nature of Things,* trans. H. A. J. Munro, 2 vols. (Cambridge: Deighton, Bell, 1864), 1:26, 28. This was the authoritative edition that Eliot, Maxwell, and other educated Victorians read.

44. As Michael North writes, "Though Maxwell was no more capable of actually observing an atom than Lucretius had been, he did have sophisticated methods of representing the aggregate facets of gas molecules—methods that, because they were probabilistic in nature, gave the random a new and apparently scientific basis." North, *Novelty: A History of the New* (Chicago: University of Chicago Press, 2015), 85. On Lucretius in Victorian Britain, see Frank Turner, "Ancient Materialism and Modern Science: Lucretius among the Victorians," in *Contesting Cultural Authority,* 262–83.

45. James Clerk Maxwell to Hugh Andrew Johnstone Munro, 7 February 1866, in James Clerk Maxwell, *The Scientific Letters and Papers of James Clerk Maxwell,* ed. P. M. Harman, 2 vols. (Cambridge: Cambridge University Press, 1990–95), 2:250. On this letter and on Maxwell's debt to Lucretius, see Brown, *The Poetry of Victorian Scientists,* 168–69.

46. Maxwell, "Molecules," in *The Scientific Papers of James Clerk Maxwell,* 2:373. As Porter observes, Maxwell had read the proofs of Fleeming Jenkin's article about Lucretius, which were sent to Maxwell before the *North British Review* published it in 1868. Porter, *The Rise of Statistical Thinking,* 203. This was the article that Eliot read in her preparations for *Middlemarch.*

47. James Clerk Maxwell, "On the Dynamical Theory of Gases," *Philosophical Transactions of the Royal Society of London* 157 (1867): 50.

48. Tyndall, *Fragments of Science,* 2:131, 146. As Harman writes, "In seeking to contest the claims of Tyndall's materialism, [Maxwell] did not advocate a form of scientific obscurantism. He . . . centered his rebuttal of materialism on the argument that molecular physics did not imply determinism." Harman, introduction to vol. 3 of Maxwell, *Scientific Letters and Papers,* 3:15. For an account of the tensions between Maxwell's circle and Tyndall's see Brown, *The Poetry of Victorian Scientists,* 164–83. More generally on the professional and methodological contrasts between London-based scientific naturalists like Tyndall, Huxley, and Clifford and North British

scientists like Maxwell and Tait, see Smith, *The Science of Energy,* 190–211; also see Dawson and Lightman, introduction to *Victorian Scientific Naturalism.*

49. Brown, *The Poetry of Victorian Scientists,* 167–68.

50. James Clerk Maxwell, "Notes of the President's Address," *Blackwood's Edinburgh Magazine* 116 (1874): 583.

51. Quoted in Brown, *The Poetry of Victorian Scientists,* 170. Brown points out that the phrase "fortuitous concourse" comes from the English translation of Cicero's commentary on Lucretius (170).

52. Maxwell, "Introductory Lecture on Experimental Physics," in *Scientific Letters and Papers,* 2:253.

53. N. Katherine Hayles, *Chaos Bound: Orderly Disorder in Contemporary Literature and Science* (Ithaca, NY: Cornell University Press, 1990), 32.

54. James Clerk Maxwell to Peter Guthrie Tait, 11 December 1867, in Maxwell, *Scientific Letters and Papers,* 2:332.

55. This was a claim that Maxwell underscored in his entry on "Diffusion" for the ninth edition of the *Encyclopedia Britannica:* "The notion of dissipated energy could not occur to a being," wrote Maxwell, "who could trace the motion of every molecule and seize it at the right moment. It is only to a being in the intermediate stage, who can lay hold of some forms of energy while others elude his grasp, that energy appears to be passing from the available to the dissipated state." Maxwell, "Diffusion," in *Encyclopedia Britannica,* 9th ed. (Edinburgh: A. and C. Black, 1875), 3:216.

56. George Eliot, *Adam Bede,* ed. Carol A. Martin (New York: Oxford University Press, 2008), 338.

57. Jesse Rosenthal, *Good Form: The Ethical Experience of the Victorian Novel* (Princeton, NJ: Princeton University Press, 2016), 158–59.

58. John Tyndall, "Appendix to Lecture XII," in *Heat Considered as a Mode of Motion: Being a Course of Twelve Lectures Delivered at the Royal Institution of Great Britain in the Season of 1862* (New York: Appleton, 1863), 452.

59. William Thomson, preliminary draft for the "Dynamical Theory of Heat," quoted in Crosbie Smith and N. Norton Wise, *Energy and Empire: A Biographical Study of Lord Kelvin* (Cambridge: Cambridge University Press, 1989), 329.

60. Balfour Stewart, *The Conservation of Energy: Being an Elementary Treatise on Energy and Its Laws* (London: Henry S. King, 1873), 36.

61. Hemmo and Shenker, *The Road to Maxwell's Demon,* 16.

62. Raymond Williams, *The Country and the City* (New York: Oxford University Press, 1975), 165.

63. C. S. Pierce, "Illustrations of the Logic of Science: The Doctrine of Chances," in *Writings of Charles S. Pierce, A Chronological Edition,* ed. Pierce Edition Project (Bloomington: Indiana University Press, 1982), 3:285; Grove, "On the Correlation of Physical Forces," in *The Correlation and Conservation of Forces,* 22.

64. I draw here on language from Rosenthal's reading of *Daniel Deronda,* which contends that the novel distinguishes between individual and group domains in sta-

tistical terms: instead of a holistic social panorama, he writes, the novel "imagines two nearly separate realms: in one, we find individual characters and actions; in the other, the large-scale movements of social aggregates." *Middlemarch* also resists the integrative impulse of the bildungsroman, though my interest resides distinctively with the novel's conditional "vision of probabilities" and the physics of variation that informed it. Rosenthal, *Good Form,* 155.

65. For a related reading that interprets the passage as an account of the "narrator as auctioneer," see Monk, *Standard Deviations,* 59.

66. E. M. Forster, *Aspects of the Novel,* ed. Oliver Stallybrass (Harmondsworth: Penguin, 1976), 62.

67. Henry James, "Middlemarch," review of *Middlemarch,* by George Eliot, in *George Eliot: The Critical Heritage,* ed. David Carroll (London: Routledge, 2009), 359.

68. Eliot, "Leaves from a Note-Book," in *Essays of George Eliot,* 451.

69. On Lydgate and nineteenth-century medicine, see Greenberg, "Plexuses and Ganglia"; Mason, "*Middlemarch* and Science"; Rothfield, *Vital Signs;* and Tambling, "*Middlemarch,* Realism, and the Birth of the Clinic."

70. Shuttleworth, *George Eliot and Nineteenth-Century Science,* 159.

71. Tyndall explains: "Whether [matter and force] recombine in the furnace of the steam-engine or in the animal body, the origin of the power they produce is the same. In this sense we are all 'souls of fire and children of the sun.' But, as remarked by Helmholtz, we must be content to share our celestial pedigree with the meanest of living things." John Tyndall, "Matter and Force: A Lecture to the Working Men of Dundee," in *Fragments of Science,* 1:91–92.

72. Brody, "Physics in *Middlemarch,*" 48.

73. See Levine, "George Eliot's Hypothesis of Reality," 14.

74. John Tyndall, "The Constitution of Nature: An Essay," in *Fragments of Science,* 1:8.

75. Maxwell, unpublished fragment on statistical regularity, quoted in *Maxwell on Molecules and Gases,* ed. Elizabeth Garber, Stephen G. Brush, and C. W. F. Everitt (Cambridge, MA: MIT Press, 1986), 260.

76. Eliot, "Leaves from a Note-Book," in *Essays of George Eliot,* 451 (emphasis mine).

77. Maxwell, "Molecules," in *The Scientific Papers of James Clerk Maxwell,* 2:373.

78. Miller, *Narrative and Its Discontents,* 193.

79. R. H. Hutton wrote in his 1871 review of book 1 in the *Spectator,* "The first sketch is full of power and originality, but so much must depend on the melancholy working-out which George Eliot's not very pleasant, and for her somewhat pedantic, 'Prelude' hints at, that it is impossible to say whether it would be most unfair to the author or to the critic to deal with the augury as if it were the event." Quoted in Carroll, *George Eliot: The Critical Heritage,* 286–87. For initial readers, including Hutton, the question of whether Eliot could convincingly bring the story to completion was part of *Middlemarch*'s dramatic appeal.

80. Richard Feynman, *The Character of Physical Law* (Cambridge, MA: MIT Press, 1965), 116.

81. Avrom Fleishman, *George Eliot's Intellectual Life* (Cambridge: Cambridge University Press, 2010), 173.

82. Maxwell, "Does the Progress of Physical Science Tend to Give Any Advantage to the Opinion of Necessity," in Campbell and Garnett, *The Life of James Clerk Maxwell*, 438.

83. Herschel, "Quetelet on Probabilities," 7.

84. Hacking, *The Taming of Chance*, xi.

85. Eliot's transcription of Maxwell suggests a continuing interest in statistics: "Even in our ordinary experiments on very finely divided matter we find that the substance is beginning to lose the properties which it exhibits when in a large mass, & that effects depending on the individual action of molecules are beginning to be prominent," George Eliot, *George Eliot's "Daniel Deronda" Notebooks,* ed. Jane Irwin (Cambridge: Cambridge University Press, 1996), 21. The source was Maxwell's 1870 "Address to the Mathematical and Physical Sections of the British Association," in *The Scientific Papers of James Clerk Maxwell*, 2:222.

86. George Eliot, *Daniel Deronda*, ed. Graham Handley (Oxford: Clarendon, 1984), 36.

87. Rosenthal, *Good Form*, 170. The rhetoric alludes to Maxwell's 1865 paper "On the Dynamical Theory of Gases," which presented an early version of his statistical physics. On the significance of Maxwell's paper, see Harman, *The Natural Philosophy of James Clerk Maxwell*, 188–208; Purrington, *Physics in the Nineteenth Century*, 138–40.

CONCLUSION

1. Porter, *The Rise of Statistical Thinking*, 319.

2. Huxley, "Evolution and Ethics," in *Collected Essays*, 9:50.

3. See Porter, *The Rise of Statistical Thinking*, 103–9; Hacking, *The Taming of Chance*, 105–14.

4. Francis Galton, *Hereditary Genius: An Inquiry into Its Laws and Consequences* (London: Macmillan, 1869), 337.

5. Karl Pearson, *The Grammar of Science* (London: Adam and Charles Black, 1892), 149–50.

6. On Herschel's influence on Maxwell's mathematics, see Porter, *The Rise of Statistical Thinking*, 118–22; on Herschel and Darwin, see Schweber, "John Herschel and Charles Darwin."

7. Brenda Silver, "The Reflecting Reader in *Villette*," in Abel, Hirsch, and Langland, *The Voyage In*, 90–111, 107.

8. Thomas Hardy, *The Return of the Native*, ed. Nancy Barrineau (New York: Oxford University Press, 2009), 13, 9.

9. Beer, "The Reader's Wager: Lots, Sorts, and Futures," in *Open Fields*, 273–94, 294.

10. Thomas Hardy, *Two on a Tower*, ed. Suleiman M. Ahmad (New York: Oxford University Press, 1999), 3.

11. Olive Schreiner, *The Story of an African Farm*, ed. Joseph Bristow (New York: Oxford University Press, 1999), 80, 116.

12. J. Willard Gibbs, *Elementary Principles in Statistical Mechanics* (New York: Scribner, 1902), 15.

13. Norbert Wiener, *The Human Use of Human Beings: Cybernetics and Society,* rev. ed. (Boston: Houghton Mifflin, 1954), 10; Hayles, *How We Became Posthuman,* 89.

14. The relations between Gills and Maxwell were mutual: the latter devoted a chapter to Gibbs's formative contributions in the expanded fourth edition of his *Theory of Heat* in 1875. James Clerk Maxwell, *Theory of Heat,* 4th ed. (London: Longmans, Green, 1875), 195–208. On Maxwell's 1881 paper, see Porter, "Statistics and Physical Theories," 499.

15. Stephen Kern, *The Culture of Time and Space, 1880–1918* (Cambridge, MA: Harvard University Press, 1983), 19.

16. Ernst Cassirer, *Substance and Function and Einstein's Theory of Relativity,* trans. William Curtis Swabey and Marie Collins Swabey (London: Open Court, 1923), 172.

17. John Stuart Mill, "William Hamilton's Philosophy," in *Collected Works of John Stuart Mill,* 9:4.

18. Christopher Herbert, *Victorian Relativity: Radical Thought and Scientific Discovery* (Chicago: University of Chicago Press, 2001).

19. I borrow here from Kern's account of the Michelson-Morley experiment in *The Culture of Time and Space,* 18.

20. Timothy Morton, *Hyperobjects: Philosophy and Ecology after the End of the World* (Minneapolis: University of Minnesota Press, 2013), 20, 10.

21. Diana Coole and Samantha Frost, eds., *New Materialisms: Ontology, Agency, and Politics* (Durham, NC: Duke University Press, 2010), 12, 13.

22. Stuart Hampshire, *Innocence and Experience* (Cambridge, MA: Harvard University Press, 1991); Geoffrey Hawthorn, *Plausible Worlds: Possibility and Understanding in History and the Social Sciences* (Cambridge: Cambridge University Press, 1993); Ferguson, *Virtual History;* H. R. Trevor-Roper, "History and Imagination," in *History and Imagination: Essays in Honor of H. R. Trevor-Roper,* ed. Hugh Lloyd-Jones, Valerie Pearl, and Blair Worden (London: Duckworth, 1981), 356–69, 364; E. H. Carr, *The Idea of History* (London: Vintage, 1967), 127.

23. Herschel, "Quetelet on Probabilities," 1.

Bibliography

Abel, Elizabeth, Marianne Hirsch, and Elizabeth Langland, eds. *The Voyage In: Fictions of Female Development*. Hanover, NH: University Press of New England, 1983.

Ablow, Rachel. *The Marriage of Minds: Reading Sympathy in the Victorian Marriage Plot*. Stanford, CA: Stanford University Press, 2007.

Acton, John. "Mr. Buckle's Philosophy of History." *Rambler* 23 (August 1858): 88–104.

———. "Mr. Buckle's Thesis and Method." *Rambler* 22 (July 1858): 27–42.

Acton, William. *The Functions and Disorders of the Reproductive Organs in Childhood, Youth, Adult Age, and Advanced Life*. 3rd ed. London: John Churchill, 1865.

Agamben, Giorgio. *Potentialities: Collected Essays in Philosophy*. Translated by Daniel Heller-Roazen. Stanford, CA: Stanford University Press, 2000.

Alborn, Timothy. *Regulated Lives: Life Insurance and British Society, 1800–1914*. Toronto: University of Toronto Press, 2009.

Allen, Emily. "A Shock to the System: *Richard Feverel* and the Actress in the House." *Victorian Literature and Culture* 35 (2007): 81–101.

Aristotle. *Poetics*. Translated by Anthony Kenny. New York: Oxford University Press, 2013.

"*Armadale*." Unsigned review of *Armadale,* by Wilkie Collins. *Saturday Review,* 16 June 1866, 726–27.

Armstrong, Nancy. *Desire and Domestic Fiction: A Political History of the Novel*. New York: Oxford University Press, 1987.

Arnold, Matthew. *The Complete Prose Works of Matthew Arnold*. Edited by R. H. Super. 11 vols. Ann Arbor: University of Michigan Press, 1962.

Babbage, Charles. *The Ninth Bridgewater Treatise*. London: Murray, 1838.

Baily, Francis. "Report on the New Standard Scale of This Society. Drawn Up at the Request of the Council, by F. Baily, and One of the Vice-Presidents of the Society. Presented December 11, 1835." *Memoirs of the Royal Astronomical Society* 9 (1836): 35–184.

Bain, Alexander. *The Senses and the Intellect*. London: Longmans, 1855.

Barad, Karen. *Meeting the Universe Halfway: Quantum Physics and the Entanglement of Matter and Meaning*. Durham, NC: Duke University Press, 2007.

Barlow, G. W., and J. Silverberg, eds. *Sociobiology: Beyond Nature/Nurture?* Boulder, CO: Westview, 1980.

Barthes, Roland. "An Introduction to the Structural Analysis of Narrative." Translated by Lionel Duisit. *New Literary History* 6 (1975): 237–72.

Beatty, Jerome. "Chance and Natural Selection." *Philosophy of Science* 51 (1984): 183–211.

Beer, Gillian. *Darwin's Plots: Evolutionary Narrative in Darwin, George Eliot and Nineteenth-Century Fiction.* Cambridge: Cambridge University Press, 1981.

———. *Open Fields: Science in Cultural Encounter.* New York: Oxford University Press, 1996.

Bennett, Jane. *Vibrant Matter: A Political Ecology of Things.* Durham, NC: Duke University Press, 2010.

Bessel, Friedrich, and Carl Gauss. *Briefwechsel zwischen Gauss und Bessel.* Leipzig: Veranlassung der Koniglich Preussischen Akademie der Wissenschaften, 1880.

Berlant, Lauren. *Cruel Optimism.* Durham, NC: Duke University Press, 2011.

Bloch, Ernst. *The Principle of Hope.* Translated by Neville Plaice, Stephen Plaice, and Paul Knight. 2 vols. Cambridge, MA: MIT Press, 1983.

Bogost, Ian. *Alien Phenomenology, or What It's Like to Be a Thing.* Minneapolis: University of Minnesota Press, 2012.

Boring, Edward. *A History of Experimental Psychology.* New York: Appleton, 1950.

Braidotti, Rosi. *The Posthuman.* Malden, MA: Polity, 2013.

Brantlinger, Patrick, ed. *Energy and Entropy: Science and Culture in Victorian Britain: Essays from Victorian Studies.* Bloomington: Indiana University Press, 1989.

Brantlinger, Patrick, and William B. Thesing, eds. *A Companion to the Victorian Novel.* Oxford: Blackwell, 2002.

Bray, Alan. *The Friend.* Chicago: University of Chicago Press, 2003.

Brilmyer, S. Pearl. "Plasticity, Form, and the Matter of Character in *Middlemarch.*" *Representations* 130 (2015): 60–83.

Broda, Englebert. *Ludwig Boltzmann: Man, Physicist, Philosopher.* Woodbridge, CT: Ox Bow, 1983.

Brody, Selma B. "Physics in *Middlemarch:* Gas Molecules and Ethereal Atoms." *Modern Philology* 85 (1987): 42–53.

Brooks, Peter. *Reading for the Plot: Design and Intention in Narrative.* Cambridge, MA: Harvard University Press, 1992.

Brown, Daniel. *The Poetry of Victorian Scientists: Style, Science, and Nonsense.* Cambridge: Cambridge University Press, 2013.

Browning, Elizabeth Barrett. *Aurora Leigh.* Edited by Kerry McSweeney. New York: Oxford University Press, 1993.

Buckland, Adelene. *Novel Science: Fiction and the Invention of Nineteenth-Century Geology.* Chicago: University of Chicago Press, 2013.

Buckle, Henry Thomas. *History of Civilization in England.* 2 vols. London: Parker, Son and Bourn, 1857–61.

Buckley, Jerome H., ed. *The Worlds of Victorian Fiction.* Cambridge, MA: Harvard University Press, 1975.

Bunzl, Martin. "Counterfactual History: A User's Guide." *American Historical Review* 109 (2004): 845–58.

Butler, Judith. *Gender Trouble: Feminism and the Subversion of Identity.* London: Routledge, 1990.

Campbell, Lewis, and William Garnett. *The Life of James Clerk Maxwell, with a Selection from His Correspondence and Occasional Writings.* London: Macmillan, 1882.

Campe, Rüdiger. *The Game of Probability: Literature and Calculation from Pascal to Kleist.* Translated by Ellwood Wiggins. Stanford, CA: Stanford University Press, 2012.

Canales, Jimena. "Sensational Differences: Individuality in Observation, Experimentation, and Representation (France 1853–1895)." Ph.D. diss., Harvard University, 2003.

———. *A Tenth of a Second: A History.* Chicago: University of Chicago Press, 2011.

Canquilhem, Georges. *The Normal and the Pathological.* Translated by Carolyn R. Fawcett. New York: Zone Books, 1991.

Cantor, Geoffrey, Gowan Dawson, Graeme Gooday, Richard Noakes, Sally Shuttleworth, and Jonathan R. Topham, eds. *Science in the Nineteenth-Century Periodical.* Cambridge: Cambridge University Press, 2004.

Cantor, Geoffrey, and Sally Shuttleworth, eds. *Science Serialized: Representations of the Sciences in Nineteenth-Century Periodicals.* Cambridge, MA: MIT Press, 2004.

Carpenter, William. *Mechanical Philosophy, Horology, and Astronomy.* London: W. S. Orr, 1844.

Carr, E. H. *The Idea of History.* London: Vintage, 1967.

Carroll, David, ed. *George Eliot: The Critical Heritage.* London: Routledge, 2009.

Caserio, Robert L., and Clement Hawes, eds. *The Cambridge History of the English Novel.* Cambridge: Cambridge University Press, 2012.

Cassirer, Ernst. *Substance and Function and Einstein's Theory of Relativity.* Translated by William Curtis Swabey and Marie Collins Swabey. London: Open Court, 1923.

Castle, Gregory. *Reading the Modernist Bildungsroman.* Gainesville: University Press of Florida, 2006.

Choi, Tina. "Natural History's Hypothetical Moments: Narratives of Contingency in Victorian Culture." *Victorian Studies* 51 (2009): 275–97.

Clagett, Marshall, ed. *Critical Problems in the History of Science: Proceedings of the Institute for the History of Science.* Madison: University of Wisconsin Press, 1959.

Clapperton, Jane Hume. *Scientific Meliorism and the Evolution of Happiness.* London: Kegan Paul, Trench, 1885.

Clark, Robert. "Riddling the Family Firm: The Sexual Economy in *Dombey and Son.*" *ELH* 51 (1984): 69–84.

Cleere, Eileen. *Avuncularism: Capitalism, Patriarchy, and Nineteenth-Century English Culture.* Stanford, CA: Stanford University Press, 2004.

Clifford, W. K. *Lectures and Essays.* Edited by Leslie Stephen and Frederick Pollock. 2 vols. London: Macmillan, 1879.

Cohn, Elisha. *Still Life: Suspended Development in the Victorian Novel.* New York: Oxford University Press, 2015.

Colebrook, Claire. "Queer Vitalism." *New Formations* 68 (2009): 77–91.

Collini, Stefan. *Public Moralists: Political Thought and Intellectual Life in Britain, 1850–1930.* Oxford: Clarendon, 1991.

Collins, Wilkie. *Armadale*. Edited by Catherine Peters. 2nd ed. New York: Oxford University Press, 1999.

———. *The Dead Secret*. Edited by Ira B. Nadel. New York: Oxford University Press, 1997.

———. *The Woman in White*. Edited by John Sutherland. New York: Oxford University Press, 2008.

Coole, Diana, and Samantha Frost, eds. *New Materialisms: Ontology, Agency, and Politics*. Durham, NC: Duke University Press, 2010.

Cronin, Helena. *The Ant and the Peacock: Altruism and Sexual Selection from Darwin to Today*. Cambridge: Cambridge University Press, 1993.

Crombie, A. C., ed. *Scientific Change: Historical Studies in the Intellectual, Social, and Technical Conditions for Scientific Discovery and Technical Invention*. New York: Basic Books, 1963.

Cross, J. W. *George Eliot's Life: As Related in Her Letters and Journals*. Edinburgh: Blackwood, 1885.

Dale, Peter Allen. *In Pursuit of a Scientific Culture: Science, Art, and Society in the Victorian Age*. Madison: University of Wisconsin Press, 1989.

Daly, Nicholas. "Railway Novels: Sensation Fiction and the Modernization of the Senses." *ELH* 66 (1999): 461–87.

Dames, Nicholas. *The Physiology of the Novel: Reading, Neural Science, and the Form of Victorian Fiction*. New York: Oxford University Press, 2007.

Dannenberg, Hillary P. *Coincidence and Counterfactuality: Plotting Time and Space in Narrative Fiction*. Lincoln: University of Nebraska Press, 2008.

Darwin, Charles. *Charles Darwin's Natural Selection, Being the Second Part of His Big Species Book Written from 1856–1858*. Edited by R. Stauffer. Cambridge: Cambridge University Press, 1975.

———. *Charles Darwin's Notebooks, 1836–1844: Geology, Transmutation of Species, Metaphysical Enquiries*. Edited by Paul H. Barrett, Peter J. Gautrey, Sandra Herbert, David Kohn, and Sydney Smith. Cambridge: Cambridge University Press, 1987.

———. *The Complete Work of Charles Darwin Online*. Edited by John van Wyhe. Accessed 10 October 2015, http://darwin-online.org.uk.

———. *The Correspondence of Charles Darwin*. Edited by Frederick Burkhardt et al. 26 vols. Cambridge: Cambridge University Press, 1985–2017.

———. *The Descent of Man, and Selection in Relation to Sex*. 2 vols. London: Murray, 1871.

———. *The Origin of Species: A Variorum Text*. Edited by Morse Peckham. Philadelphia: University of Pennsylvania Press, 1959.

Daston, Lorraine J. *Classical Probability in the Enlightenment*. Princeton, NJ: Princeton University Press, 1995.

Daston, Lorraine J., and Peter Galison. *Objectivity*. London: Zone Books, 2007.

Dawson, Gowan. *Darwin, Literature, and Victorian Respectability*. Cambridge: Cambridge University Press, 2007.

Dawson, Gowan, and Bernard Lightman, eds. *Victorian Scientific Naturalism: Community, Identity, Continuity*. Chicago: University of Chicago Press, 2014.

Deleuze, Gilles, and Félix Guattari. *Anti-Oedipus: Capitalism and Schizophrenia*. Translated by Robert Hurley, Mark Seem, and Helen R. Lane. Minneapolis: University of Minnesota Press, 1983.

Dellamora, Richard. *Friendship's Bonds: Democracy and the Novel in Victorian Britain*. Philadelphia: University of Pennsylvania Press, 2004.

De Moivre, Abraham. *The Doctrine of Chances*. London: Pearson, 1738.

De Morgan, Augustus. *An Essay on Probabilities*. London: Longman, 1838.

Desmond, Adrian, and James Moore. *Darwin: The Life of a Tormented Evolutionist*. New York: W. W. Norton, 1991.

Dickens, Charles. *Dombey and Son*. Edited by Andrew Sanders. New York: Penguin, 2002.

———. *Hard Times*. Edited by Paul Schlicke. New York: Oxford University Press, 2008.

———. *Martin Chuzzlewit*. Edited by Margaret Caldwell. Oxford: Clarendon, 1982.

———. *Master Humphrey's Clock*. 3 vols. London: Chapman and Hall, 1840–41.

Dinshaw, Carolyn. *How Soon Is Now? Medieval Texts, Amateur Readers, and the Queerness of Time*. Durham, NC: Duke University Press, 2012.

Dixon, Thomas. *The Invention of Altruism: Making Moral Meanings in Victorian Britain*. New York: Oxford University Press, 2008.

Dolezel, Lubomír. *Heterocosmica: Fiction and Possible Worlds*. Baltimore: Johns Hopkins University Press, 2000.

Donkin, Edwin. *The Midnight Sky: Familiar Notes on the Planets*. Cambridge: Cambridge University Press, 2010.

———. "On Some Peculiar Instances of Personal Equation in Zenith Distance Observations." *Memoirs of the Royal Astronomical Society*, vol. 34. London: Strangeways and Walden, 1866. 17–24.

Drummond, Henry. *The Lowell Lectures on the Ascent of Man*. London: Hodder and Stoughton, 1894.

Duncan, Ian. "George Eliot's Science Fiction." *Representations* 125 (2014): 15–39.

Eliot, George. *Adam Bede*. Edited by Carol A. Martin. New York: Oxford University Press, 2008.

———"Belles Lettres and Art." *Westminster Review* 67 (1856): 638–39.

———. *Daniel Deronda*. Edited by Graham Handley. Oxford: Clarendon, 1984.

———. *Essays of George Eliot*. Edited by Thomas Pinney. New York: Columbia University Press, 1963.

———. *George Eliot's "Daniel Deronda" Notebooks*. Edited by Jane Irwin. Cambridge: Cambridge University Press, 1996.

———. *Middlemarch*. Edited by David Carroll. Oxford: Clarendon, 1986.

———. "The Shaving of Shagpat." Review of *The Shaving of Shagpat*, by George Meredith. *Leader* 7 (1856): 13–17.

Ellis, Lorna. *Appearing to Diminish: Female Development and the British Bildungsroman, 1750–1850*. Lewisburg, PA: Bucknell University Press, 1999.

Ernst, Waltraud, ed. *Histories of the Normal and the Abnormal: Social and Cultural Histories of Norms and Normativity*. New York: Routledge, 2007.

Esty, Jed. *Unseasonable Youth: Modernism, Colonialism, and the Fiction of Development.* New York: Oxford University Press, 2012.

Felski, Rita. *Beyond Feminist Aesthetics: Feminist Literature and Social Change.* Cambridge, MA: Harvard University Press, 1989.

———. *The Limits of Critique.* Chicago: University of Chicago Press, 2015.

Ferguson, Niall, ed. *Virtual History: Counterfactuals and Alternatives.* New York: Basic Books, 2000.

Feynman, Richard. *The Character of Physical Law.* Cambridge, MA: MIT Press, 1965.

Fitzgerald, Percy. *The Life of Charles Dickens as Revealed in His Writings.* London: Chatto and Windus, 1905.

Fleishman, Avrom. *George Eliot's Intellectual Life.* Cambridge: Cambridge University Press, 2010.

Flood, Raymond, Mark McCartney, and Andrew Witaker, eds. *James Clerk Maxwell: Perspectives on His Life and Work.* New York: Oxford University Press, 2014.

Forman, Maurice. *A Bibliography of the Writings in Prose and Verse of George Meredith.* Edinburgh: Dundin, 1922.

Forster, E. M. *Aspects of the Novel.* Edited by Oliver Stallybrass. Harmondsworth: Penguin, 1976.

Foster, David E. "Rhetorical Strategy in *Richard Feverel.*" *Nineteenth-Century Fiction* 26 (1971): 185–95.

Foucault, Michel. *Abnormal: Lectures at the Collège de France, 1974–1975.* Translated by Graham Burchell. Edited by Valerio Marchetti and Antonella Salomoni. New York: Picador, 2003.

———. *Discipline and Punish: The Birth of the Prison.* Translated by Alan Sheridan. New York: Pantheon, 1977.

———. *Language, Counter-Memory, Practice: Selected Essays and Interviews.* Edited by D. F. Bouchard. Ithaca, NY: Cornell University Press, 1977.

———. *Security, Territory, Population: Lectures at the Collège de France 1977–1978.* Translated by Graham Burchell. Edited by Michel Senellart. New York: Picador, 2007.

Fraiman, Susan. *Unbecoming Women: British Women Writers and the Novel of Development.* New York: Columbia University Press, 1983.

François, Anne-Lise. *Open Secrets: The Literature of Uncounted Experience.* Stanford, CA: Stanford University Press, 2007.

Frederickson, Kathleen. *The Ploy of Instinct: Victorian Sciences of Nature and Sexuality in Liberal Governance.* New York: Fordham University Press, 2014.

Freedgood, Elaine. *Victorian Writing about Risk.* Cambridge: Cambridge University Press, 2001.

Freeman, Elizabeth. *Time Bends: Queer Temporalities, Queer Histories.* Durham, NC: Duke University Press, 2010.

Furneaux, Holly. *Queer Dickens: Erotics, Families, Masculinities.* New York: Oxford University Press, 2009.

Fyfe, Paul. *By Accident or Design: Writing the Victorian Metropolis.* New York: Oxford University Press, 2015.

Gallagher, Catherine. *The Body Economic: Life, Death, and Sensation in Political Economy and the Victorian Novel*. Princeton, NJ: Princeton University Press, 2008.

———. *The Industrial Reformation of English Fiction: Social Discourse and Narrative Form, 1832–1867*. Chicago: University of Chicago Press, 1988.

———. "What Would Napoleon Do? Historical, Fictional, and Counterfactual Characters." *New Literary History* 42 (2011): 315–36.

———. "When Did the Confederate States of America Free the Slaves?" *Representations* 98 (2007): 53–61.

Galperin, William. "Describing What Never Happened: Jane Austen and the History of Missed Opportunities." *ELH* 73 (2006): 355–82.

Galton, Francis. *Hereditary Genius: An Inquiry into Its Laws and Consequences*. London: Macmillan, 1869.

———. *Natural Inheritance*. London: Macmillan, 1889.

Garber, Elizabeth, Stephen G. Brush, and C. W. F. Everitt, eds. *Maxwell on Molecules and Gases*. Cambridge, MA: MIT Press, 1986.

Geddes, Patrick, and J. Arthur Thomson. *The Evolution of Sex*. London: Walter Scott, 1889.

Gibbs, J. Willard. *Elementary Principles in Statistical Mechanics*. New York: Scribner's, 1902.

Gigerenzer, Gerd, Zeno Swijtink, Theodore Porter, Lorraine Daston, John Beatty, and Lorenz Krüger. *The Empire of Chance: How Probability Changed Science and Everyday Life*. Cambridge: Cambridge University Press, 1989.

Gillham, Nicholas. *A Life of Sir Francis Galton*. New York: Oxford University Press, 2001.

Gold, Barri. *ThermoPoetics*. Cambridge, MA: MIT Press, 2011.

Goodlad, Lauren. *The Victorian Geopolitical Aesthetic: Realism, Sovereignty, and Transnational Experience*. New York: Oxford University Press, 2015.

Grabar, Terry. "'Scientific' Education and *Richard Feverel*." *Victorian Studies* 14 (1970): 129–41.

Greenberg, Robert A. "Plexuses and Ganglia: Scientific Allusion in *Middlemarch*." *Nineteenth-Century Fiction* 30 (1975): 33–52.

Griffiths, Devin. *The Age of Analogy: Science and Literature between the Darwins*. Baltimore: Johns Hopkins University Press, 2016.

Grosz, Elizabeth. *Time Travels: Feminism, Nature, Power*. Durham, NC: Duke University Press, 2005.

Hacking, Ian. *The Taming of Chance*. Cambridge: Cambridge University Press, 1990.

Hadley, Elaine. *Living Liberalism: Practical Citizenship in Mid-Victorian Britain*. Chicago: University of Chicago Press, 2010.

Hamilton, Ross. *Accident: A Philosophical and Literary History*. Chicago: University of Chicago Press, 2007.

Hampshire, Stuart. *Innocence and Experience*. Cambridge, MA: Harvard University Press, 1991.

Haraway, Donna. *Simians, Cyborgs, and Women: The Reinvention of Nature*. New York: Routledge, 1991.

Hardy, Thomas. *The Return of the Native*. Edited by Nancy Barrineau. New York: Oxford University Press, 2009.

———. *Two on a Tower.* Edited by Suleiman M. Ahmad. New York: Oxford University Press, 1999.

Harman, P. M. *Energy, Force, and Matter: The Conceptual Development of Nineteenth-Century Physics.* Cambridge: Cambridge University Press, 1982.

———. *Metaphysics and Natural Philosophy: The Problem of Substance in Classical Physics.* New York: Barnes and Noble Books, 1982.

———. *The Natural Philosophy of James Clerk Maxwell.* Cambridge: Cambridge University Press, 2001.

Harootunian, Harry. "Remembering the Historical Present." *Critical Inquiry* 33 (2007): 471–94.

Harrison, Kimberly, and Richard Fantina, eds. *Victorian Sensations: Essays on a Scandalous Genre.* Columbus: Ohio State University Press, 2006.

Hayles, N. Katherine. *Chaos Bound: Orderly Disorder in Contemporary Literature and Science.* Ithaca, NY: Cornell University Press, 1990.

———. *How We Became Posthuman: Virtual Bodies in Cybernetics, Literature, and Informatics.* Chicago: University of Chicago Press, 1999.

Hayot, Eric. *On Literary Worlds.* New York: Oxford University Press, 2012.

Hawthorn, Geoffrey. *Plausible Worlds: Possibility and Understanding in History and the Social Sciences.* Cambridge: Cambridge University Press, 1993.

Heidelberger, Michael, Lorenz Krüger, and Rosemarie Rheinward. *Probability since 1800: Interdisciplinary Studies of Scientific Development.* Bielefeld: B. Kleine Verlag, 1983.

Hemmo, Meir, and Orly R. Shenker. *The Road to Maxwell's Demon: Conceptual Foundations of Statistical Mechanics.* Cambridge: Cambridge University Press, 2012.

Hensley, Nathan K. "*Armadale* and the Logic of Liberalism." *Victorian Studies* 59 (2009): 607–32.

Herbert, Christopher. *Victorian Relativity: Radical Thought and Scientific Discovery.* Chicago: University of Chicago Press, 2001.

Herring, Paul D. "The Number Plans for *Dombey and Son:* Some Further Observations." *Modern Philology* 68 (1970): 151–87.

Herschel, John. *Essays from the Edinburgh and Quarterly Reviews, with Addresses and Other Pieces.* London: Longman, Brown, Green, Longmans, and Roberts, 1857.

———. "Quetelet on Probabilities." *Edinburgh Review* 92 (October 1850): 1–57.

Hesketh, Ian. *The Science of History in Victorian Britain.* London: Pickering and Chatto, 2011.

Hoffman, Christoph. "Constant Differences: Friedrich Wilhelm Bessel, the Concept of the Observer in Early Nineteenth-Century Practical Astronomy and the History of the Personal Equation." *British Journal for the History of Science* 40 (2007): 333–65.

Hughes, Winifred. *Maniac in the Cellar: Sensation Novels of the 1860s.* Princeton, NJ: Princeton University Press, 1980.

Hutton, Richard Holt. *Criticisms on Contemporary Thought and Thinkers: Selected from "The Spectator."* 2 vols. London: Macmillan, 1894.

Huxley, Leonard, ed. *Life and Letters of Thomas H. Huxley.* 2 vols. New York: Appleton, 1901.

Huxley, T. H. *Collected Essays.* 9 vols. London: Macmillan, 1893–95.

———. *Lay Sermons, Addresses, and Reviews.* London: Macmillan, 1870.

Inman, Billie. *Walter Pater and His Reading, 1874–1877, with a Bibliography of His Library Borrowings, 1878–1894.* New York: Garland, 1990.

Jaffe, Audrey. *The Affective Life of the Average Man.* Columbus: Ohio State University Press, 2010.

———. *Scenes of Sympathy: Identity and Representation in Victorian Fiction.* Ithaca, NY: Cornell University Press, 2000.

James, Henry. *The Novels and Tales of Henry James.* New York ed. 24 vols. New York: Scribner's, 1908.

Jameson, Fredric. *The Political Unconscious: Narrative as Socially Symbolic Act.* Ithaca, NY: Cornell University Press, 1982.

Jastrow, Joseph. *The Time-Relations of Mental Phenomena.* New York: N. D. C. Hodges, 1890.

Jenkins, Alice. *Space and the "March of Mind."* New York: Oxford University Press, 2007.

Johnson, Curtis. *Darwin's Dice: The Idea of Chance in the Thought of Charles Darwin.* Cambridge: Cambridge University Press, 2014.

Jones, Anna Maria. "Conservation of Energy, Individual Agency, and Gothic Terror in Richard Marsh's *The Beetle,* or, What's Scarier Than an Ancient, Evil, Shape-Shifting Bug?" *Victorian Literature and Culture* 39 (2011): 65–85.

———. *Problem Novels: Victorian Fiction Theorizes the Sensational Self.* Columbus: Ohio State University Press, 2007.

Jones, Bence. *The Life and Letters of Michael Faraday.* 2 vols. London: Longmans, 1870.

Keller, Evelyn Fox. *Reflections on Gender and Science.* New Haven, CT: Yale University Press, 1995.

Kent, Christopher. "The Average Victorian: Constructing and Contesting Reality." *Browning Institute Studies* 17 (1989): 41–52.

Kern, Stephen. *The Culture of Time and Space, 1880–1918.* Cambridge, MA: Harvard University Press, 1983.

Kirby, William, and William Spence. *An Introduction to Entomology: Or Elements of the Natural History of Insects.* 2 vols. London: Longman, 1826.

Knoepflmacher, U. C. *Laughter and Despair: Readings in Ten Novels of the Victorian Era.* Berkeley: University of California Press, 1973.

———. "*Middlemarch:* An Avuncular View." *Nineteenth-Century Fiction* 30 (1975): 53–81.

———. *Religious Humanism and the Victorian Novel.* Princeton, NJ: Princeton University Press, 1965.

Kohn, David, ed. *The Darwinian Heritage.* Princeton, NJ: Princeton University Press, 1985.

Koselleck, Reinhart. *Futures Past: On the Semantics of Historical Time.* Translated by Keith Tribe. Cambridge, MA: MIT Press, 1985.

Kripke, Saul A. *Naming and Necessity.* Cambridge, MA: Harvard University Press, 1980.

Kropotkin, Peter. *Mutual Aid: A Factor in Evolution.* Harmondsworth: Penguin, 1939.

Krüger, Lorenz, Lorraine Daston, Gerd Gigerenzer, Michael Heidelberger, and Mary S. Morgan, eds. *The Probabilistic Revolution*. 2 vols. Cambridge, MA: MIT Press, 1987.

Kuhn, Thomas. *The Structure of Scientific Revolutions*. Chicago: University of Chicago Press, 1962.

Laplace, Pierre-Simon. *Philosophical Essay on Probabilities*. Translated by F. W. Truscott and F. L. Emory. New York: Wiley, 1902.

Latour, Bruno. *Reassembling the Social: An Introduction to Actor-Network-Theory*. Oxford: Oxford University Press, 2005.

Leavis, F. R. *Two Cultures? The Significance of C. P. Snow*. Cambridge: Cambridge University Press, 2013.

Lee, Maurice S. *Uncertain Chances: Science, Skepticism, and Belief in Nineteenth-Century American Literature*. New York: Oxford University Press, 2012.

Levine, Caroline. *Forms: Whole, Rhythm, Hierarchy, Network*. Princeton, NJ: Princeton University Press, 2015.

———. *The Serious Pleasures of Suspense*. Charlottesville: University of Virginia Press, 2003.

Levine, George. *Darwin and the Novelists: Patterns of Science in Victorian Fiction*. Chicago: University of Chicago Press, 1988.

———. *Dying to Know: Scientific Epistemology and Narrative in Victorian England*. Chicago: University of Chicago Press, 2002.

———. "George Eliot's Hypothesis of Reality." *Nineteenth-Century Fiction* 35 (1980): 1–28.

———, ed. *One Culture: Essays on Science and Literature*. Madison: University of Wisconsin Press, 1987.

Lewes, George Henry. "Mr. Buckle's Scientific Errors." *Blackwood's Edinburgh Magazine* 90 (1861): 582–96.

———. *Problems of Life and Mind*. 2 vols. London: Trübner, 1874.

Lightman, Bernard. *The Origins of Agnosticism*. Baltimore: Johns Hopkins University Press, 1987.

———. *Victorian Popularizers of Science: Designing Nature for New Audiences*. Chicago: University of Chicago Press, 2010.

Lloyd-Jones, Hugh, Valerie Pearl, and Blair Worden, eds. *History and Imagination: Essays in Honor of H. R. Trevor-Roper*. London: Duckworth, 1981.

Locke, John. *An Essay Concerning Human Understanding*. Edited by Peter Nidditch. Oxford: Oxford University Press, 1979.

Lohrli, Anne, ed. *Household Words: A Weekly Journal, 1850–1859*. Toronto: University of Toronto Press, 1973.

Love, Heather. *Feeling Backward: Loss and the Politics of Queer History*. Cambridge, MA: Harvard University Press, 2007.

Lubbock, John, and John Drinkwater. *On Probability*. London: Baldwin and Cradock, 1830.

Lucretius. *On the Nature of Things*. Translated by H. A. J. Munro. 2 vols. Cambridge: Deighton Bell, 1864.

Lukács, Georg. *The Historical Novel*. Translated by Hannah Mitchell and Stanley Mitchell. Lincoln: University of Nebraska Press, 1962.

―――. *The Theory of the Novel: A Historico-Philosophical Essay on the Forms of Great Epic Literature.* Translated by Anna Bostock. Cambridge, MA: MIT Press, 1971.

―――. *Writer and Critic and Other Essays.* Translated and edited by Arthur Kahn. London: Merlin, 1970.

MacDuffie, Allan. *Victorian Literature, Energy, and the Ecological Imagination.* Cambridge: Cambridge University Press, 2014.

Macpherson, Sandra. *Harm's Way: Tragic Responsibility and the Novel Form.* Baltimore: Johns Hopkins University Press, 2009.

Mao, Douglas. *Fateful Beauty: Aesthetic Environments, Juvenile Development, and Literature, 1860–1960.* Princeton, NJ: Princeton University Press, 2008.

Marcus, Sharon. *Between Women: Friendship, Desire, and Marriage in Victorian England.* Princeton, NJ: Princeton University Press, 2007.

Marx, Karl, and Friedrich Engels. *The German Ideology.* Edited by C. J. Arthur. New York: International, 1970.

Mason, Michael York. "*Middlemarch* and Science: Problems of Life and Mind." *Review of English Studies* 22 (1971): 151–69.

Maudsley, Henry. *The Physiology and Psychology of the Mind.* London: Routledge, 1993.

Maxwell, James Clerk. "Diffusion." In *Encyclopedia Britannica,* 9th ed. Edinburgh: A. and C. Black, 1875.

―――."Notes of the President's Address." *Blackwood's Edinburgh Magazine* 116 (1874): 583.

―――. "On the Dynamical Theory of Gases." *Philosophical Transactions of the Royal Society of London* 157 (1867): 49–88.

―――. *The Scientific Letters and Papers of James Clerk Maxwell.* Edited by P. M. Harman. 2 vols. Cambridge: Cambridge University Press, 1990–95.

―――. *The Scientific Papers of James Clerk Maxwell.* Edited by W. D. Niven. 2 vols. New York: Dover, 1890.

―――. *Theory of Heat.* 4th ed. London: Longmans, Green, 1875.

Mayr, Ernst. *The Growth of Biological Thought: Diversity, Evolution, and Inheritance.* Cambridge, MA: Harvard University Press, 1982.

Menke, Richard. "Fiction as Vivisection: G. H. Lewes and George Eliot." *ELH* 67 (2000): 617–53.

Meredith, George. *The Ordeal of Richard Feverel: A History of Father and Son.* Edited by Edward Mendelson. New York: Penguin, 1999.

Merrill, Lynn L. *The Romance of Victorian Natural History.* Oxford: Oxford University Press, 1989.

Mill, John Stuart. *Collected Works of John Stuart Mill.* Edited by J. M. Robson. 19 vols. Toronto: University of Toronto Press, 1963.

Miller, Andrew H. *The Burdens of Perfection: On Ethics and Reading in Nineteenth-Century British Literature.* Ithaca, NY: Cornell University Press, 2008.

Miller, D. A. *Narrative and Its Discontents: Problems of Closure in the Traditional Novel.* Princeton, NJ: Princeton University Press, 1981.

―――. *The Novel and the Police.* Berkeley: University of California Press, 1988.

Miller, Elizabeth. *Slow Print: Literary Radicalism and Late-Victorian Print Culture*. Stanford, CA: Stanford University Press, 2013.

Molesworth, Jesse. *Chance and the Eighteenth-Century Novel: Realism, Probability, Magic*. Cambridge: Cambridge University Press, 2010.

Monk, Leland. *Standard Deviations: Chance and the Modern British Novel*. Stanford, CA: Stanford University Press, 1993.

Moretti, Franco, ed. *The Novel*. 2 vols. Princeton, NJ: Princeton University Press, 2006.

———. *The Way of the World: The Bildungsroman in European Culture*. London: Verso, 1987.

Morris, John W. "Inherent Principles of Order in *The Ordeal of Richard Feverel*." *PMLA* 78 (1963): 333–40.

Morton, Timothy. *Hyperobjects: Philosophy and Ecology after the End of the World*. Minneapolis: University of Minnesota Press, 2013.

Morus, Iwan. *When Physics Became King*. Chicago: University of Chicago Press, 2005.

Mueller, William R. "Theological Dualism and the 'System' in *Richard Feverel*." *ELH* 18 (1951): 138–54.

Müller, Johannes. *Elements of Physiology*. Translated by William Baly. 2 vols. London: Taylor and Walton, 1838.

Newton, Isaac. *The Principia: Mathematical Principles of Natural Philosophy*. Translated by I. Bernard Cohen, Anne Whitman, and Julia Budenz. Berkeley: University of California Press, 1999.

North, Michael. *Novelty: A History of the New*. Chicago: University of Chicago Press, 2015.

Nye, Mary Jo, ed. *The Cambridge History of Science*. Vol. 5, *The Modern Physical and Mathematical Sciences*. Cambridge: Cambridge University Press, 2002.

Ospovat, Dov. *The Development of Darwin's Theory, 1838–1859*. Cambridge: Cambridge University Press, 1981.

Paley, William. *Principles of Moral and Political Philosophy*. Indianapolis: Liberty Fund, 2012.

Pandora, Katherine. "Knowledge Held in Common: Tales of Luther Burbank and Science in the American Vernacular." *Isis* 92 (2001): 484–516.

Pater, Walter. "The Poems of William Morris." *Westminster Review* 150 (1868): 300–312.

———. *The Renaissance: Studies in Art and Poetry*. Edited by Donald L. Hill. Berkeley: University of California Press, 1980.

Patey, Douglas. *Probability and Literary Form: Philosophic Theory and Literary Practice in the Augustan Age*. Cambridge: Cambridge University Press, 1984.

Pattison, Mark. "*The History of Civilization in England*." Review of *History of Civilization in England*, by Henry Thomas Buckle. *Westminster Review* 68 (1857): 375–99.

Pavel, Thomas G. *Fictional Worlds*. Cambridge, MA: Harvard University Press, 1989.

Pearson, Karl. *The Grammar of Science*. London: Adam and Charles Black, 1892.

Pierce, Charles S. *Writings of Charles S. Pierce: A Chronological Edition*. Edited by Pierce Edition Project. 8 vols. Bloomington: Indiana University Press, 1982–2010.

Pond, John. *Astronomical Observations Made at the Royal Observatory at Greenwich in the Year 1832*. Part 5, *Supplement*. London: T. Bensley, 1833.

Poovey, Mary. *A History of the Modern Fact*. Chicago: University of Chicago Press, 1998.

Porter, Theodore. *The Rise of Statistical Thinking, 1820–1900*. Princeton, NJ: Princeton University Press, 1986.

———. "A Statistical Survey of Gases: Maxwell's Social Physics." *Historical Studies in the Physical Sciences* 12 (1981): 77–116.

Priestley, Joseph. *The Doctrine of Philosophical Necessity Illustrated*. London: J. Johnson, 1777.

Purrington, Robert D. *Physics in the Nineteenth Century*. New Brunswick, NJ: Rutgers University Press, 1997.

Puskar, Jason. *Accident Society: Fiction, Collectivity, and the Production of Chance*. Stanford, CA: Stanford University Press, 2012.

Pykett, Lyn. "*Dombey and Son*: A Sentimental Family Romance." *Studies in the Novel* 19 (1986): 16–30.

Quetelet, Adolphe. *A Treatise on Man and His Faculties*. Edinburgh: Chambers, 1842.

Richards, Robert J. *Darwin and the Emergence of Evolutionary Theories of Mind and Behavior*. Chicago: University of Chicago Press, 1987.

Ricoeur, Paul. *Time and Narrative*. Translated by Kathleen McLaughlin and David Pellauer, 2 vols. Chicago: University of Chicago Press, 1984.

Rieber, Robert, and David K. Robinson, eds. *Wilhelm Wundt in History*. New York: Kluwer Academic, 2001.

Roberts, M. J. D. "Morals, Art, and the Law: The Passing of the Obscene Publications Act, 1857." *Victorian Studies* 28 (1985): 609–29.

Ronen, Ruth. *Possible Worlds in Literary Theory*. Cambridge: Cambridge University Press, 1994.

Rosenthal, Jesse. *Good Form: The Ethical Experience of the Victorian Novel*. Princeton, NJ: Princeton University Press, 2016.

Rothfield, Lawrence. *Vital Signs: Medical Realism in Nineteenth-Century Fiction*. Princeton, NJ: Princeton University Press, 1994.

Ruse, Michael, and Robert J. Richards. *The Cambridge Companion to the "Origin of Species."* Cambridge: Cambridge University Press, 2009.

Ryan, Marie-Laure. *Possible Worlds, Artificial Intelligence, and Narrative Theory*. Bloomington: University of Indiana Press, 1994.

Rylance, Rick. *Victorian Psychology and British Culture, 1850–1880*. New York: Oxford University Press, 2000.

Sadoff, Diane. *Monsters of Affection: Dickens, Eliot, and Bronte on Fatherhood*. Baltimore: Johns Hopkins University Press, 1982.

Sadrin, Amy. *Parentage and Inheritance in the Novels of Charles Dickens*. Cambridge: Cambridge University Press, 1994.

Schaffer, Simon. "Astronomers Mark Time: Discipline and the Personal Equation." *Science in Context* 2 (1988): 116–19.

Schmidgen, Henning. *The Helmholtz Curves: Tracing Lost Time*. New York: Fordham University Press, 2014.

Schmitt, Cannon. "Interpret or Describe?" *Representations* 135 (2016): 102–18.

Schor, Hilary. *Dickens and the Daughter of the House.* Cambridge: Cambridge University Press, 1999.

Schreiner, Olive. *The Story of an African Farm.* Edited by Joseph Bristow. New York: Oxford University Press, 1999.

Schweber, S. S. "John Herschel and Charles Darwin: A Study of Parallel Lives." *Journal of the History of Biology* 22 (1989): 1–71.

Sedgwick, Eve. *Touching Feeling: Affect, Pedagogy, Performativity.* Durham, NC: Duke University Press, 2003.

Shuttleworth, Sally. *George Eliot and Nineteenth-Century Science: The Make-Believe of a Beginning.* Cambridge: Cambridge University Press, 1984.

———. *The Mind of the Child: Child Development in Literature, Science, and Medicine, 1840–1900.* New York: Oxford University Press, 2011.

Slaughter, Joseph R. *Human Rights, Inc.: The World Novel, Narrative Form, and International Law.* New York: Fordham University Press, 2007.

Small, Helen, and Trudi Tate, eds. *Literature, Science, Psychoanalysis, 1830–1970.* New York: Oxford University Press, 2003.

Smith, Crosbie. *The Science of Energy: A Cultural History of Energy Physics in Victorian Britain.* Chicago: University of Chicago Press, 1998.

Smith, Crosbie, and N. Norton Wise. *Energy and Empire: A Biographical Study of Lord Kelvin.* Cambridge: Cambridge University Press, 1989.

Snyder, Katherine V. *Bachelors, Manhood, and the Novel, 1850–1925.* Cambridge: Cambridge University Press, 1999.

Somerville, Mary. *On the Connexion of the Physical Sciences.* London: Murray, 1834.

Somkin, Fred. "The Contributions of Sir John Lubbock, F.R.S. to the *Origin of Species*: Some Annotations to Darwin." *Notes and Records of the Royal Society of London* 17 (1962): 183–91.

Spanberg, Sven-Johan. "The Theme of Sexuality in *The Ordeal of Richard Feverel.*" *Studia Neophilologica* 46 (1974): 202–24.

Stack, David. *The First Darwinian Left: Socialism and Darwinism, 1859–1914.* Cheltenham: New Clarion, 2003.

Stephen, James Fitzjames. "Buckle's History of Civilization in England." Review of *History of Civilization in England,* by Henry Thomas Buckle. *Blackwood's Edinburgh Review* 107 (1858): 465–512.

———. "The Study of History." *Cornhill Magazine* 3 (1861): 666–80.

Stephen, Leslie. *The Science of Ethics.* London: Smith, Elder, 1882.

Stevenson, Richard C. *The Experimental Impulse in the Novels of George Meredith.* Lewisburg, PA: Bucknell University Press, 2004.

Stewart, Balfour. *The Conservation of Energy: Being an Elementary Treatise on Energy and Its Laws.* London: Henry S. King, 1873.

Stewart, Balfour, and William Tait. *The Unseen Universe.* London: Macmillan, 1875.

Stewart, Garrett. *Novel Violence: A Narrotography of Victorian Fiction.* Chicago: University of Chicago, 2009.

Stone, Donald D. *Novelists in a Changing World*. Cambridge, MA: Harvard University Press, 1972.

Sully, James. *Sensation and Intuition: Studies in Psychology and Aesthetics*. London: H. S. King, 1874.

Taine, Hippolyte. *On Intelligence*. Translated by T. D. Haye. London: Reeve, 1871.

Tait, Peter Guthrie. *Lectures on Some Recent Advances in Physical Science, with a Special Lecture on Force*. London: Macmillan, 1876.

Tambling, Jeremy. "*Middlemarch*, Realism, and the Birth of the Clinic." *ELH* 57 (1990): 939–69.

Taylor, Jenny Bourne. *In the Secret Theatre of Home*. New York: Oxford University Press, 1987.

Tondre, Michael. "The Impassive Novel: 'Brain-Building' in Walter Pater's *Marius the Epicurean*." *PMLA* 133 (forthcoming).

Turner, Frank. *Contesting Cultural Authority: Essays in Victorian Intellectual Life*. Cambridge: Cambridge University Press, 1993.

Tyndall, John. *Fragments of Science for Unscientific People: A Series of Detached Essays, Lectures, and Reviews*. 2 vols. London: Longmans, Green, 1871.

———. *Heat Considered as a Mode of Motion: Being a Course of Twelve Lectures Delivered at the Royal Institution of Great Britain in the Season of 1862*. New York: Appleton, 1863.

Venn, John. *The Logic of Chance: An Essay on the Foundations and Province of the Theory of Probability*. London: Macmillan, 1866.

Vicinus, Martha. *Intimate Friends: Women Who Loved Women, 1778–1928*. Chicago: University of Chicago Press, 2004.

Wallace, Alfred Russel. *Letters and Reminiscences*. Edited by James Marchant. 2 vols. London: Cassell, 1916.

Warwick, Andrew. *Masters of Theory: Cambridge and the Rise of Mathematical Physics*. Chicago: University of Chicago Press, 2003.

Wells, H. G. *"The Time Machine" and "The Island of Doctor Moreau."* Edited by Patrick Parrinder. New York: Oxford University Press, 1996.

White, Hayden. *Metahistory: The Historical Imagination in Nineteenth-Century Europe*. Baltimore: Johns Hopkins University Press, 1973.

Wiener, Norbert. *The Human Use of Human Beings: Cybernetics and Society*. Rev. ed. Boston: Houghton Mifflin, 1954.

Williams, Ioan, ed. *Meredith: The Critical Heritage*. New York: Barnes and Noble, 1973.

Williams, Raymond. *The Country and the City*. New York: Oxford University Press, 1975.

Winter, Alison. *Mesmerized: Powers of Mind in Victorian Britain*. Chicago: University of Chicago Press, 1998.

Woloch, Alex. *The One vs. the Many: Minor Characters and the Space of the Protagonist in the Novel*. Princeton, NJ: Princeton University Press, 2004.

Wright, Walter. *Art and Substance in George Meredith*. New York: Greenwood, 1980.

Yeo, Richard. *Defining Science: William Whewell, Natural Knowledge and Public Debate in Early Victorian Britain*. Cambridge: Cambridge University Press, 1993.

Youmans, Edward L., ed. *The Correlation and Conservation of Forces: A Series of Expositions by Prof. Grove, Prof. Helmholtz, Dr. Mayer, Dr. Faraday, Prof. Liebig and Dr. Carpenter.* New York: Appleton, 1865.

Young, Kay. *Imagining Minds: The Neuro-Aesthetics of Austen, Eliot, and Hardy.* Columbus: Ohio State University Press, 2010.

Zeitz, Lisa M., and Peter Thoms. "Collins's Use of the Strasbourg Clock in *Armadale.*" *Nineteenth-Century Literature* 45 (1991): 495–503.

Zemka, Sue. *Time and the Moment in Victorian Literature and Society.* Cambridge: Cambridge University Press, 2012.

Zola, Émile. *Oeuvres Complètes.* Edited by Menri Mitterand. 15 vols. Paris: Cercle du Livre Précieux, 1969.

Index

Abbott, Edwin, *Flatland,* 171
Acton, John, 39, 183n20
Acton, William, 42, 46, 52
adoptive attachments, 5, 111, 116, 120
aestheticism, 7, 15, 59, 63, 83, 163, 194n5;
    aesthetic formalism, 127–29
Airy, John, 66, 70
Allen, Grant, 25
alternative masculinities, 5, 17; in *Richard
    Feverel,* 42
alternative kinship networks, 123, 192n43
alternative possibilities, 2, 4, 10, 29, 52,
    139, 152, 166. *See also* counterfactuals
    and counterlives; nonhappenings; time
    and temporality
altruism, 95–96, 103–4, 110, 113, 122,
    189n3
Aristotle, 59–60
Armadale (Collins), 14, 61–94, 167; com-
    pared with *Dombey and Son,* 114;
    compared with *Middlemarch,* 147, 159;
    compared with *Richard Feverel,* 86, 89;
    composition and publication in install-
    ments of, 75–76; dream as plot vehicle
    in, 84–85, 189n59; ensemble effects
    in, 60, 93; hero's hesitation in, 14, 16,
    62, 75, 83–84, 86–87, 91; hesitation of
    Lydia Gwilt in, 87–88, 90, 92; inward-
    ness and masculinity in, 77–78, 85–87;
    irresolution as attribute of male novel-
    ist in, 93–94; mathematical models of
    time in, 80; postponement in, 72–75,

77, 90–91; multiple temporalities in,
    62, 73, 78–79, 80, 82–84, 86, 88, 90,
    92–93, 129, 169, 185n4; narrative res-
    olution in, 93; negated potential and,
    43, 64, 86; nonreproduction in, 147
Armstrong, Nancy, 131
Arnold, Matthew, 128–29, 163, 194nn5–6;
    "Literature and Science," 194n6
artificial selection, 104–5
astronomers and astronomy, 14, 32, 62,
    64–66, 152, 168, 185n3; astronomer's
    error law, 33, 65, 135, 158–59, 169
atomism, 132, 134–35, 141–42, 153–55,
    170
Austen, Jane, 72
average man, 23, 34, 137, 167–69, 182n10

Babbage, Charles, 10, 99, 162; *Ninth
    Bridgewater Treatise,* 10, 20–21, 34
bachelors, 96, 110, 114, 122–23, 169,
    190n5, 192n43
Bagehot, Walter, 39
Baily, Francis, 80
Bain, Alexander, 68, 73; *The Senses and the
    Intellect,* 67
Barad, Karen, 8
Barrett Browning, Elizabeth, 5
Barthes, Roland, 11, 51
Bayes, Thomas, 32
Beer, Gillian, 106, 170, 192n36
Benjamin, Walter, 61
Bennett, Jane, 5

Bergson, Henri, 172

Berkeley, George, 3, 21

Berlant, Lauren, 63, 188–89n57

Bernoulli, Jacob, 32

Bessel, Friedrich, 64–66, 70

Bethune, John Elliot Drinkwater, 34, 184n2; *On Probability,* 52

Bichat, Marie François Xavier, 154

bildungsroman: as experimental construct, 4, 6, 16, 30, 42, 108, 113, 131, 144, 161, 167, 176n14, 188n43, 199n64; Goethean tradition of, 26, 108; juvenile maturation and, 26–27, 47; Victorian tropes of, 6, 26–27, 46, 129, 167. *See also* connections between physical sciences, mathematics, and fiction; counterfactuals and counterlives; digressions and deviance in narrative; realism; Victorian novels

Bloch, Ernst, 27

Bohr, Niels, 171

Boltzmann, Ludwig, 136

Boole, George, 135

Boring, Edward, 185n3

British Association for the Advancement of Science, 20, 99, 134, 140

Brody, Selma B., 155

Brontë, Charlotte, 6, 27; *Villette,* 49, 170

Brontë, Emily, 27

Brooks, Peter, 5, 16, 152

Brown, Daniel, 140, 142, 198n51

Buckle, Henry: on "average man," 165, 167, 168; Darwin and, 39; Eliot and, 39, 135, 137–38; *History of Civilization in England,* 13, 38–39, 99, 134, 135; Maxwell and, 135–38, 169, 180n63, 194n4; on Napoleon, 40; Victorian critiques of, 41, 166, 169

Burney, Frances, 55

Butler, Judith, 56

Cambridge Apostles, 138, 175n4

Campbell, John, 54

Canales, Jimena, 68, 185n3

Carnot, Sadie, 19

Carpenter, Edward, 192n30

Carpenter, William, 5, 66–67, 70; *Mechanical Philosophy, Horology, and Astronomy,* 66

Carr, E. H., 172

Cassirer, Ernst, 171

Cavendish Laboratory (Cambridge), 8, 12, 20, 138

censorship, 26, 30

chance, 9–10, 31–33, 166; chance variation, 98–100, 103, 105, 108; Darwinism and, 14, 98–99, 191n20; doctrine of chances vs. calculus of probabilities, 31–33; Herschel on, 35; religious accounts of, 34; risk management, 177n20; subjective view of chance, 33. *See also* determinism; indeterminism; probabilistic thinking

chaos and complexity theory, 172

Choi, Tina, 98, 101

Clapperton, Jane Hume, 123

Clarendon Laboratory (Oxford), 128

Clark, J. C. D., 44

class relations, 27, 116

Clausius, Rudolf, 19, 132–33, 134, 136

Clay, E. R., 172

Cleere, Eileen, 190n5

Clifford, William, 5, 9, 23, 24, 74, 137, 177n25; compared with North British scientists, 197–98n48

Cohen, I. Bernard, 2–3

Cohn, Elisha, 6, 74, 180–81n70, 182n2

Colebrook, Claire, 17

Collins, Wilkie, 6, 16; as antibourgeois bohemian, 17; *The Dead Secret,* 74; *The Moonstone,* 75; personal motto of, 61, 62; postponement in fiction of, 62, 75; scientific professionals in novels of, 25; visiting Strasbourg clock, 81; *The Woman in White,* 75. See also *Armadale*

coming of age. *See* bildungsroman; maturation

compassionate marriage plot, 16, 170. *See also* marriage in Victorian novels

Connolly, Joseph, 88
connections between physical sciences, mathematics, and fiction, 8, 12–13, 166, 177–78n27, 181n71; British intellectual commons and, 17, 25, 106, 166, 180n68; Eliot's understanding of, 128, 129, 137, 162–63; energy science and, 132; "trails of associations" and, 40
conservation, law of, 132, 154
Coole, Diana, 172
Cornhill Magazine, 39, 41, 76
counterfactuals and counterlives, 4, 7–8, 12–13, 30, 35, 39–40, 42–52, 117, 139, 161, 166, 170
Cronin, Helena, 96, 189n3

Daly, Nicholas, 61
Dames, Nicholas, 185n2
Dannenberg, Hillary P., 48
Darwin, Charles, 95–106; on accidental change, 101; on altruism and self-sacrifice, 95–96, 103–4, 189–90n3; Buckle and, 39; on chance variation, 5, 98–100, 103, 105, 191n20; on connection between sciences of life and matter, 97; *The Descent of Man,* 97, 99–100, 103, 105, 117; Dickens and, 14–15, 105–6, 115, 117, 169, 191n25, 192n36, 192n43; *The Expression of the Emotions in Man and Animals,* 117; Herschel and, 10, 99, 102, 135, 169; Huxley on Darwinian chance, 100, 123; on individual struggle in theory of natural selection, 102; on moral transformation, 123; on nonreproduction and sterility, 95–96, 103–5, 190n3, 191–92n30; *On the Origin of Species,* 95, 98, 101–2, 104, 105; Paley and, 102; Wallace and, 189n2
Daston, Lorraine J., 68, 93
Defoe, Daniel, 26, 48, 129; *Robinson Crusoe,* 108
delay. *See* slowness and postponement
Deleuze, Gilles, 131

de Moivre, Abraham, *The Doctrine of Chances,* 32
De Morgan, Augustus, 34, 36–38, 43, 52, 64, 99, 137, 162, 182n15; *Essay on Probabilities,* 36; *Treatise on Probability,* 36
Descartes, René, 3
Desmond, Adrian, 105
determinism: defense of, 139; historical, 11, 38; ontological, 142; rejection of, 19, 39, 139
Dickens, Charles: avuncular bachelors in novels of, 122–25, 169, 190n5, 192n43; *Barnaby Rudge,* 107; *Bleak House,* 115; *Christmas Stories,* 44; *David Copperfield,* 75, 124; Darwin and, 14–15, 105–6, 115, 117, 169, 191n25, 192n36, 192n43; *Household Words* (magazine), 106; *Little Dorrit,* 115; *Martin Chuzzlewit,* 106, 107; *Nicholas Nickleby,* 124, 192n43; physical sciences and, 25; visit to Strasbourg clock, 81; *A Tale of Two Cities,* 192n43; on unconventional family structures, 17. See also *Dombey and Son*
diffusion: acceptance of Maxwell's work on, 16, 136, 163; diffusive reading, 128, 162; law of universal diffusion, 126–27, 129, 132, 143; in *Middlemarch,* 16, 126–29, 144–63; redemptive diffusion in Victorian culture, 137–44, 151, 160–61, 163; salutary outcomes of, 133, 139, 149
digressions and deviance in narrative, 5, 11, 111–12, 149, 165. *See also* counterfactuals and counterlives
Dinshaw, Carolyn, 63
Dixon, Thomas, 96, 189n3
Dombey and Son (Dickens), 105–25; adoptive arrangements in, 111, 116, 120; altruism in, 110, 113, 122; autobiographical form of, 124; bachelors in, 96, 110, 114, 122–25; chance variation and, 108; communal evolution in, 16, 106, 107–25, 167; compared with *Armadale,* 114; compared with *Middlemarch,* 147, 159; compared with *Richard Feverel,*

Dombey and Son (*continued*)
114; competition in, 105, 107, 110,
112–13, 122, 123; Darwinism and, 15,
115, 169; Dick Whittington story, allusions to, 114–15, 192n44; egoism in,
96, 102, 107, 112, 114, 118, 169; moral
transformation in, 116–19; masculinity
in, 112; reproduction and nonreproduction in, 107, 109, 110–15, 122,
124–25, 147; writing plan for, 107
Donders, Franciscus, 71
Drinkwater, John Eliot, 34, 184n42; *On
Probability*, 52
Drummond, Henry, 123

Edgeworth, Francis, 5
Edinburgh Review subjects (1850s), 10, 35,
39, 177–78n27
egoism: in *Dombey and Son*, 96, 102, 107,
112, 114, 118; in *Middlemarch*, 144, 145,
147, 163
Einstein, Albert, 171
Eliot, George: *Adam Bede*, 143, 144; Arnold
and, 194n5; Buckle and, 39, 135, 137–38;
criticism of, 199n79; *Daniel Deronda*,
143–44, 163, 198–99n64; energy science
and, 132, 133; on entropy, 195n10; on
fiction's diffusive influence, 16; on
fiction's nonutilitarian value, 16; "A
Fine Excess: Feeling Is Energy," 129–30,
134, 140; Grove and, 132; *Impressions of
Theophrastus Such*, 163; Jenkin's article
about Lucretius and, 197n46; Maxwell
and, 134–44, 163, 200n85; Meredith and,
41, 129; *Mill on the Floss*, 49; resistance
to classical bildungsroman, 6, 131;
scientific interests of, 10, 127; scientific
professionals in novels of, 25, 155; *The
Spanish Gypsy*, 130; sympathetic feeling
and, 127, 130; thermodynamics and,
144; on unproductive expenditures of
characters, 130–31. See also *Middlemarch*
energy science, 19, 22, 23, 129–37,
193–94n2, 194n7, 195n10, 195n15; dis-

tinction between "force" and "energy,"
133–34; Faraday on distribution of
forces in, 140; Maxwell's application of
probabilistic thinking to, 134–36, 138;
natural philosophers on, 147; statistical
studies of energy, 134
Engels, Friedrich, 27
Enlightenment, 3, 129, 172
ensemble effects: in *Armadale*, 60, 93, 167;
in *Dombey and Son*, 167; Maxwell and,
171; meaning of, 11, 23; in *Middlemarch*, 167; in *Richard Feverel*, 45, 167;
statistical ensemble and, 11, 170–71; in
Victorian novels, 11–12, 167
entropy law (second law of thermodynamics), 15, 132–33, 135, 148, 194n7.
See also diffusion
epic literature, 16, 60, 82, 124, 145–46
error law, 33, 65, 135, 158–59, 169
ether principle, 155
ethics: of fiction, 1, 43, 60, 116–19,
127–28, 149–50; moral certainty, 37;
natural history of, 97–106
eugenics, 168
evolutionism, 5, 12, 97, 103; Austen and,
72; as continuum of possibilities,
14–15; nonreproduction and, 95. *See
also* Darwin, Charles; nonreproduction; Wallace, A. R.
Exner, Sigmund, 71

Faraday, Michael, 19, 21, 132, 197n41;
"On the Physical Character of the
Lines of Magnetic Force," 140
Felski, Rita, 6, 25–26
Ferguson, Niall, 40–41, 172
Feynman, Richard, 160
Fielding, Henry, 26; *Tom Jones*, 108
Fielding, Sarah, 129
Fleishman, Avrom, 161
formalism: aesthetic formalism, 127–29;
in criticism, 181n71; formalist doc-
trines of art for art's sake, 12
Foucault, Michel, 8, 61, 63, 97

Fraiman, Susan, 5, 6, 131
François, Anne-Lise, 14
Frederickson, Kathleen, 105, 191–92n30
Freeman, Elizabeth, 17, 63, 93
friendship, 5; in *Armadale*, 62, 79, 94; Darwin's writing on, 102, 190n5; in *Dombey and Son*, 108–9, 121, 169; in *Middlemarch*, 154; in *Richard Feverel*, 47–48
Frost, Samantha, 172
Furneaux, Holly, 190n5, 192n43

Galison, Peter, 68, 93
Gallagher, Catherine, 12, 104, 119
Galperin, William, 48
Galton, Francis, 24, 32, 71, 168, 180n65; *Hereditary Genius*, 168
gambler's fallacy, 40
gambling, 31, 144, 149, 150
Gauss, Carl Friedrich, and Gaussian distribution, 65, 169
Geddes, Patrick, 123
gender: antifoundationalist accounts of, 17; in *Armadale* (Collins), 14; female formation and, 17, 27, 49; norms in fiction of, 27, 45–47, 51, 56; queer vitalism, 17, 27; in *Richard Feverel*, 4, 14, 42–43, 45–47, 55–58; Victorian norms of, 16, 30, 57; youthful development and, 16, 46–47. *See also* alternative masculinities; masculinity
genealogical critique, 62–63
geology: Dickens's novels and, 106; Scott's historical novels and, 73. *See also* Lyell, Charles; uniformitarian theories
Gibbs, Josiah Willard, 170–71
Gold, Barri, 140, 180n68
gothic fiction, 16, 88
Gould, Stephen Jay, 189n3
Griffiths, Devin, 99
Grosz, Elizabeth, 15, 97
Grove, William, 19, 21, 24, 132–34, 150, 195n18; *On the Correlation of Physical Forces*, 22–23
Guattari, Félix, 131

Hacking, Ian, 2–3, 31, 162
Hadley, Elaine, 35
Hamilton, William, 171
Hamilton, William Rowan, 19
Hampshire, Stuart, 172
Haraway, Donna, 8
Hardy, Thomas: *The Return of the Native*, 12, 170; *Two on a Tower*, 170
Harman, P. M., 179n49, 197n48
Harootunian, Harry, 90
Hasenöhrl, Friedrich, 136, 196n27
Hawthorn, Geoffrey, 172
Hayles, N. Katherine, 8, 171
Hayot, Eric, 4, 181n71
Heisenberg, Werner, 171
Helmholtz, Hermann von, 62, 67, 132, 154, 187n24, 199n71
Hemmo, Meir, 184n41
Herbert, Christopher, 171
Herschel, John, 24, 35–37, 66, 177–78n27; counterfactuals in work of, 35, 45, 168; Darwin and, 10, 99, 102, 135, 169; De Morgan and, 37; Eliot and, 137; Maxwell and, 10, 135, 137, 169, 200n6; Quetelet and, 34–35; "Quetelet on Probabilities," 10–11, 135
Hinton, C. H., 171
historical fiction, 16
historiography, 166, 169–70, 172–73; linguistic turn in, 40–41, 183n26
Hughes, Tom, *Tom Brown's Schooldays*, 48
Hume, David, 21
Hutton, Richard Holt, 199n79; "The 'Sociology' of Ants," 123
Huxley, T. H., 5, 9, 17, 179n48; Arnold and, 194n6; compared with North British scientists, 197–98n48; compared with Pater, 74; Darwin and, 100, 123; "Evolution and Ethics," 74; vs. materialist reductionism, 74; on "nebulous potentiality," 17, 27, 166; "On the Physical Basis of Life," 9; popularization of science and, 25; proposals for physical science education, 129; "Science and Culture," 194n6

idealism, 41, 74, 148
indeterminism, 8, 10; quantum indeterminism, 17; ultimate indeterminism, 162
individualism, 47, 157
insanity, 72, 89. *See also* psychological science
intelligent design, 118

Jaffe, Audrey, 182n10
James, Henry, 1, 152, 194n5
James, William, 172
Jameson, Fredric, 6
Jastrow, Joseph, 72
Jenkin, Fleeming, 132, 141, 179n48, 197n46
Jenkins, Alice, 179n52
Johnson, Curtis, 101
Jones, Anna Maria, 188n43
Jones, Bence, *The Life and Letters of Faraday*, 132
Joule, James, 19, 154, 179n48

Kant, Immanuel, 21
Keller, Evelyn Fox, 8
Kent, Christopher, 182n10
Kern, Stephen, 171, 201n19
Kirby, William, and William Spence, *An Introduction to Entomology*, 104, 191n25
Knoepflmacher, U. C., 46, 190n5, 194n5
Koselleck, Reinhart, 9, 14
Kraepelin, Emil, 71
Kripke, Saul, 181n71
Krönig, August, 134
Kropotkin, Peter, 123, 192n30
Kuhn, Thomas, 19

Laplace, Pierre-Simon, 31–33, 65; *Philosophical Essay on Probabilities*, 21, 31, 143
Latour, Bruno, 13, 25, 40, 168
Leibniz, Gottfried, 21
Levine, Caroline, 13, 16, 25–26, 84, 187n28

Levine, George, 115, 192n36, 192n46
Lewes, George Henry, 10, 39, 41, 68, 137; "Mr. Buckle's Scientific Errors," 137; *Problems of Life and Mind*, 137, 195n18
Lightman, Bernard, 25
Locke, John, 3, 70
Love, Heather, 86
Lubbock, John, 34, 99; *On Probability*, 52
Lucas, Samuel, 29
Lucretius, 132, 141–42, 197n44, 198n51; *On the Nature of Things*, 141, 197n43
Lukács, Georg, 124; "Narrate or Describe?," 81–82, 188n54
Lunar Society, 19
Lyell, Charles, 99, 100

Macaulay, Thomas Babington, 39
Mach, Ernst, *The Science of Mechanics*, 172
Macintosh, James, 102
Malthus, Thomas Robert, 95, 100–101, 104, 105, 191n20
Marcus, Sharon, 25–26
marriage in Victorian novels, 47–48, 170; in *Dombey and Son*, 124; in *Richard Feverel*, 42–44. *See also* compassionate marriage plot
Martineau, Harriet, 102
Marx, Karl, 27
masculinity: irresolution as attribute of male novelist, 93–94; male hysteria, 168; postponement as sign of effeminacy, 14, 62, 69, 70; self-control, 70, 91, 112. *See also* alternative masculinities; gender; maturation
materialism, 8–13, 179n56; mathematical principles and, 9; North British scientists vs. London naturalists on, 179n48; scientific materialism, 9, 74, 177n23, 179n48; Tyndall and, 74, 142, 196n30, 197n48
mathematical principles: deviation from the norm, 68, 70, 165, 168; empirical observation and, 9; mathematics of probability, 32, 34

Mathematical Tripos program (University of Cambridge), 3, 19, 135
maturation, 6, 16, 167; in *Armadale*, 86–87, 114, 129; in *Dombey and Son*, 110, 114, 129; in *Middlemarch*, 147; in *Richard Feverel*, 26, 46–47, 114, 129
Maudsley, Henry, 25, 69–72, 73, 93, 168; *The Physiology and Pathology of Mind*, 69
Maxwell, James Clerk, 3–4, 5, 134–44, 162; "Atom" entry in *Encyclopedia Britannica*, 142; Buckle and, 135–38, 169, 180n63, 194n4; chance, understanding of, 10; compared with Tyndall and London-based scientists, 179nn48–49, 197–98n48; creative writings of, 24; demon paradox of, 142–43; determinism, rejection of, 19, 139; "Diffusion" entry in *Encyclopedia Britannica*, 198n55; Eliot and, 134–44, 163, 200n85; energy science and, 198n55; ensemble concept and, 171; entropy law and, 15–16; Faraday and, 140, 197n41; Herschel and, 10, 135, 137, 169, 200n6; Jenkin and, 197n46; law of averages and, 23–24; Lucretius and, 141; Maxwell speed distribution, 134; "Molecules" lecture, 24, 141; "Notes of the President's Address," 142; "On Faraday's Lines of Force," 197n41; "On the Dynamical Theory of Gases," 134, 141, 200n87; "A Paradoxical Ode (After Shelley)," 139; "Report on Tait's Lecture on Force," 140; statistics of diffusion and, 128, 155; *Theory of Heat*, 134, 196n20, 201n14; thermodynamics and, 24, 158; *Treatise on Electricity and Magnetism*, 140; Tyndall and, 141–42, 179nn48–49, 196n30
melodrama, 14, 16, 87, 106
medical science: Maudsley vs. Pater on postponement, 73–74; in *Middlemarch*, 154. *See also* psychological science
Meredith, George: accidents in fiction of, 29, 43, 60; avant-garde aesthetics of, 17; criticism of, 13, 29; *The Egoist*, 170;

Eliot and, 41, 129; failed marriage of, 41–42; *Modern Love*, 41; *The Shaving of Shagpat*, 41; writing career of, 41. *See also The Ordeal of Richard Feverel*
Michelson, Albert, 172
middle class: conventionalism, 3, 5, 112, 170; domesticity, 48, 89; ethics, 19, 86, 161; reading markets, 34, 70; reification of time in culture of, 83
Middlemarch (Eliot), 126–29, 137, 143–63; avuncular bachelors in, 190n5; compared with *Armadale*, 147, 159; compared with *Dombey and Son*, 147, 159; compared with *Richard Feverel*, 159; diffusion and, 16, 126–29, 144–63; energy and lost potential in, 134–37, 145–46, 149–50, 154, 156–57; entropy law and, 15–16, 143, 148; experiments of time in, 165, 167; finale of, 126, 153–58, 160–61; marriage in, 148; Maxwell and, 137, 169; observations of Henry James on, 152; obstructed development in, 6, 15–16, 144, 145; Raffles subplot, 150–51; realism of, 143, 148, 159, 161, 163; Saint Theresa and, 145–46, 157; social life and scientific concerns connected in, 156, 158–59, 162; sympathetic feelings inhibited in, 153–54, 157; Victorian social imaginary and, 153–63
Mill, John Stuart, 36, 39, 129, 171; *System of Logic*, 39, 135
Miller, Andrew H., 12, 48
Miller, D. A., 131, 159, 185n2
Miller, J. Hillis, 128
modal arc, 12
modal stratifications, 11
modernism: and classical development plot, 6; emergence of modern physics, 171–72; mid-Victorian cultural origins of, 8; sensation novels and, 185n2
molecules and molecular knowledge, 15, 20, 131, 135, 143, 155, 171, 197n44. *See also* atomism

Moore, James, 105
Moretti, Franco, 6
Morley, Edward, 172
Morton, Timothy, 172
Müller, Johannes, *Elements of Physiology,* 67

Napoleon, 39–40
natural history of morals, 97–106, 118
naturalism, 170
natural philosophy, 18, 19, 23, 147
negated potential: in *Armadale,* 43, 64, 86;
   in *The Ordeal of Richard Feverel,* 16, 30,
   43–48, 51, 53–60, 59, 129, 167
Newtonianism, 8, 20, 24, 100, 133, 172,
   179n56
nonhappenings, 26, 31–42, 60, 168
nonreproduction, nineteenth-century
   theories of, 95–96, 103–6, 190n3,
   191–92n30
normal curve. *See* Gauss, Carl Friedrich
normalization, power of, 8, 167
North, Michael, 197n44
North British scientists, 18, 179n48,
   197–98n48

Obscene Publications Act (1857), 30, 54,
   184n44
Ordeal of Richard Feverel, The (Meredith),
   13–14, 29–60; alternative temporalities and, 52, 56; autobiographical
   associations of, 41–42; Buckle and,
   169; compared with *Armadale,* 86, 89;
   compared with *Dombey and Son,* 114;
   compared with *Middlemarch,* 159;
   distinction between "consecutiveness
   and consequence" in, 51–52; counterlives in, 13, 42–52, 170; critical reviews
   of, 29; gender norms and deviations
   in, 4, 14, 30, 42–43, 45–47, 54–58; marriage in, 42–44, 49, 51; mimetic desire
   in, 50; negated potential and, 16, 30,
   43–48, 51, 53–60, 129, 167; nonhappenings, theory of, 31–42; nostalgia
   in, 44; probability in, 50; satire in, 45,

54; scientific system of education in,
   25, 42, 46, 182n2; "temporal unity of
   the whole" and, 30, 41, 59; Victorian
   conduct codes and, 45, 47, 54–55,
   184–85n47
Ospovot, Dov, 101, 191n20

Paley, William, 118; *The Principles of
   Moral and Political Philosophy,* 102
Pandora, Katherine, 25
Pater, Walter, 73–74, 83, 128, 194n5; *The
   Renaissance,* 74
Patey, Douglas, 59
Pavel, Thomas, 181n71
Pearson, Karl, 32, 168, 171; *The Grammar
   of Science,* 165
Peirce, C. S., 33
personal equation, 32, 65–66
physical science: early nineteenth-century
   conceptions of, 3; Maxwell on future
   of, 24, 138–139; in Victorian Britain,
   18–24, 166
physics: emergence as discipline, 12, 18,
   128, 161, 172; Maxwell speed distribu-
   tion as statistical law in, 134; particle
   physics, 172; statistical ensemble, 171.
   See also physical science; physics of
   possibility; science; thermodynamics
physics of possibility: British novels and,
   4, 166; progressive politics and, 168; as
   Victorian conceptual legacy, 18, 172
Pierce, C. S., 150
Pigott, Edward, 76
Planck, Max, 171
Poisson, Siméon Denis, 33–34
Pond, John, 66
Porter, Theodore, 2–3, 31, 34, 40, 135,
   136, 165, 182n11, 182n15, 197n46
possibility. *See* alternative possibilities;
   chance; counterhistories and counterlives; physics of possibility; probabilistic thinking
postponement. *See* slowness and postponement

Pratt-Smith, Stella, 139
present: *Armadale* and alienation from, 62–63, 78–79, 82–84, 86, 88; history of the present and, 63; Huxley on, 74; "multitemporal world of the now," 63; plural understanding of, 63; role in modern medicine, 89; skeptical accounts of, 84. *See also* standard time
Priestley, Joseph, *The Doctrine of Philosophical Necessity Illustrated,* 21, 139
probabilistic thinking: in astronomers' error curve, 33, 65, 135; on "behavior of things," 64; "calculus of probabilities" (Laplace), 31, 32, 33; in Britain vs. France, 34; chance and, 9–10; classic probability distribution and, 32; "probabilistic revolution," 1–2, 32, 172; Darwin and, 99; Eliot and, 137–38; energy science and, 134–36; fiction and, 152; law of probability, 39; mathematical demonstration of, 32, 34; Maxwell and, 137–38; in Meredith's fiction, 29, 128; origins of probability theory and, 18–19, 30–31, 66; philosophical implications of, 36; retrodiction and, 184n41; sensation and, 69, 70; Smollett and, 184n43. *See also* Babbage, Charles; Bessel, Friedrich; chance; Darwin, Charles; De Morgan, Augustus; Drinkwater, John Eliot; Gauss, Carl Friedrich; Herschel, John; Laplace, Pierre-Simon; mathematical principles; Maxwell, James Clerk; Poisson, Siméon Denis; statistics
psychological science: critique of established mental models in *Armadale,* 90; Leipzig Institute, opening of (1879), 93; on mental confusion and drug consumption, 71–72; and pathology, 70, 83; physiological psychology and, 185n3, 188n48; on postponement as "individual difference," 68; on postponement as symptom of malaise, 62–63, 70–71; sanitarium as institutional site for, 88–90. *See also* medical science
Purrington, Robert D., 136
Pykett, Lyn, 113

quantum determinism and indeterminism, 8, 17
quantum mechanics, 171–72
queer vitalism, 17, 27
Quetelet, Adolphe, 23, 34–35, 38, 165, 167, 182n10

reaction time. *See* slowness and postponement
reading: diffusive reading, 128, 162; middle class market for, 34, 70; physics of variation and, 173; redemptive diffusion and, 160–61
realism: bildungsroman and, 127; demon paradox of Maxwell and, 143; mathematics and, 37, 52; in novels and physical sciences, 4; utopian potential and, 7
reductionism, 74, 179n49
religion. *See* spirituality and religion
reparative criticism, 26, 180–81n70
reproduction and sexuality in Victorian discourse, 97, 104, 121. *See also* nonreproduction
Richard Feverel. See Ordeal of Richard Feverel, The
Richards, Robert J., 96, 104, 189n3
Richardson, Samuel, 48; *The History of Sir Charles Grandison,* 53
Ricoeur, Paul, 41
Robertson, Howard Percy, 171
Ronen, Ruth, 11, 181n71
Rosenthal, Jesse, 143–44, 163, 198–99n64
Rousseau, Jean-Jacques, 42; *Confessions,* 53
Royal Astronomical Society, 36
Royal Institution, 19, 21, 22
Rutherford, Ernest, 20
Ryan, Marie-Laure, 181n71
Rylance, Rick, 72

Sadoff, Diane, 120
Sanders, Andrew, 119
Schaffer, Simon, 66
Schmidgen, Henning, 187n24
Schor, Hilary, 120
Schreiner, Olive, *Story of an African Farm,* 5, 170
Schrödinger, Erwin, 171, 196n27
science: increasing specialization of, 12; popularization of, 25; statistical studies and, 3. *See also* astronomers and astronomy; energy science; evolutionism; geology; medical science; physics; physical science; probabilistic thinking; psychological science
scientific materialism, 9
Scott, Walter, 73
Sedgwick, Eve, 25–26, 180n70
sensation: postponement and duration of, 67–68; rhetoric of statistics and, 68; scientific definition of, 61
sensation fiction, 61, 63, 81, 170, 185n2
sequence, 59, 139, 155; "consecutiveness and consequence" and bildungsroman, 51–52
Shakespeare, William, 46, 53, 142
Shuttleworth, Sally, 46
Silver, Brenda, 170
Simmel, Georg, 61
slowness and postponement: definitions of postponement, 66, 68; delayed reactor and, 69, 71; masculinity and, 14, 62, 69, 70; personal equation and, 65–66; reaction-time experiments in, 71; sensation in terms of, 61–62, 68–69; as symptom of mental malaise, 62–63, 70–71; in Victorian print culture, 187n41
Smith, Adam, 47
Smith, Crosbie, 179n48, 193n2
Smith, Goldwin, 39
Smollett, Tobias, 26, 48, 184n43; *The Adventures of Roderick Random,* 53–54, 108

Snow, C. P., 20, 194n6
Snyder, Katherine V., 190n5
Society for the Diffusion of Useful Knowledge, 19
sociology of science, 13
Somerville, Mary, *On the Connexion of the Physical Sciences,* 22
Spanberg, Sven-Johan, 46
speed of sensation, 61–62; impossible to calculate, 67
Spencer, Herbert, 9, 25, 42, 68, 123, 171
Spinoza, Baruch, 21
spirituality and religion, 16, 102, 105, 115, 131, 195n10
Stack, David, 96
Stallo, J. M., 171
standard time, 80–83. *See also* present; time and temporality
statistical mechanics, 24, 136, 153
Statistical Society of London, 19, 99
statistics: accuracy in, according to Clifford, 177n25; developments in, 9, 18, 23–24; as distinct domain in Britain, 2, 18; Eliot and, 143–44, 200n85; law of averages and, 23–24, 36, 38, 165, 180n65; meaning of, 30–31, 36; science in relation to, 3, 31; statistical ensembles, 11, 170–71; unification with thermodynamics, 134, 136
Stephen, James Fitzjames, 39–40, 46–47, 52, 137
Stephen, Leslie, *The Science of Ethics,* 123
Sterne, Laurence, 55, 129
Stevenson, Richard C., 184–85n47
Stewart, Balfour, 23, 148, 195n10
Stewart, Garrett, 111
suicide, 38, 91–92
Sully, James, 67–68, 73; *Sensation and Intuition,* 67–68

Taine, Hippolyte, 68–69, 172; *On Intelligence,* 68
Tait, Peter Guthrie, 23; creative writings of, 24; determinism, rejection of, 19;

energy science and, 133, 140, 195n10; as North British scientist, 179n48, 198n48

Taylor, Jenny Bourne, 88, 185n2, 188n48, 189n59

Tennyson, Alfred, 72–73

Thackery, William Makepeace, *Pendennis*, 75

Theresa, Saint, 145–46, 157

thermodynamics, 3, 5, 12–15, 132–33; codification of, 19, 132; cultural history of, 180n68; Eliot and *Middlemarch* and, 144, 146, 155, 161, 169; Maxwell's "Molecules" lecture and, 24; Maxwell's statistical thermodynamics, 169; origins of, 22, 132; Tennyson and, 73; unification of statistics with, 136. *See also* conservation, law of; energy science; entropy law; physics; statistical mechanics

Thoms, Peter, 188n51

Thomson, J. Arthur, 123

Thomson, J. J., 20

Thomson, James, 179n48

Thomson, William, 19, 147, 179n48, 195n10; *Treatise on Natural Philosophy*, 19

time and temporality: alternatives to the present, 18, 52, 62, 73, 78–79, 80, 82–84, 86, 88, 90, 92–93, 129, 167, 169, 172, 185n4; deceleration of time, 172; Einstein's theory of relativity and, 171–72; Enlightenment-era views of, 3; feminist and queer accounts of, 63; Greenwich Mean Time, 82; homogeneous time, assumption of, 40; Huxley on temporalities of speech and writing, 74; Maudsley on "time-rate," 69–72; nonlinear temporalities in fiction, 63, 74, 82; nonlinear temporalities in probability theory, 52; personal time, causes of, 66, 68, 80; relation to reading acts, 83; shifting significance of temporal possibilities in Victorian discourse, 52, 69; "temporal unity of the whole" in historiography, 30, 41,

59; time-asymmetric phenomenon, 149; varying experiments of time, 128, 165, 167, 172. *See also* present; slowness and postponement; standard time

tragedy, 59–60, 152

Trevor-Roper, Hugh, 172; "History and Imagination," 165

Trollope, Anthony, *Phineas Finn*, 75

Tyndall, John, 9, 19, 23, 74, 137, 154, 179nn48–49, 187n39; Belfast Address (1874), 141–42; compared with North British scientists, 197–98n48; energy science and, 133, 144, 199n71; *Fragments of Science for Unscientific People*, 132, 155; *Heat: A Mode of Motion*, 147, 196n30; higher materialism and, 74, 142, 196n30, 197n48; Lucretius and, 141–42; Maxwell and, 141–42, 179nn48–49, 196n30

Unger, Roberto, 13

uniformitarian theories, 106

University of Cambridge: Mathematical Tripos program, 3, 19, 135; psychological laboratory, 72

utopia, 7, 27, 168

Venn, John, 170; *The Logic of Chance*, 36, 64

Victorian novels: chance, role in, 10; ensemble effects in, 11–12; ideological constraint in, 130–31; intellectual commons shaped by, 25, 180n68; Henry James's critique of, 1; nonhappenings in, 26, 35, 37, 60, 168; pleasures of suspense in, 84; plot and narrative intent in, 152; probabilistic concepts in, 12, 17, 152, 175n3; scientific orientations of, 2, 4, 5, 7, 24–27, 32, 166–69; sensation novels and, 61, 63, 81, 185n2; unlived lives in, 12. *See also* bildungsroman; compassionate marriage plot; connections between physical sciences, mathematics, and fiction; counterfactuals and counterlives;

Victorian novels (*continued*)
  digressions and deviance in narrative;
  realism; sensation fiction
von Mayer, Julius, 19

Wallace, A. R., 95, 105, 189n2
Weiner, Norbert, 171
Wells, H. G., *The Time Machine,* 133
Westminster Review, 41
Whewell, William, 18, 66, 102, 118
White, Hayden, 183n26
Wilde, Oscar, 83, 128; *The Picture of
  Dorian Gray,* 5

Williams, Raymond, 150
Winter, Alison, 61, 185n2
Woloch, Alex, 111
"worlding," 181n71. *See also* connections
  between physical sciences, mathematics, and fiction; counterfactuals
  and counterlives; modal arc; modal
  stratifications
Wundt, Wilhelm, 71, 93

Zeitz, Lisa M., 188n51
Zemka, Sue, 81, 82, 188n56
Zola, Émile, 82